NURTURING SOCIAL CAPITAL IN EXCLUDED COMMUNITIES

Nurturing Social Capital in Excluded Communities
A kind of higher education

JULIA PREECE
University of Surrey

ANN-MARIE HOUGHTON
University of Lancaster

Ashgate
Aldershot • Burlington USA • Singapore • Sydney

© Julia Preece and Ann-Marie Houghton 2000

All rights reserved. No part of this publication may be reproduced, stored in a retrieval system, or transmitted in any form or by any means, electronic, mechanical, photocopying, recording or otherwise without the prior permission of the publisher.

Published by
Ashgate Publishing Ltd
Gower House
Croft Road
Aldershot
Hampshire GU11 3HR
England

Ashgate Publishing Company
131 Main Street
Burlington, VT 05401-5600
USA

Ashgate website: http://www.ashgate.com

British Library Cataloguing in Publication Data
Preece, Julia
    Nurturing social capital in excluded communities : a kind of higher education
    1. Education, Higher - Social aspects - Great Britain
    2. Adult education - Social aspects - Great Britain 3. Social isolation - Great Britain
    I. Title II. Houghton, Ann-Marie
    374.9'41

Library of Congress Control Number: 00-134840

ISBN 0 7546 1465 4

Printed and bound by Athenaeum Press, Ltd.,
Gateshead, Tyne & Wear.

Contents

List of Tables *vi*
Preface *vii*
Acknowledgements *ix*

PART I: THE CONTEXT

Introduction 3
1 A Kind of Higher Education 5
2 Action and Research 21
3 Surveying the Provision 37

PART II: EXPLORING THE KIND OF HIGHER EDUCATION DEBATES

4 Skills and Lifelong Learning in the Community 59
5 A Curriculum Off-limits: Social and Cultural Relevance 77
6 Educational Guidance: Customer or Citizen? 91
7 Technology in the Community 108

PART III: THE LEARNERS' STORIES

Introduction 127
8 Nurturing Social Capital in Communities: Women in East Lancs 133
9 Nurturing Social Capital in Communities: The DAB Centre 145
10 Nurturing Social Capital in Communities: The Bridge Centre 160
11 But is it Higher? 174

Appendices *187*
Bibliography *195*
Index *211*

List of Tables

Table 1 *Features of Community Groups* 41

Table 2 *How Participants Spend Their Spare Time* 44

Table 3 *Future Study Plans* 50

Table 4 *Features Identified as Required for Future Study* 52

Preface

This book presents action research findings on two contemporary issues: how to create an accessible and relevant higher education for adults and how to document the wider social and non economic benefits of learning amongst people who do not contribute directly to the nation's wealth creation through waged work.

The book starts from the premise that full employment in the conventional sense is unlikely to be a future reality. Nevertheless, pressures of globalisation and economic competitiveness drive policy makers to find solutions to the human problem of unequal participation in modern society. The book argues that for some adult learners their contribution to globalised systems must stem from individuals having a strong sense of self stemming from a local identity. This means education must recognise different and multiple identities, communities and cultures by strengthening social capital from the grass roots. The distinctive qualities of higher education have an essential role to play in nurturing the skills, knowledge and understanding necessary for regenerating communities. In order to reach the people most in need of these qualities, their experience must be local to those communities. But this higher learning must also equip people for the inevitable influences and demands of globalisation in a modern, changing world. It must be accredited, transportable, quality assured and useful.

The engagement with communities must also be understood in their social and historical contexts. Social capital, for example, is fluid, complex and interfaces with citizenship status. The relationship between education and social capital is contingent upon how power differentials of class, race, age, gender, disability are constructed and played out by individuals, their communities and wider society. Participation is contingent on how people are positioned in society at various stages in their lives. Cumulative effects of this positioning and the related discourses affect how easily people enter the educational arena and how easily they stay there. It is also dependent on how minorities and their identities are allowed space in the new globalisation discourses for integration and convergence. Learning provision needs to take account of these issues in order to address existing inequalities which exclude them. A future kind of higher education must be flexible enough to accommodate these contingencies if it is to be accessible to the many.

Acknowledgements

This book and its research would not have been possible without the support, insights, knowledge and contributions at all levels of the community access programme from Wendy Rogerson. She has been key to its ongoing success. In addition we would also like to thank Helen Ali, Raana Bokhari, Mollie Mason and Nalini Patel for their invaluable involvement and feedback at various stages of the project.

It would be remiss, of course, if we did not also thank the many students and tutors who have contributed to the programme and directly to the research. In the interests of confidentiality they must remain anonymous but they all provided us with much new knowledge and stimulated many new ideas which have been reflected in the project throughout its evolution.

Finally thanks are also due to Stephen McNair and Rennie Johnston for their helpful comments on earlier chapter drafts.

We must take responsibility, however, for any errors of judgement or other inaccuracies in the final publication.

PART I:
THE CONTEXT

Introduction

Globalisation, new technologies and changing work demands are moving higher education (HE) towards becoming a mass system. Adults and excluded communities are increasingly a focus of attention in the new participation discourses. This book looks at one way in which UK higher education might be accessed and valued by people who have hitherto been excluded from its very gates. It explores how HE might become de-institutionalised, engage directly with adults in their communities, but still remain 'higher'. It also looks at the different social and cultural contexts surrounding such participation.

The book takes its title from a 1993 NIACE policy discussion document on adult learners and higher education. The NIACE debate is expanded with reference to more recent commentary on the future shape of higher education. The emergence of this system is contextualised in the rapidly growing literature on globalisation, citizenship, social capital and social exclusion. The book consequently tries to put higher education for adults into a modern (as in 'up-to-date') but inclusive, lifelong learning context which privileges difference and local interests. It asks questions, for instance about what is distinctive about higher education when it engages with mass participation. What are the qualities of a flexible credit programme in a higher education framework? What are the implications for teaching and learning when learning takes place amongst people with disparate starting points? Indeed, how do we square the localised, less-technological learning worlds with the fast moving systems of communication to which higher education aspires?

We, the authors, have been working with adult learners in their community settings for between five and seven years. At the time of our action research we were based in the Educational Research department of Lancaster University. Our work comprised both course provision in negotiation with a number of community groups and a range of systematic inquiries into the nature and effectiveness of that provision. We do not claim to have answers to all the questions concerning the move towards a mass and inclusive higher education system, but we do have a story to tell. Some of the ideas in this book will be of relevance to providers across the post-compulsory system. Others are specific to the struggle to find a distinctive, but inclusive role for higher education in post modernity.

The book divides into three parts. The first part provides the book's context. Chapter one introduces the global and localised context for a future higher education system. It discusses recent influences and debates on the relationship between education and human and social capital. It asks: What kind of higher education is envisioned for the twenty first century and what are the implications for those least involved in its provision so far? From the literature, we draw some conclusions about rationales and ways forward for HE institutions' engagement with adults most on the margins, introducing the themes for the rest of the book. Chapter two introduces our project - its function within the university and how we went about combining action with research - making provision and analysing what worked and why. Chapter three provides an overview of the community locations, interlaced with commentary on a questionnaire survey of the project's most regular learners.

The second part of the book explores four of the more practical aspects of our higher education provision. We expand on some of the themes of chapter one and three and explain how those themes interface with current debates about adult learners and higher education. In particular we look at the core skills debate, technology, curriculum and guidance issues. In other words, what, if anything, has been distinctively higher about university intervention for the learners; and what are the distinctive needs of new higher learners? Part three looks more theoretically at the learners' experiences in a life history context and in relation to what they want for themselves from a future higher education system. We take some individual stories and follow through what learning in the community has meant for them in their social and historical contexts. This section interfaces with debates on the relationship between education, social capital, citizenship, globalisation and learner identities and how these relate to a broader lifelong learning agenda. For instance, how does HE contribute to nurturing the community sense of self and cultural identity? The last chapter offers some thoughts on the implications and costs of community based higher education. We summarise the key debates and suggest strategies for a higher learning policy for the millennium.

1 A Kind of Higher Education

> Mass enrolments in further and higher education have spawned highly innovative curricular changes. Courses have been modularised. Access to further and higher education has been widened. Systems of credit accumulation and transfer have been developed. Education institutions themselves have grown in scale and complexity and older subject boundaries have been and are eroding. Stronger links between the worlds of work and education and the interests and needs of students are taken much more seriously than they once were. There remains none the less, a wide divide between what has been and what might yet be achieved (Williamson, 1998: 53).

Introduction

Much has been written in the last decade about what our future higher education system might look like. Several themes have precipitated these debates and they are introduced in this first chapter. Amongst the most prominent is the impact of globalisation, manifested by a technologically shrinking world and increased competitiveness. There is an assumption that increased educational participation will contribute to economic, and therefore competitive, advancement - though some question the proven evidence for this (Edwards, 1997). There is also a feeling that people need to be better prepared for the new, fast moving world of uncertainty and change:

> A new kind of society is emerging, which is global in its reach, market driven, socially and culturally fragmented, individualistic in its moral commitments and powered by the technology of an information revolution (Williamson, 1998: 116).

The argument nowadays is that in order to fit into this kind of society. We can no longer afford to train people for one skill only. The one-off specific practical or academic training of the past needs to be supplemented by ongoing updating and the nurturing of higher skills of adaptability and flexibility. People across all social groups are now required to be better prepared intellectually for unpredictable employment patterns. Alongside this challenge it seems that old styles of university elitism are proving more expensive than inclusion might prove to be. Whilst elitism is out of fashion universities have a correlated need for more public money to pay for its expanding services. But for the HE system to secure the public support it needs to survive, it must be seen to be playing a stronger part in the everyday lives of ordinary people. Williamson claims that one way forward is for universities to develop closer links with regional and local, as well as global communities:

> They will reduce their vulnerability to the state if they are seen to have a unique place in the cultural life of society as a whole (1998: 126).

It is never easy to change, of course - especially if you have already decided that what you do is, quite simply, excellent. So, universities must first convince themselves that there is a need for change. Many are doing so, and the notion of terms like the 'adult university' and the 'learning university' are now embedded in the literature (for example Duke, 1992, Bourgeois et al., 1999). But universities are also struggling to defend what is 'higher' about their system, particularly in relation to efforts for radical change. The challenge is to find a distinctive role for universities - in a world with increasingly fewer boundaries between levels of provision. Indeed, part of the problem for universities in a mass HE system lies in the increasingly blurred boundaries for what, precisely, HE stands for if it is no longer the prerogative of the privileged few.

Before discussing this point further, however, it is worth digressing into some of the wider debates, trends and influences on the changing HE scene. These are presented under three broad themes: the relationship between globalisation and local communities; the relationships between education, notions of citizenship and social capital; policy considerations for addressing social exclusion.

Globalisation and Local Communities

There is insufficient space here to explore all the complexities of globalisation, but there are some significant features which directly impact on how HE positions itself in the future, as well as how local communities interface with the process of globalisation. In summary this process reflects the constriction of time and space brought about by the rise of the 'network society' (Castells, 1996). We are now part of a global economy, mediated primarily by information technology. The extent to which economies, politics and cultures are converging, or not, is open to debate (Robertson, 1992; Waters, 1995; Held et al., 1999; Hirst and Thompson, 1996). Most are agreed, however, on the effects of globalisation (the recasting of national communication boundaries, increasing mobility and transnational companies operating independently of national policy, the formation of new kinds of compressed time-space boundaries, relationships and hierarchies). These impact on countries, regions and communities. Some talk about the concept of a global village - where distant events can have their effect on different locations across the world (Waters, 1995: 35). In other words there is 'an intensified consciousness of the world as a whole' (Robertson, 1992: 8). Robertson suggests that people are moving from a sense of 'Gemeinschaft' (community) to one of 'Gesellschaft' (society) (ibid: 11). Bauman (1998) proposes that the reaction of people on the receiving end of these processes is to regroup, forming new, localised identities. It is Friedman (1994) however, who most explicitly unpacks the relationship between global trends and 'local' behaviour. Whilst no-one specifically defines precisely what 'local' means, Friedman at least explains that 'local' is not self contained. It depends on its interface with other locales and wider networks. He suggests that where global trends may try and influence the culture of the local, the local also appropriates these trends for its own gain (p.12). An unknown tribe in danger of extinction, for example, may interact with tourism networks and become a tourist feature in order to preserve its heritage. However, as globalisation increases, people and their communities may re-fragment to retain their distinctiveness: 'Cultural fragmentation and modernist homogenisation are two constitutive trends of global reality' (ibid. p.102). People want to shape what they consume in order to fit their own identity and needs. This means, of course, that people and communities position themselves differently in response to global interference. Higher education is geographically positioned within local communities but also interfaces, through a ripple effect, with its region and the wider world. It needs to be sensitive to the economic and political consequences of attending to all these. It is also an investment resource (now competing with other players) for the development of society's future human capital (the skills and knowledge required for wealth creation).

The economic need to maximise the nation's wealth creating resources and minimise the demands from its loss-making dependency population has led to an increasing political interest in the causational relationship between education and the labour market. The European agenda for lifelong learning, taken on board by the UK Government, is to increase people's labour skills and mobility, thereby reducing this dependency, now named 'social exclusion'. The solution has been to devise a range of strategies to decrease welfare dependency by increasing work capacity. The focus of these strategies has been on building human capital (See, for example, DfEE, 1999). In order to achieve this it is necessary to generate a lifelong learning culture whereby individuals develop an expectation that they will return to formal skills and knowledge learning throughout their lives as circumstances change. These rationales leave unaddressed the value of learning for unwaged work and for those who do not have a prospect of employment. Although a connection is not overtly made in public policy, interest is now also growing in the potential link between continuous learning and people's involvement in local activities - of a citizenship or social nature. This coincides with the globalisation theorists' perceptions of people's inclinations to re-group in the face of global re-ordering of society. There is therefore a renewed focus, in the UK at least, in the 'local'. UK policies are now seeking the 'non economic benefits' of learning, particularly in local communities (DfEE, 1999a). This might be measured in terms of increased citizenship activity or some kind of reduction of demands on welfare agencies as a result of increasing participation in learning. One way of interpreting the economic value of such community resourcing is to see it as social capital.

Social Capital and Citizenship

Part three discusses these aspects in relation to the learners more directly, but a brief introduction is relevant here. The discussions revolve around a sense that there is a problematic relationship between education, employment and the economic value of individual learning for society as a whole. It is addressed differentially by educationists and sociologists. Giddens (1998) and Beck, for instance, focus on a view of employment which gives political status to currently unrecognised 'work'. They argue for a definition of employment and wealth creation which recognises active participation in voluntary organisations as an alternative to employment and also as a contribution to citizenship:

> Those who commit themselves to voluntary organisations are no longer available for the labour market and in this sense are no longer 'unemployed'. They are active citizens (Beck, 1998: 63).

By giving grass roots social action a credible visibility within the discourse for inclusion, such activity gains 'economic organisational and political weight' (ibid: 63-4). Giddens calls this kind of activity 'social capital'. Capital in this sense becomes a reserve of social skills which have exchange value to society as a whole and which therefore may provide indirect economic gains:

> Conventional poverty programmes need to be replaced with community focused programmes which permit more democratic participation as well as being more effective. Community building emphasises support networks, self help and the cultivation of social capital as a means to generate economic renewal in low income neighbourhoods (Giddens, 1998: 110).

Demonstration of social capital, it is argued, provides added value to individuals who might otherwise not be seen as contributing directly to the country's wealth creation. Giddens and Beck claim there is a need to recognise the reality of the non-waged employed as a sector of society. Giddens calls this the 'beyond the work society' (1998: 105). From this perspective strong links are made between civic behaviour (citizenship) and ideas of community as a form of social stability and means of sharing social values. The economic capital generated from such activity is justified through its indirect reduction in social welfare costs to the wider social world. These arguments have a direct bearing on the lives of many of the participants in this project.

Putnam (1995) also sees a relationship between 'civic engagement' (p.667) and social capital. He and others (Coleman, 1988; 1994; Schuller and Field, 1998) have been searching for links between social capital and educational achievement. Understanding how people acquire such social capital through educational participation, however, is problematic. Indeed the concept of social capital itself is open to interpretation, as this book will emphasise. Coleman (1994) defines the constituents of social capital as a set of social structures and social relations which are based on three forms of behaviour. These derive from connections with, and activity in, social networks such as clubs, societies or community projects. These forms of behaviour consist of *obligations and expectations* developed through mutual activity and a common purpose. This ultimately entails reciprocal arrangements between members and the development of mutual trust. The outcome is a network of communication - *information channels* - which can be called upon outside their original social purpose. Over time *norms of collective interest* evolve which are internalised and act as self-defining sanctions on the behaviours of other members. Field and Spence (2000) note that Coleman and Putnam see social capital in slightly different ways. Coleman's emphasis is on bonds between school, family, church and neighbourhood, whereas Putnam's focus for achieving social capital is less on educational resources and more on systems of communication and co-operation between social groups (Field and Spence, 2000: 34-5). Schuller and Field (1998) found that people who are members of certain well-established social networks were more likely to have initially high human capital (employability skills) but the relationship between social capital and lifelong learning was less established. Field and Spence's further analysis of the link between social capital and lifelong learning suggested that in Northern Ireland bonds and families ties are often strong. In these cases formal education and training were often marginalised in favour of informal learning arrangements. The concept of social capital and its relationship to lifelong learning therefore is complex, though the theorists still argue that there is a causal link between accumulated social capital and the indirect gains derived from lifelong learning.

Notions of social capital and citizenship are not necessarily interdependent concepts but the dominant discourse of citizenship suggests that social capital qualities provide the foundations for 'civic engagement' (Jordan, 1996). Whilst citizenship can be defined as a legal status with associated personal rights, citizenship is also about the self responsibilities of civil society (Beck, 1998). It is seen in relationship to its political affiliation with the nation state and therefore its association with formal political institutions. Social and collective behaviour is of citizenship status if it conforms to the current political system of a particular nation. Citizenship implies political integration and participation in 'collective self rule' which is invested in a certain type of 'moral and political order' (Jordan, 1996: 102). As such, Jordan argues the public discourse of citizenship does not take account of divergent beliefs and practices of separate social groups: 'Citizenship is a concept that serves to define members and exclude non members' (p.104). In other words not all social activities seem to count for the public status of citizenship or social capital. Definitions of both citizenship and social capital, then, already prescribe what forms of self discipline or collective action are valued in society. A more inclusive model of society, Beck suggests, would be one where the social action itself is given 'organisational and political weight' (1998: 64) before its real benefits can be measured.

A telling additional clue to this suggestion lies in feminist literature which discusses citizenship values. Oommen (1997) and Brine (1999) argue that the whole definition of citizenship is class dominated and gender blind, often ignoring the absence of women from those activities most highly regarded for active citizenship: 'The young, the lower class and women are not equal citizens in the context of public participation' (Oommen 1997: 10). Indeed the title of citizen is not even a right for migrant communities. Ackers (1998) and Lister (1997) argue for a feminist citizenship 'which gives due accord to women's agency' (Lister, 1997: 5) and which acknowledges their private spheres of activity such as caring.

They also apply this argument to other minority groups such as black or disabled people. It is these latter points which suggest the complexity of measuring educational achievement and social participation amongst groups that are now frequently described in political terms as 'socially excluded'.

Social Exclusion and Policies for Inclusion

Social exclusion is often equated with people who are on a continuum between poverty and unemployment. It is also described as a multifaceted phenomenon which has to do with social processes which exclude people 'from systems which facilitate social integration' (Howarth and Kenway, 1998: 80). Under that definition the socially excluded may be 'unemployed', 'homeless', 'disabled', 'disaffected youth' or some such other category. Policy initiatives attempt to address social exclusion by normalising such groups into a homogenised notion of human behaviour (Preece, 1999). In this respect they may be responding to globalisation trends for convergence but they potentially deny some people's need for a local identity and opportunity to create a sense of citizenship on their own terms (Beck, 1998). There is therefore a need to explore social inclusion as a more broad based pluralistic strategy.

Recent UK initiatives have focused almost exclusively on developing human capital through a discourse of individualism and employability. Opinion is now growing, however, that employability skills alone will not generate the collectivity and sense of mutual obligation required for sustaining the citizenship values necessary in a fragile labour market (OECD, 1999). (Indeed, it might more cynically be argued that a discourse which counts voluntary activity as 'employed' will also reduce unemployment statistics). The government is now looking for 'non economic' or indirect economic benefits of non formal, non vocational, learning (DfEE, 1999a). Currently, the role of higher education (HE) in general community learning is not part of the government's agenda. UK HE is encouraged to widen participation on an institutional 'access' basis (HEFCE, 1999) where input and output of new university students can be measured as a result of direct intervention to recruit certain social groups. There is evidence to suggest, however, that HE in the community can also contribute to the 'capacity building' of those communities at a local level (McNair et al, 1999). Whilst such arguments have always been documented (Fordham et al., 1976; Ward and Taylor, 1986), other literature (for example, Trotman and Pudner, 1998) places such activity in its modern context - one of endemic unemployment, pluralism, demand for qualifications and increasingly stark divisions between the well-off and poor. The community project described in this book undertook a learning model which engaged with both human capital and social capital goals. It has openly provided an off-campus service but in doing so has appropriated current discourses for an adult and a distinctively 'higher' education.

So what does the literature say about positioning our HE system in a lifelong learning context, fit for the many, rather than the few? And what in particular might HE have to offer our adult population, the majority of whom have absorbed a very traditional concept of HE - and the majority of whom were not members of its privileged elite? The rest of this chapter offers an argument for HE in the community which addresses its distinctiveness as 'higher' but also adopts, for the benefit of local communities, the concept of a fragmenting HE.

In this context we explore a number of questions. Firstly, what kind of HE are we currently critiquing? What are the perceived essential qualities and primary purposes of HE which should be preserved? Alongside this, what are the anxieties about possible future directions for mass HE which might threaten those purposes within the current concept of lifelong learning? Finally we discuss a number of visions for the future shape of an inclusive HE for adults. From these visions we draw up, in the ensuing chapters, our own understanding of community based HE provision, the place where most inclusive education starts. Here will be the test for the reality of a new kind of adult HE.

The Primary Purposes of Higher Education

There is some consensus that university missions generally have been to do with research and scholarship, teaching and learning and contributing to services 'outside' the university (Duke, 1992). In this context Duke (1992) points out that universities have in the past been more focused on preparing their students for HE than the wider world. Barnett (1990) suggests that the universities' principle domains of knowledge (research and scholarship) are in reality only constructions of self interest: 'Ideologies serving hidden social interests and fundamental concepts of man and society' (p.37). In spite of these caveats of purpose, Barnett in particular identifies some 'essential conditions' which make higher education 'higher' than other forms of learning. He claims that education:

> Only becomes higher when the student is able to form an independent evaluation of what he or she has learned ... to put it into some kind of perspective ... see its strengths but also its limitations (1990: 165).

Higher learning takes a broad view of knowledge; the university student is encouraged to make independent judgements about knowledge based on an informed understanding from several perspectives. To place this experience in the higher domain of learning, Barnett identifies some of the essential conditions which achieve that goal as a 'deep' understanding and 'radical critique' of knowledge claims. These include the ability to conduct some form of independent inquiry and present that critique in open dialogue, alongside critical self reflection (p.203). The essence of learning at this level is the application of a 'critical spirit' in the rehearsal of established truths.

Other writers tend to support the notion that universities have historically been about the creation, testing and transmission of knowledge (McNair, 1997a; 1997b) and that graduate skills include the ability to analyse, synthesise, reason critically and think creatively (Knapper and Cropley, 1995) though there is still a tendency to see these processes in the context of university defined subject disciplines (Barnett, 1997a; 1997b). The definition of knowledge poses both potential and problems for the new higher education. Even the concepts of 'critical' and 'inquiry' and 'continuous learning' often come across in the literature as self-defining norms for the university experience. It has been argued elsewhere, however (Preece, 1999; 1999a), that critical thinking takes place in a context which allows only certain viewpoints, usually through authorised text. New knowledge is allowed but only if it is approved by those already in the system. The contesting of knowledge, as proposed by McNair, is consequently self defining as it can only be done from within established frameworks and through the use of peer authorised texts. Knowledge, therefore, is defined by and according to the social and cultural milieu of those who already create it. Even writers looking specifically for new directions in HE base their goals on a set of value laden terms such as truth, objectivity and freedom of thought (Coffield and Williamson, 1997). Nevertheless these concepts provide a starting point from which to build the new vision.

Higher Education and Lifelong Learning

Most of the new visions are written in the wake of recently generalised conceptions of a 'learning age' (DfEE, 1998; Dearing, 1997) and precipitated by a drive for the now common catch phrase of 'lifelong learning'. Both these terms suffer from a fuzziness of definition, though a concept of lifelong learning is beginning to be shared by political and economic discourses. At the more liberal end Knapper and Cropley (1995) suggest that lifelong learning is about bridging the gap between education and the outside world, linking education with everyday life needs. Higher education's new role, they suggest, is to 'equip people with lifelong learning skills' (p.45). They define these as the ability to set personal objectives, apply knowledge, evaluate personal learning, skills of information retrieval and interpretation of materials from different subject areas (p.45). Such a goal would surely appeal to a mass HE system and enable inclusivity.

The fragility of this goal in the context of the above values for HE are apparent. On the one hand there is a European driven focus for lifelong learning which is vocationally oriented. This is being adopted by some sectors for instrumental purposes and primarily focuses on skills updating programmes. The narrow emphasis on such an instrumentalist form of learning is critiqued by a number of writers. Hake (1997) suggests that the European focus on lifelong learning for predictable economic imperatives - labour mobility, employability and education and training - ignore the very requirements of education for a risk society on which the more open, critical thinking aspects of HE should be concentrating. Korsgaard (1997) too claims that the labour market imperative has meant that 'other goals have receded' (p.18). They voice anxieties about the potential direction for HE as a contributor to this form of lifelong learning. Scott (1995) suggests that a mass HE system in these domains will become less autonomous. Barnett (1990) expresses concern about a potential skills emphasis on instrumentalism and vocationalism rather than his perceived emancipatory elements of HE. Edwards (1997) challenges the current discourse of lifelong learning which forefronts 'self reliance and economic competitiveness' at the expense of wider societal goals (p.179). He suggests that such a discourse is a strategy for blurring the old boundaries between education and training - a way of marginalising previously acceptable differentials between the two styles of provision. The effect of this is to reconfigure what constitutes today's learning society (p.78).

Amongst these concerns is a consensus that the new university requires a different perception of itself and its relationship to the local as well as global world. McPherson (1991) suggests this might mean that HE becomes a stage, rather than level, of learning in the new lifelong learning models. Here the emphasis shifts from seeing HE as a natural progression from the school accreditation and learning system. It will be more focused on a style of provision accompanied by extensive student support services, open admissions policies, flexible programmes, the promotion of underrepresented groups as well as the continued promotion of excellence. The key to the new HE is to see it as a contributor to lifelong learning, rather than a particular phase in the life cycle. Higher education will be something which is open to all, a learning organisation in itself which relates to and responds to the wider society in which it operates (Longworth, 1997).

So how will this new university look? Lifelong learning visions for HE now oscillate between an emphasis on vocationalism (the European White Paper, 1995 for example) and concerns for the need to maintain a finger on the pulse of social democracy (Williamson, 1998, for example). Nevertheless almost all are in agreement that the new university must be seen within a lifelong learning perspective of continuous learning throughout the adult lifespan, which will have to deal with a more heterogeneous student body than previously, alongside a concern by some that universities need a stronger regional role and accountability to the public (Williamson and Coffield, 1997).

A New Higher Education

Adults are now the majority in HE. The nature of full time and part time study is already changing. The campus university has already diversified:

> The adult university represents a major paradigm shift in demand on the mission of the university, sits squarely at the centre of this contested redefinition of purpose and angst over identity (Bourgeois et al., 1999: 20).

Equally, justifications for HE study for other than work reasons are also being mooted in the predicted 'post-full-employment society' (ibid: 28). HE, it is argued, has additional roles for its citizens.

The race is on to come up with a notion of HE which is not itself marginalised - one which embraces plurality and goes beyond practical perceptions of labour market needs. So what are the challenges to the new HE? What aspects of today's society are predicating the need for change? Middlehurst (1997) suggests universities need a broader definition of quality. Quality is also about accountability to the wider public. Rather than assessing quality on the basis of entry requirements into specific degree programmes with predefined outcomes, quality should include looking at the process of quality enhancement of the learning experience. Coffield and Williamson (1997) and Scott (1997) point to the issue of knowledge itself. Where universities were once the main producers of knowledge, defined by their own theoretical boundaries, experiential knowledge is now a competitive commodity, defined and produced by people outside of the university. So Coffield and Williamson (1997) point out that HE is no longer the main producer of knowledge; it no longer produces universal truths (if it ever did) and the public are no longer prepared to tolerate a system of education which makes few links with them. To ensure wider public support HE institutions need to meet more diverse public needs. Robertson (1997), too, claims that universities need to make friends with the public at large in order to remain a leader in the field of higher learning. McNair (1997a) interprets this as universities needing to embrace a wider field of knowledge. Coffield and Williamson suggest that one way forward is to equip a broader range of students with an understanding of how to learn for themselves, rather than transmit knowledge itself. Barnett (1997a, 1997b, 1998) suggests that the old emphasis on discipline based critical thinking skills needs to be broadened to include more attention to critical action, the use of 'the lived experience' and self reflection abilities (1997b: 69). The university must concentrate on preparing students to understand a world of super complexity (Barnett, 2000). He suggests the new student needs to acquire 'metabilities' to stimulate change, not just respond to it. The challenge is to enlist HE: 'To develop human beings capable not just of living in a world of uncertainty, but of contributing actively to it' (Barnett, 1998: 21). It might be said that it is the very complexity of the world today which needs to be translated into the higher learning abilities of the new HE student.

There is no shortage of suggestions about how this broader purpose of HE might function, ranging from the conceptual to the organisational. Barnett's (1997a) vision is broadly conceptual. He suggests that if HE's role is to problematise knowledge then the new institution should build an environment which emphasises critical learning, rather than teaching. He even proposes that no topic should be 'off limits' in HE (1997b: 2). He states that we need a new concept of HE: 'Which starts from the understanding that the world is unknowable in any serious sense' (1997a: 43). The new metabilities to be developed will combine the traditional academic domain of critical thinking with a greater exploration of the role of self (reflexivity) in dialogue, and application of practical understanding (praxis) - resulting in 'metacritique' (p.42). He is one of the few writers to attempt a description of how the new learning experience might function. He suggests, for instance that:

> Students are challenged through the interpersonal character of their experiences to justify themselves and to come up with creative formulations in both their thinking and their actions (1997b: 167).

Unlike the more traditional notion of objectivity, where the authoritative text is the medium for analysing knowledge, Barnett goes beyond this. He proposes a synthesis of critique between knowledge, the self and the world: 'Critical being means investing something of yourself' (1997b: 172).

This is a more radical concept than the one produced by the officially commissioned Dearing report (1997) to propose a model of HE for the twenty first century, but Dearing and Barnett's models are both relevant to the engagement of adult learners, as future chapters will show. Dearing essentially followed a practice based approach responsive to the demands of industry. So Dearing proposed the development of broad intellectual skills rather than subject specialisms at an early stage in the undergraduate programme, and the incorporation of work experience, with flexible, modularised teaching. Such an environment would operate within a national qualifications framework to facilitate portability of qualifications and the opportunity to stop and re-start HE at various points in the life-cycle. Whilst chapter three will look more specifically at core skills as a learning framework for community education it is worth noting here that Dearing's original, and longer, list of skills included many that have already been cited as essential to the HE learning experience, such as critical thinking, information appreciation and management, problem identification and solving.

Ironically, in view of Dearing's focus on the professionalisation of university teaching, for the most part writers on behalf of the future university have emphasised its need to concentrate on the development of learning rather than teaching (Longworth, 1997; Watson and Taylor, 1998; McNair, 1998). Of these publications the latter two attempt a more organisational concept of the future university and with particular reference to adult learners. Watson and Taylor (1998) identify some key features which they see as inevitable for the HE system - ranging from a notion that all universities should still retain a sense that they are the conscience of democratic society, to a recognition that the sector as a whole will continue in the foreseeable future to consist of hierarchical differentiation including diversity of missions and research emphases. The new HE system is envisaged, nevertheless, to be inclined to a stronger focus on work experience elements in its curriculum. This includes attention to a wider, more interdisciplinary curriculum base, probably devised more collaboratively, and in closer interaction with the wider community. It will belong to a credit rated system involving flexible teaching which leans more towards facilitation of learning rather than a traditionally top down imposed teaching style. To this Williamson and Coffield (1997) add that universities will need to demonstrate a clearer transparency of purpose and more emphasis on collaboration with outside agencies in devising and accrediting learning, partly as a result of the need for diversified funding of programmes. In spite of these leanings towards the local community there is an implicit assumption - particularly amongst the more recent writers - that HE will still provide its curriculum from the central campus. So Johnstone (1999), for instance, talks about the virtual university where space is virtual and teaching is digital, but the curriculum implicitly comes from the campus. Alternatively the adult university means adult students are brought into the existing university infrastructure (Brennan et al., 1999; Bourgeois et al., 1999). Even though Bourgeois et al. acknowledge that the continuing education model is often peripatetic, the idea is generally to access the campus curriculum.

McNair (1997a, 1998), following the NIACE (1993) policy document, more specifically focuses on the relationship between the student experience and knowledge - which links back to Barnett's notion of critical being. He suggests that adult learners will bring their own experience and understanding to the traditional curriculum. This will mean a stronger student engagement in knowledge creation, challenging its traditional 'monopoly over the validity of knowledge' (p.36). The result will be a curriculum which inevitably relates more closely to the outside world and meets many needs, with outcomes which are achievement led, rather than leading to the traditional three year degree programme. He also, more openly than most, suggests that 'higher' education may not necessarily happen solely within the university. It will be a kind of education which is made explicit by its style rather than content or place of learning. As is already the case in most continuing education programmes, quality of candidate will not be defined by initial entry requirements, but on outcomes and achievements of individual students. Taking aside funding issues for the time being, he cites three key features which will underpin the new HE system. Firstly a skills based core curriculum would consist of analysis, critical thinking, problem solving and communication. Secondly there would also be a strong learner support and guidance system. A learner, rather than subject centred curriculum would require tutoring and guidance as their central function, rather than act as bolt on services. Thirdly a credit framework which enables maximum flexibility and mobility of students would be modular and have clearly defined learning goals. Indeed Bourgeois et al (1999) provide evidence of campus activity on these lines. These features are explored in chapters four to seven in terms of their practicalities for community based learners.

From these proposals it is possible to conceive of some form of generic approach for a new kind of HE. There will be an emphasis on forefronting the learner experience, combining theory, reflection and practice and a closer dialogue with the outside world, including the public at large. Higher education, if it is to survive, has to become more relevant to the paymasters, but also has to identify and make transparent its distinctive contribution to knowledge creation. What is missing from these visions is a reality perspective of how the macro will translate into the micro. How can HE enter into a dialogue with its community at its most local level? What aspects of learner identity must be considered for this to take place? How do we engage with a credit system which focuses on achievement and works with open entry from a disenfranchised adult public? How can 'higher' translate into 'mass', so that it includes the most excluded? How do we develop a lifelong learning curriculum for those who are already outside the labour market? How does HE begin to deconstruct its traditional knowledge bases to engage with experiential knowledge? What is the interface between these experiences and social capital? What does a curriculum 'off limits' look like? How does a higher learning experience which forefronts guidance rather than knowledge transmission really work? What is higher education progression in this context?

The following chapters attempt to answer these questions by putting the above theoretical perspectives into a reality context. They describe and analyse community learning which involves underrepresented groups, addresses modularisation, credit accumulation, assessable outcomes, an HE skills framework and accountability to the local region. They also explore some of the issues around the two speed world of those with and those without information technology. Then the learners themselves put such learning into their own life history contexts and demonstrate how their HE learning experience both builds on existing social networks and feeds into new forms of social capital. The goal of this book is to engage with the practical reality of some of the above notions of a kind of HE and look at some possible ways forward for disenfranchised groups, based on our own experience of attempting to address this issue.

But we do not wish to delude ourselves that we are straying too far from the dominant discourses of our time. Whatever our solutions they will necessarily be constrained by language which already defines what counts as synthesis, creativity and knowledge creation. In the words of Edwards:

> A discourse of access to provision may well increase and widen participation, but this will be within certain cultural boundaries, signifying specific exercises of power. Indeed part of that power is precisely in constructing questions of participation and non participation as cultural - that participation can be extended through the technical alteration to the delivery of the curriculum alone. This combines technical and practical rationality, thereby limiting the challenge to established practices and dominant norms (Edwards, 1997: 115).

Nevertheless we think we have gone further than most in looking at how HE might meet the needs of those currently least involved in its programmes.

2 Action and Research

Research processes are rarely detailed in book publications. As our research design was inextricably interwoven with the project's activities, we felt it important to explain these connections. This chapter therefore does two things. It reviews the contextual background for the Community Access Programme (CAP). It also examines the relationship between action research and the practice of widening provision with local community groups.

CAP provides a link between the university with its international global connections and the localised context of community groups. The programme undertakes two distinctive but complementary functions. Firstly, it provides tailor made courses in collaboration with community partners. Although course validation systems were consistent with university quality assurance procedures a number of distinctive features were developed for our purpose. The programme's generic features outlined in this chapter are expanded upon in section two where we examine some specific adaptations concerning curriculum content, key skills and guidance provision. The second and complementary function undertaken by CAP was our evaluation of the impact of HE intervention on adult learners as well as an exploration of the academic and personal support needs of adult learners who don't have a history of higher education participation. In essence this second function was concerned with extending our understanding of the issues and improving our own and others' provision. The action (courses) and research were both clearly influenced by the adult learners with whom we worked. We therefore give here a snapshot of the gender, age, ethnicity, disability and educational and employment histories of all CAP learners. More details about three specific groups of learners are provided in section three of the book.

In writing this chapter we were conscious of the web of policies, significant events, communities, cultures, attitudes, values, beliefs, experiences, and people that interfaced with the programme. Teasing out issues from this complex web of factors was not easy. For the purposes of this discussion however, we have divided the web into four sections -

background context, our programme, our action research model, and the adult learners and their communities.

Background Context

Three external factors influenced the general development of community adult education provision during 1993-95. Firstly, the shift toward accreditation, a challenge imposed by the Higher Education Funding Council for England (HEFCE, 1995/96a) and one that was to be tackled in a myriad of ways by continuing education providers throughout the UK (Hunter, 1995; Hunter et al., 1995). Due to its focus on outreach CAP was largely unaffected by this development. Courses continued to be offered without credit although an optional higher education skills framework was developed to accredit those courses for students who wished to work toward HE access level credits (see chapter four for further details).

The second external factor was the funding impetus provided in 1995, again from HEFCE (1995/96b). This was in the form of a four-year initiative to widen provision in higher education. This initiative included two strands, each designed to enhance and widen provision in the existing higher education system. The first strand was intended to develop liberal adult education. In many cases it maintained support for the existing traditional continuing education students. The second strand that provided valuable financial support for our programme focused on non-award bearing provision. In this initiative courses were required to be accessible and relevant to those least able to benefit from higher education.

CAP tackled this work by developing partnerships with a variety of statutory and voluntary agencies. The latter included local branches of larger organisations such as Age Concern. There were also groups formed by local people, either on a self-help basis or to support a targeted group. CAP adopted a course development model that was typical of many community development initiatives (Elliot et al., 1996; Johnston, 1992; Stuart, 1996; Stuart and Thomson, 1997; Ward, 1996). We established effective channels of communication by drawing on programme staff members' previous life and work experiences. In reality the world of the university and community were very different. For effective collaboration it was essential that interaction with the cultures of both kinds of communities acquired the viewpoint and language of each community in order to be accepted (Brown and Duguid, 1996). This was especially important during the process of preparing courses for validation or when employing tutors who work for other education and training providers.

The third external factor that influenced our work and that of others in continuing education was the European Social Fund (ESF). Whilst our approach to course development remained constant during this period, our entrée into seeking and securing funding from ESF influenced the geographical location, student participation and some aspects of course administration! Retrospectively it is clear that each of the aforementioned factors engendered its' own combination of benefits and constraints, some of which were not as obvious at the commencement of the funding grant. For example, a one-year ESF programme with the long-term unemployed adults enabled us to develop a model of guidance that could be used with subsequent students. It also imposed certain constraints. These were associated with ESF administrative requirements, which will be all too familiar to anyone in receipt of ESF funding.

These external factors not only influenced our programme but also national debates about the purpose of higher education and continuing education. For instance, the impetus for awarding credit in continuing education was driven by notions of human capital. Accreditation supplied the mechanism for ensuring that higher education was able to serve those seeking continuing professional development or retraining for alternative employment. The widening provision initiative re-opened the debate about the profile of adult learners. The non award bearing strand not only gave prominence to people not usually represented within the HE mainstream it provided opportunities for enhancing the human capital of adults who might otherwise be a drain on the welfare system. Finally Europe provided financial incentives which were a useful, albeit a highly prescriptive, source of income for educational providers looking to enhance the employability of the unemployed. To varying degrees all factors offered opportunities to increase the country's economic success in a rapidly changing global economy.

This then, was the backdrop for institutional initiatives that involved the accreditation of courses and development of appropriate support mechanisms to meet a more diverse student population. We now move on to describe the key features of our programme.

Our Programme

The Community Access Programme is based in Lancaster University's Department of Educational Research. The adult learners targeted by CAP included people who had left school with minimal qualifications and usually came from socio-economic groups four and five. Additionally these adults belonged to some form of community group or agency designed to meet the particular needs of older adults, members of a minority ethnic community, as long-term unemployed or people who had a disability. This cohort of adult learners described in the early nineties as 'non participants' (McGivney, 1990), contrasted with the educated, white, middle class students who typically enrolled on the university's liberal adult education courses. (For further information about the origins of the programme see (Preece, 1999; Preece, 1999a). A summary of the CAP student profile is described later in this chapter.

For the duration of this project CAP was an action research project staffed by a team of women with diverse personal and professional backgrounds. Our collective personal profiles, educational and life histories afforded us opportunities to enter into and make connections with working class, minority ethnic and disability groups. Although we tended to work primarily with the groups for whom we might be considered to be a role model, our collaborative team approach enabled us all to work with groups interchangeably. By 1995 the programme had grown in size to include one full time lecturer/programme manager, one full and one part time research associate; all of whom acted as community co-ordinators with specific areas of expertise. The programme was also fortunate to have an administrative assistant who skilfully assisted members of the programme, liaised with a variety of community contacts and juggled the diverse range of material generated from the courses and research. In addition to the core and centrally located team of co-ordinators the programme employed community tutors, the majority of whom were also role models, familiar with the learner group and living locally to the adult learners.

The main action component of CAP's work was collaboration with local communities in order to provide short courses for adult groups. Throughout the project we collaborated with a variety of community organisations. In summary our partnerships with these organisations involved work with:

- learners from minority ethnic communities, predominately women of Asian heritage;
- members of self help and statutory disability groups, including people with physical, sensory disabilities, chronic illness and two groups with learning difficulties;
- young people working with the youth service;
- older adults attending their local Age Concern centres;
- 'women returners' attending women's groups, community centres and their local primary school;
- people who were long term unemployed;

- and one group of prisoners.

Courses were developed in each case for a particular group of learners. Consequently, each course provided the learners with a culturally or socially relevant curriculum and an opportunity to gain optional credit. In addition the courses were intended to enable adults to move into higher level study through staged progression. To achieve these goals CAP had to span two very different worlds – the university and the community. To facilitate the course validation process it was necessary to create systems that allowed CAP to be responsive to the needs of the adult learners whilst still complying with university course validation requirements.

A course validation procedure was devised that involved considerable consultation with community organisations and the intended participants. Course proposal forms (appendix one) were designed to prompt those responsible for developing and ultimately validating the courses to consider in detail the relevance and rationale of all aspects of a course for each group of learners. Aspects of course delivery that are frequently taken for granted such as the time, place and pace of learning were therefore carefully scrutinised. In addition consultation procedures and potential study support needs were incorporated in the course proposal forms. These included childcare, British Sign Language or Bi-lingual translation, single sex provision, accessible venue and assistance with transport. Over time sections addressing issues of employability and educational guidance were integrated into the form. This had the effect of ensuring that course tutors and those validating the course considered such matters. The validation procedure followed the standard university model of scrutiny by departmental colleagues. The feedback systems, however, were modified to enable courses to be validated more quickly and be responsive to local needs.

Courses fell into two main categories. Firstly, pre-access courses introduced a group into education after a long absence of involvement and allowed the tutor to identify with the learners their ability to cope with more academic courses. Although categorised as pre access in level these courses were different from others available in the community, which tended to be more practical. CAP courses were distinctive in terms of curriculum content which was not typical of campus university education but offered learners an opportunity to reflect on and analyse their own experience. In addition the courses focused on developing learners' ability to think critically and acquire good study habits. The second type of CAP course offered optional credit and was based on one of four foundation credit frameworks. These foundation credit frameworks enabled learners to develop skills relevant to higher education. Content was framed as personal development, study, investigation or enterprise related. Chapter four provides further discussion about the foundation credit frameworks in terms of their potential for enhancing higher education skills, level of learning, the outcomes for the students and the teaching and learning process.

There were other distinctive features relating to CAP course delivery. Wherever possible we employed role model tutors who shared something in common with the learners. They formed the bridge between a community organisation and the university. They complemented the role assumed by CAP staff. Community co-ordinators and tutors tended to have closer links with a community and might be described as 'insiders', whereas the CAP university based staff tended to live at a distance and thus retained their 'outsider' status (Cruikshank, 1994). Regardless of their status within the community tutors and CAP co-ordinators alike operated as 'street level bureaucrats' (Hudson, 1993) mediating between the different communication and administration strategies and organisational cultures. This was important as their ability to understand and satisfy the requirements of community *and* university was vital if the courses were to be regarded as credible by all participants.

Other aspects of CAP's quality assurance procedure were also adapted to take account of the adult learners' life and educational experiences. Course evaluation forms included a host of progression indicators that enabled learners to indicate personal achievement and development. The indicators moved beyond the simple attainment of certification that tend to be the only measure recognised by supporters of a human capital approach. So for instance becoming a member of or increasing use of the library, participation in the community organisations activities, more regular course attendance, and subjective measures relating to confidence and assertiveness were all listed on the evaluation forms. (See chapter three for a breakdown of these progression indicators.) Similarly the educational guidance forms, developed in consultation with tutors, formed the basis of a more comprehensive and student centred recording mechanism for learner support issues. (See chapter six for further details.)

In addition to developing courses CAP was keen to pursue a range of research activities that were relevant to the theme of educational equality. The research we undertook was closely related to our action and was designed to increase our own understanding about the participation of adults with limited experience of education since leaving school. Like our course design it was necessary to develop a research strategy that served a number of purposes and addressed issues that related to our action.

Our Action Research Model

Predominately action research models are based on a cyclical approach, usually with a variety of feedback loops that involve, to a greater or lesser extent, practitioners themselves as researchers. Although it would have been interesting to embark on a fully participatory model whereby we involved our tutors in all stages of the research, constraints of time and funding meant this was not practical.

In collaboration with students and tutors we researched the impact of *our* action and intervention. We decided to have two research strands. The first focused on attitudes towards, and perceptions of higher education. This strand enabled students and tutors to consider to what extent CAP intervention and contact with community tutors and university personnel influenced or affected their perceptions about higher education. The second explored the educational guidance and support needs of the adult learners with whom we worked. Additionally and perhaps more importantly it sought to explore tutors' understanding of the guidance terminology and the strategies they used to deliver guidance in the community. Although there was considerable overlap between the issues covered each strand involved its own action-research cycle. The distinctive features of each strand are outlined briefly here.

Educational Experience and Attitudes Toward Higher Education

This was the most complex strand. We concentrated on in-depth, semi-structured interviews from three groups of learners: older adults, women of Asian heritage and adults with physical and sensory disabilities. These distinctive and clearly differentiated groups were invited to take part in the more focused strand of the research. They were chosen for a number of reasons. Firstly, their collective group characteristics, secondly their geographical location - South Cumbria, North and East Lancashire - and finally, the established relationships of the agency contacts with the community access programme. In almost all cases the learners were currently on a low income or claiming benefit. They had left school at the earliest opportunity, with no or very few qualifications. Furthermore they would be considered by some, including themselves, as least likely to benefit from higher education.

We also referred to information on enrolment and evaluation forms plus records of CAP staff meetings, course proposal forms, student assignments and 'head notes' (Barton and Hamilton, 1998) of community visits and discussions with learners, tutors and community contacts. Each of these data sources has enabled us to contextualise issues emerging in the learners' personal stories.

We supplemented these interviews with more quantitative data from participants across the programme. A postal questionnaire was sent to all our widening provision course participants (approximately 400). The questionnaire included key issues relating to their educational experience, involvement and attitudes about CAP courses, future educational plans and progression routes. Given the diversity of our students' backgrounds, life and educational experiences there were some difficulties involved in designing a generic questionnaire, primarily related to the use of language. Despite this caveat, the results obtained from this postal questionnaire reveal some interesting patterns. They are discussed in chapter three, which also reviews the characteristics of community groups.

Educational Guidance and Learner Support

The guidance and learner support strand involved all groups of learners. We utilised information from educational guidance forms that were developed in consultation with tutors and incorporated into the programme's quality assurance procedure. These forms required tutors to record pre-course, on course as well as end of course needs. In addition to this statistical data, each group of learners was invited to participate in an end of course, focus group discussion, which used a semi-structured framework of questions. The CAP team conducted semi-structured interviews with tutors and community contacts. These provided a significant amount of information about the terminology used within the area of guidance. Chapter six draws upon this information to illustrate how tutors identified learner needs and integrated guidance activities into the curriculum.

It is worth discussing in more detail the distinctive process of our action-research engagement in the context of this particular programme as it significantly influences our ability to reach marginalised voices.

Reinharz (1992) cites the work of action researcher Crystal Eastman who advocates the importance of a plan of action prior to commencement of the research. She contends that the research process involves change that is designed to improve the situation under investigation. External agencies undoubtedly influenced our action plans. For instance the remit outlined in the aims and objectives of our HEFCE widening provision project determined the groups and course targets that we were expected to meet. In addition we integrated the personal and collective goals of the programme team. Essentially these related to social justice, recognising and valuing difference and enabling individuals to realise their full potential. Like Lather our intention was to:

> Empower through empirical research, designs which maximise a dialogic, dialectically educative encounter between researcher and researched. ... What I suggest is that our intent more consciously be to use our research to help participants understand and change their situations (Lather, 1988 in Reinharz, 1992: 175).

To this, we would want to add the caveat that change of situation is the choice and responsibility of the individual learners as well as ourselves. We sought to stimulate change by utilising our research findings to inform and encourage policy makers, funding agencies and practitioners to take account of the diverse needs of adult learners. Many of the students expressed an interest in participating in this kind of higher education, providing it was able to respond to their needs. A responsive HE needs to address institutional barriers that relate to personal, cultural and structural issues. For the individual learners, increasing understanding of their situation, especially in respect of their guidance and support needs, is an essential prerequisite to personal change and future progression. We return to the issues associated with educational guidance in chapter six. The cyclical nature of action research, together with the relationships we endeavoured to establish, allowed us to incorporate feedback from our tutors and community contacts into subsequent provision. This process was a positive learning encounter for us, and we hope our tutors.

Cynthia Chertos (1987), cited by Reinharz (1992:179) stresses the importance of 'usable research'. Usability is a prime concern for CAP in terms of improving our own provision. The research approach we ultimately adopted contained aspects of an action research model that presents action and evaluation as proceeding simultaneously (Kelly, 1985, Smail et al., 1982). We disseminated the research findings to our community contacts and the wider community of professional practitioners to whom we belong. This strategy proved useful as it allowed our findings to be used, evaluated, modified and reused. Staff development sessions, for instance, provided tutors with an opportunity to comment upon issues emerging from the research. The events also encouraged tutors to exchange personal as well as pedagogical ideas with other practitioners committed to providing higher education in a community context. Likewise the research process assisted individual tutors in evaluating and refining their own teaching, learning and guidance practice. The benefits of enabling participants (in this case tutors) to use the research process for their own goals is discussed elsewhere (Houghton, 1998b).

We used this action and evaluation model to modify and improve aspects of our data collection strategies. For example, the focus group discussions influenced the educational guidance research strand, and the strategies used to gain access to our interviewees within the HE strand.

It has been argued that there are inadequate strategies for representing the voice of adults who are considered least likely to benefit from higher education. In effect this perpetuates their powerlessness and reduces the possibility of change that is responsive to these learners needs (Reinharz, 1992). Tutors and community contacts responded positively to our invitation to become involved. They recognised that they had valuable contributions to make, but few opportunities or forums in which to share their expertise. Consequently, tutors welcomed the opportunity to be involved in this additional aspect of CAP's work. The commitment of these key informants and gatekeepers was equally significant in aiding our access to the adult learners whose voices we were particularly keen to hear.

There were many complexities and dilemmas associated with trying to give greater prominence to the voices of our tutors, community contacts and adult learners. Kay Standing in her chapter entitled: 'Writing the voices of the less powerful' highlights many of the dilemmas we faced. For instance, the terminology we used in writing up this research, the format of transcribed statements, their selection and position in the final text was in the final analysis our decision (Standing, 1998). We recognised the inherent tension between our desire to let the adult learners speak and produce an academically acceptable text. Faced, like others, with the desire to span the community of academia and less powerful communities, we opted in this context to use their words to support the themes that emerged during our process of analysis. In other forums, the voice of our students, tutors and community contacts is presented in a more direct and less processed form. For example, students delivered CAP's presentation at the Northern Network of Non Award Bearing Continuing Education Conference - Voices in the Community (Houghton and Ali, 1998). However, it is worth noting that over time their words have become part of our own way of thinking about and expressing particular messages concerning attitudes about higher education, guidance and learner support needs. Conversely the students have adopted our phrases and terminology, so that in some cases it is unclear where the words originated. Perhaps this is a feature of the cyclical action research process?

Returning to the commonalties of our research strands tutors and agency contacts, operating as 'key informants', provided additional background information about CAP provision - especially in relation to learning contexts, teaching styles and the impact on some adults of this type of educational intervention. In some cases tutors shared additional insights about the learners that could be pursued within the individual interviews for the higher education research strand. For instance, when tutors interviewed the students they often used their insider knowledge to good effect, by probing and enabling the students to describe experiences that they knew would be of interest to us as researchers. Alternatively, the tutor interviews and on-going dialogue with members of the CAP team alerted us to issues worthy of further discussion with the students. The existing relationships between our key informants and the students undoubtedly increased the interviewer access to information that was highly relevant to the topics under consideration, but which may not have emerged during a more objective, formalised interview approach. Another consideration was the number of times we would interview people. Barton and Hamilton (1998) in their study of 'Local Literacies' highlight the benefit of repeated interviews and the potential limitation of one-off interviews. Whilst concurring with this observation, the constraints of our project meant that it was only possible to formally interview students twice, with a year gap. Fortunately, because of the regular contact regarding course provision we obtained valuable supplementary information between interviews via a host of informal conversations with students. Additionally tutor and agency feedback enriched and helped verify the reality of the data collected during the two taped interviews.

In addition to their role as key informants, our community contacts played a pivotal role as gatekeepers to the adult learners. As alluded to earlier, they had considerable power to encourage or sabotage our attempts to get access to the adult learners. Miller's account of using gatekeepers highlights some of the potential difficulties associated with using intermediaries to access participants in the research process. These include issues of confidentiality, a lack of understanding about the research, the impact of the gatekeepers and allegiance towards them (Miller, 1998). Some of these we experienced. For example, the impact of the gatekeepers' influence on student participation in the research process was often difficult to determine. In some cases interviewees clearly wanted to be involved to please their community leader:

> I said I'd be interviewed because I was nervous, and because I thought well if this is going to help the group go ahead, then I would be interviewed (Bernadette, Bridge Centre).

Clearly students used interviews as an opportunity to offer their opinion about certain issues in confidence. The course referred to by Sarah in the following quote had two tutors whose advice regarding assignments was slightly different. This student, like others, used the confidentiality of the interview to express concern about this situation.

> The only thing I disliked about it (the course) was the goal posts changing, you didn't quite know what you were supposed to be doing. It could have been my misunderstanding, I just don't really know (Sarah, DAB Centre).

Thankfully our gatekeepers did not expect us to break confidences. Their involvement in the research also meant that their role as gatekeeper was generally an encouraging rather than a sabotaging one. The time and potential difficulties associated with gaining access especially to those not normally involved in research should not however be underestimated.

Our interview style and data analysis is the final common feature for the higher education and educational guidance research strands. Our interviews were partially interactive. The interviewer engaged in some self-disclosure and was able to share the culture of the informant (Burgess, 1982; Lather, 1991). This was particularly prevalent in those interviews where interviewer and interviewee shared, for example, personal background, religious belief, or disability status.

We chose semi-structured interviews as they provided a framework for covering certain issues but still allowed the interviewer a degree of flexibility to follow the story of the person being interviewed. The interview schedules were used to guide the discussion. So for example, the higher education strand included questions relating to the following themes: past educational experience; family involvement and encouragement in education; post school educational experience; attitudes and experience of higher education (universities); the present CAP provision and future plans. Students were interviewed twice with a year gap between each interview. Interviews lasted between forty-five and ninety minutes. People known to the student undertook the interviews that were held in familiar locations - either their home or community centre.

We made a conscious decision to use community contacts as interviewers as they were part of the social setting and known to the learners. Consequently they were well positioned to make sense as well as understand the meaning behind comments made during the interview. This decision was based on earlier research experiences of the team (Preece and Bokhari, 1996); like all research decisions, it brought with it advantages as well as disadvantages. For the women of Asian heritage it revealed information that almost certainly would not have been available to someone external to the community.

For the educational guidance strand, the interviews were slightly more structured and designed to identify specific practices used by a tutor.

Again we employed a flexible interactive approach that allowed the needs of a specific learner group to be explored in-depth. The interviews with tutors and community contacts were taped and subsequently transcribed.

We invited interviewees from both research strands to talk freely about issues. This was encouraged through a series of prompts prepared under each of the main questions. We followed up points of interest at the time, which resulted in a more naturalistic conversation. This had implications when it came to data analysis but for the less confident interviewees who thought they had to give the right answer and who were trying to please us, it meant that researcher interference was kept to a minimum. As Cottle (1978) states:

> Without allowing people to speak freely we will never know what their real intentions are, and what the true meaning of their words might be (Cottle (1978) in Burgess, 1982: 109).

The process of analysis involved repeated reading, annotation, coding and discussion about themes emerging from the transcriptions. The common educational concepts for us were core skills, educational guidance and the nature of higher education. These were considered in the light of broader themes outlined in chapter one which included social capital, citizenship and the impact of globalisation. Additionally the personal stories from three groups of learners highlighted specific issues appertaining to disability, older adults and women of Asian heritage. The commonalties of these three groups included their early school leaving age, working class status and identity associated with disability, retirement or unwaged/unemployment benefits. Earlier analysis of aspects of our data has resulted in discussions about curriculum (Preece and Bokhari, 1996); core skills (Preece, 1999b); credit frameworks (Preece, 1997); working in partnership (Houghton, 1997); educational guidance and learner support (Houghton, 1998b; Houghton and Bokhari, 1998) and action research (Houghton, 1998a).

Adult Learners and Their Communities

Before discussing our themes in more depth it would be helpful to outline the general profile of the students as far as we were able to collect this information. This summary includes student details in terms of gender, ethnicity, disability, employment status, previous educational experience and reasons for studying, qualifications gained and progression indicators other than qualifications.

During 1996 and 1998 CAP delivered 98 courses totalling 1143 enrolments. In common with many widening provision projects women account for the majority of students - 844 (74%). This included 833 (73%) white students, 277 (24%) of Asian heritage, 36 (3%) whose ethnicity was unknown or other than any of the above. Largely because of the course content and the local delivery most courses tended to have a majority of students whose ethnic, cultural background was the same. Overall 349 (31%) students declared that they had a disability. In the main these students belonged to community groups designed to help and support people who have a disability. With one exception (a group created for and with adults who have a learning disability) the groups catered for students with a range of physical and sensory disabilities often linked to chronic health conditions.

The majority of learners - 954 (83%) were unemployed, unwaged and/or claiming a state benefit. Distinctions about the length of their unemployment or reasons for unemployment were not recorded. However tutor observations about a learner's attendance, their need for travel assistance or childcare support is discussed elsewhere. Only 67 (6%) learners were in part time employment whilst studying, and courses targeted at older adults accounted for the 122 (11%) learners who were retired.

It was interesting that the majority of these students did not start with the intention of entering higher education, but were motivated more by the opportunity to enhance their employment prospects. Whatever their motivation this initial involvement was significant because as the Learning Divide Survey (Sargant et al: vii, 1997) confirms: 'Recent experience of learning is a powerful influence on whether adults expect to study in the future' (key finding 18).

Although the challenge of trying to widen provision to include adult learners who often left school early without formal qualifications and who have no recent experience of learning was built into the programme, obtaining information about previous educational experience was a complex task. The student enrolment form asked students to indicate their highest level of qualification and the date they obtained it. Although on the surface this was a straightforward question, the range of names for equivalent qualifications, such as school certificate, 'O' level, GCSE, GNVQ 2 and Open College North West Stage A added considerable complication. Perhaps more significantly, the level and comparability of overseas qualifications proved most challenging.

Despite this caveat, for students enrolled on credit courses we recorded 680 (67%) as having no formal qualifications, 212 (21%) with GCSEs and 46 (5%) with 'A' levels or equivalent. Overall 120 (11%) of learners had a professional or degree level qualification. Their involvement in CAP courses was a result of changes in their personal circumstances such as unemployment or an acquired disability (including the onset of a mental health problem). These changes in their personal situation appeared to be important in attracting them to local, culturally and socially relevant curricula delivered in bite sized pieces. Further details about CAP learners obtained from the postal questionnaire are discussed in the next chapter.

Conclusion

In this chapter we have attempted to describe what was a very complex situation. The inter- relationship between external and internal factors at a particular time clearly shaped the development of provision for adults with previously low participation in higher education. The current prominence and visible backing by the UK government and HEFCE for widening participation as well as support for the notion of lifelong learning provides a very different context to that existing in the early nineties. Yet the commitment of a four-year project for widening provision was at the time a significant step forward from earlier initiatives. The influence of the European agenda continues to be increasingly important and provides considerable ammunition for advocates of learning for human capital. Universities, albeit differentially, are now responding to calls to address issues of employability and the development of key skills and recruiting and retaining widening participation of students whose identities are largely measured in terms of their postcode. The reasons for more enthusiastic institutional support for widening participation may cynically be regarded as opportunistic. Despite this there does appear to be a greater willingness on the part of senior university personnel to take seriously the challenge to build in opportunities to widen participation. How long this support will last probably depends on funding. However, lessons from the HEFCE widening provision project highlight the importance of embedding work into the institution. Involving senior managers to encourage institutional change and staff awareness of the issues offers the possibility of change lasting beyond the lifetime of current projects. We hope to provide further ammunition for defending these policies, whilst pointing out the complexities of issues surrounding widening participation initiatives.

Explaining the rationale for our course development, validation system and the key features of our provision was difficult because we were endeavouring to make explicit issues which were crystal clear to us because we have lived them. Similarly there was a danger in providing these student profiles that we might fall into the trap of trying to label students as products whose needs can be categorised and then catered for according to predetermined solutions. For example, all unemployed people require x, or women all need y. The analysis of groups of learners' needs was a more thorough process. Course proposal forms were used to record aspects of the negotiation between a global university and local community group. The next chapter elaborates the types of groups to which the learners belonged and how community contacts sought to gain access to education for their learners.

3 Surveying the Provision

> The (Learning Divide) survey confirms that the UK still faces an enormous task in involving all its people in the learning society, and that the learning divide between the learning rich and the learning poor is growing (Sargant et al., 1997: Key finding 3).

The Learning Divide, a study of participation in adult learning in the United Kingdom conducted in 1996, is the most recent NIACE large-scale survey. It looks at the learning habits and goals of adults in the UK and many of its findings are relevant to the task of widening provision in higher education. This chapter covers many of the issues highlighted in the Learning Divide but from the perspective of one particular widening provision project, the Community Access Programme (CAP). It has three main sections. The first is an analysis of the community organisations with whom CAP worked, categorising them in order to identify key features of the learning context they provided for their adult learners. It then examines the results of a postal questionnaire that revealed further information about the previous educational experiences, current learning needs and future goals of CAP students. Finally the chapter explores themes referred to in chapter one - in particular the role of social capital - and considers to what extent it contributes to bridging the learning divide by encouraging adults to engage in learning for the first time since school.

Community Organisations

The community organisations or groups, with whom CAP worked, played a significant role in encouraging people to participate in formal education. In this process we relied heavily on the role of community gatekeepers. The relationship with each group was distinctive and, as with all collaborative arrangements, dependent upon the outcome of a complex set of factors. Community groups are categorised here according to their geographical location, organisational structure, size, objectives and the members of the community they seek to serve (see Table 1 for allocation of groups). Organisational and individual names are fictional throughout.

Organisations are located in South Cumbria (4), North (5), South (3) and East Lancashire (5). They all worked with adults who lived in relatively close proximity to their community centre. Where support with travel was required the centre would often provide transport. They operated at a local and individual level. The university on the other hand operated from local through to global level and not always with individuals.

The community groups' organisational structure and goals generally determined who participated and what kinds of courses were offered. The groups can be divided into four main categories; these included statutory funded centres (5), regional services (3), local branches of national charities (2) and finally local voluntary groups (7). Centres funded by the Prison and Social Services had members who attended as a result of an assessment of their need. Consequently, they had a potentially captive and restricted target group (disabled adults, parents having difficulties and prisoners). Primary schools funded by the LEA, however, used courses to recruit and encourage greater parental involvement and increase local support for the school. The youth service funded by the County Council is a regional service with a clear educational remit designed to empower and enable young adults and unemployed people to participate in education and society more generally. CAP also worked in partnership with FE Colleges to deliver courses for Asian heritage women in community and youth service venues. Although these women belonged to a strong local community they did not belong to a specific organisation which liaised directly with CAP. Liaising voluntary organisations consisted of local branches from national charities (Age Concern, for example). Here CAP worked in partnership with a key link person who co-ordinated the educational programme in line with members' interests. In common with the locally developed self-help groups targeted at unemployed adults or people with a disability, decisions about integrating education into the work of the organisation were normally discussed and decided by a local committee. The intricacy and degree of formality of the partnership between CAP and another organisation is without doubt an issue of considerable import in enabling some adults to access and integrate higher education into their busy lives.

The type and extent of support that each group offered inevitably depended upon a host of external and internal factors. Although funding was guaranteed for statutory organisations it was rarely allocated for education, despite the obvious health, personal, social and community benefits gained from offering courses. In charities and local self-help groups finding the necessary finances remained an ongoing challenge and strain, often leading to a rapid turn over of volunteers and workers. Inevitably this affected continuity and progression opportunities.

Elsdon et al., (1995) offered a series of typologies for categorising voluntary organisations. Two seem useful in the context of this review. The first involves seven descriptors outlining the type of organisational activities and objectives. The descriptors are: 1) social service, community development, umbrella bodies; 2) advocacy; 3) health education, mutual support, care; 4) physical activity; 5) specific interests and hobbies; 6) sociability; and 7) provision for women. Many, if not all, of these organisational activities offer the potential for developing and extending the social capital available within a local community. There was however a significant difference in the local reality of this potential. Policy makers may, in global terms, discuss and recognise the benefits of women only provision, for instance. The translation of such a policy at a local level needs to recognise that a women only course is not necessarily going to address or serve the needs of all women. It would be inaccurate to assume that Asian heritage women would automatically participate in a course because it was only for women. Other relevant factors must be taken into consideration - for example, where the course is to be held or who the tutor is. As one community co-ordinator explained, getting women from different backgrounds to attend a course was not always straightforward. At a community level there were sometimes hidden issues that would mean women living in adjacent streets would not want to attend the same course.

Elsdon's second category relates to the size of the group; 0-29 members constitute a small group, 30-99 a medium group and 100 plus is described as a large group. According to these definitions CAP worked with 5 (30%) small groups, 6 (35%) medium groups and 6 (35%) large groups. In some cases the numbers of students involved in CAP courses was very small.

The final criterion for categorising groups that worked in partnership with CAP is the type of person they seek to serve. Two community groups were age related. The youth service, which offered courses for under 25's, and Age Concern who catered for the older adults. Other community groups were linked to other distinguishing features, for example, ethnicity (4), disability (6) and unemployment (4). This type of categorisation brings with it gains and losses. As Elsdon et al., explain in their review of voluntary organisations:

> A sense of narrowing or limitation, as well as insecurity, is felt most strongly by those who are permanently or temporarily the victims of conditions or characteristics, which distinguish them from what are, or seem to be, majorities (Elsdon et al., 1995: 56).

CAP adult learners have traditionally not participated in higher education. Many of them have characteristics that distinguish them from the white eighteen year old, middle class male who until recently represented the typical university student. There is always a danger of falling into the trap of assuming that all Muslim women, or disabled adults, or any other group of learners automatically have the same learner support needs. Although conscious of this trap, CAP tended to gain access to these learners by collaboration with groups who targeted and worked primarily with people who have shared some form of identity or purpose.

Interestingly, commonalties also existed between groups relating to learner support issues rather than personal characteristics. For instance, travel was a common issue. However, for some the difficulties related to cost, whereas for others the problem was one of access or concerns about safety, particularly at night. In addition there were common features that encompassed categories of ethnicity, disability and employment status. These often related to issues associated with social capital. They included family experience of higher education, space to study, access to written information, computer facilities, or experience of making sense of educational terminology and the bureaucracy associated with university (Beinart and Smith, 1998; Brown and Lauder, 1997; CIHE, 1997; McGivney, 1990; Sargant et al., 1997). Unfortunately the underlying assumption that all adult learners are willing and able to overcome their particular barriers to learning by calling in favours and accessing help from their social networks remains prevalent within the mindset of educational providers. For example, finding and having access to funding to cover course fees, learning materials, childcare costs, travel expenses etc. is often a challenge for those on fixed or limited income. Adult learners are not alone in having concerns about hidden course costs. There is increasing evidence to suggest that these concerns are also common amongst full time undergraduate students (Walters and Baldwin, 1998).

Table 1 Features of Community Groups

Organisational Name	Location	Structure #	Objectives *	Size	Learner Group
Riverside Centre	N Lancs	SF	1,2,3,6.	Large	Disability
DAB Centre	S Cumbria	VG	1,2,3,5,6.	Large	Disability
Ash Centre	E Lancs	VG	1,2,5,6.	Medium	Unemployed
Family Centre	N Lancs	SF	1,2,3,5,6 (7)	Medium	Unemployed
Jubilee Centre	S Lancs	VG	1,2,5,6 (7)	Medium	Ethnicity
Poplar Centre	S Lancs	VG	1,2,3,6.	Small	Disability
ARC Centre	S Lancs	VG	1,2,3,5,6.	Small	Disability
Youth group	S Cumbria	RS	1,2,4,5,6.	Large	Age
Bridge Centre	N Lancs	NC	1,3,5,6.	Large	Age
Prison Service	N Lancs	SF	1,2,3,4,5,6.	Large	N/A
Dell Centre	E Lancs	VG	1,2,3,5,6 (7)	Medium	Disability
Thornhill Centre	E Lancs	RS	1,2,5,6,7.	Small	Ethnicity
Forrest School	E Lancs	SF	1,2,5,6,7.	Small	Ethnicity
Water Field Centre	E Lancs	SF	1,2,5,6 (7)	Large	Ethnicity
Community Development	N Lancs	RS	1,2,5,6.	Small	Unemployed
Deaf Association	S Cumbria	NC	1,2,3,5,6.	Medium	Disability
Family History group		VG	5,6.	Medium	Unemployed

Key to Table 1

* Objectives = Elsdon's categories of organisational activities:
1) social service, community development, umbrella bodies;
2) advocacy;
3) health education, mutual support, care;
4) physical activity;
5) specific interests, hobbies;
6) sociability;
7) provision for women.

# Structures = Elsdon's categories of organisations:
SF = statutory funded; VG = voluntary group; NC= national charity; RS= regional service.

These community groups influenced the learning environment and context for the CAP adult learners. Findings from the postal questionnaire sent to all CAP students expand on factors that characterise their difference from the student norm.

The Questionnaire

A student postal questionnaire was devised to complement the overall student profile described in chapter two and explore in more detail observations that had emerged during individual student interviews. The questionnaire also enabled a greater number of CAP students to comment on those features of course provision that they preferred. In particular it allowed them to express their views about what higher education would need to be like for them to continue studying in the future. By asking students after they participated in education, rather than before participation it was not possible to ascertain the extent of the impact of our educational intervention, though the in-depth interviews give some partial insight into this.

Of the 432 questionnaires sent 111 were returned giving a response rate of 26%. Whilst this response rate is low, it did enable us to glean some tendencies which could be substantiated, or not, by the more in-depth interviews. The profile of the people who replied showed that the majority were English - 88 (79%) and female - 76 (69%), with 56 (52%) aged between 36 and 55. Eighty (72%) of the learners had left school by the age of 16. Although this response rate covered the range of CAP students there were a few exceptions. For instance, it was not sent to the male prison students and only a few older adults replied. Despite these exceptions the questionnaire sheds light on issues of time, place and pace of learning together with the potential social capital available to students and their local communities. Percentages are calculated in terms of the number of replies for a specific question. Whilst acknowledging that the number of students for the sub groups (disability and Asian heritage) are small the responses suggest some trends which will be highlighted in the discussion of the results.

The first issue was division of time. To ascertain how students spent their time, what sort of activities they participated in and therefore gain some insight into how education featured in their lives, we asked three related questions. The first was open-ended; it asked students to describe how they spend most of their time each day. The results revealed that the majority spent their time engaged in activities that contributed to the well being of family and others in their local community. Domestic commitments, including housework and family care, accounted for 46 (44%) replies with 28 (27%) either employed or undertaking voluntary work. It may be that conventional definitions of active citizenship place considerable emphasis on the economic contribution that a person can make. Nevertheless there is increasing recognition that the unpaid home, family and voluntary based work is an equally important indicator of citizenship (Barnes, 1997; Jordan, 1997; Lister, 1997; Meekosha and Dowse, 1997).

In addition to making a valuable contribution to the resources of a local community these activities provided numerous opportunities for opening communication channels and extending the networks associated with social capital. Furthermore many of the leisure related activities (hobbies and reading/studying accounting for 46 (44%) of replies), offered the potential for communicating with other people and therefore enlarging an individual's social network.

The second question combined a closed and open-ended section; it asked students to identify how they used the rest of their time. We created a checklist of six spare time options obtained previously from face to face interviews. The replies also included additional information to this list. The total group of students reported that their spare time was spent watching television 72 (65%), attending courses 47 (42%) undertaking committee work 22 (20%), charity work 24 (22%), church/mosque activities 26 (24%) and other 15 (14%). The 'other' activities fell predominately within the study and hobby category.

If social capital is taken to include relationships based on trusting others that lead to an obligation and responsibility towards other people - then taken together the way in which students appeared to spend their time suggested that they have considerable social capital at their disposal. A further breakdown of the questionnaire findings for Asian women and students with a disability revealed that the type of activity varied according to the group of learners. Students with a disability were more likely to engage in committee and charity work, whilst Asian women spent more time undertaking activities linked to the mosque (Table 2).

Table 2 How Participants Spend Their Spare Time

Spare Time Activities	Total n 105	Disability n 29	Asian n 21
1. Committee Work	22 (20%)	10 (35%)	2 (10%)
2. Charity Work	24 (22%)	12 (42%)	2 (10%)
3. Church/Mosque	26 (24%)	3 (10%)	12 (57%)

(N.B. Some people ticked more than one activity)

Putnam (1995) regards television viewing as a key reason for the decline in civic engagement. A sizeable majority of all questionnaire students admitted to watching television. Despite this the rest of their time was spent undertaking activities that were likely to contribute to the well being of their local community and therefore enhance individual and community social capital. From the questionnaire replies it seemed that these people have access to at least one aspect of social capital. This information bears some resemblance to the findings of Field and Spence (2000) and raises a number of questions rather than answers. For instance, why then did these adults have a low level of participation in education and higher education in particular? Was it simply that having participated in one course that they suddenly gained the confidence to embark upon all these civic-based activities? Although the power and benefits of education are linked to economic growth in terms of human capital, there is no evidence to prove that the impact is that great! Since CAP's educational intervention failed to explain why students have not participated in education before, it may be that social capital like other forms of human and cultural capital, exists in many guises, not, all of which are regarded in the literature as equally useful, or valuable. It may be that the kind of social capital that non-traditional adult learners use is lacking in some way. It certainly seems that their social capital fails to provide them with the same socio-economic benefits enjoyed by educated middle class adults. Is it possible that the social capital that serves local networks, and informs local norms and sanctions is in some way inferior to that available to those citizens who operate in a wider global context? What if anything does a kind of higher education offer to combat this divide if it actually exists? The definitions of social capital are undoubtedly open and ambiguous enough to accommodate this interpretation. Does the evidence from the questionnaires also support this proposition?

Social Capital and Participation in Education

Coleman (1997) stated that social capital is productive, making possible the achievement of certain ends that in its absence would not be possible. For Putnam (1995) this involves certain relationships and behaviours such as networks, norms and mutual trust that enable individuals to act together to achieve common goals. Coleman's (1997) three forms of social capital comprising trust and obligations, information channels, norms and sanctions are said to encourage or constrain individuals to work for the benefit of their community:

> Social capital is high where people trust each other, and where this trust is exercised by the mutual acceptance of obligations (Schuller and Field, 1998: 229).

To engender trust arguably requires a sense of understanding and belonging. For adults who have not participated in education before there are inevitably feelings of apprehension, uncertainty and exclusion. Feelings and attitudes that evoke comments like 'universities are for posh, clever people', or 'young people with 'A' levels' and 'its not for the likes of us' do not signal high levels of belonging and therefore trust. These dispositional factors combine with situational and institutional deterrents to learning (McGivney, 1990: 17) with the result that adult learners without experience of higher education frequently have considerable distrust of these distant, elite institutions with their ivory tower image. One of the reasons cited by McGivney (1990) for widening participation is the breaking down of the:

> 'Negative intergenerational cycle' whereby parents with negative perceptions of education and low levels of educational attainment pass on negative perceptions and attitudes to their children (McGivney, 1990: 32).

A negative attitude towards education is however only part of the equation. Adults with limited experience of education tend to dismiss publicity and information about education as something that doesn't apply to them. They often believe that they don't have a right to education and therefore fail to find out what opportunities may be available. Hence adults with few qualifications and low levels of invested time in education (both human capital indicators) are less likely to participate in the future. Described in terms of their guidance needs these adults were operating at a pre, pre-entry phase; the issues facing them in the guidance context are discussed further in chapter six.

Whatever social capital CAP students might have, it appears that in terms of accessing education this neither converts into trust of higher education or an obligation on the part of many higher education staff to widen access. The recent shift in government policy has provided financial incentives to encourage the active engagement in further and higher education in widening participation. This is engendering in some a limited sense of obligation (Dearing, 1997; DfEE, 1998; HEFCE, 1998; HEFCE, 1999; Kennedy, 1997). Unfortunately even this commitment continues to be restricted, with some arguing for diversity of mission to enable the sector to meet the needs of 'non traditional' students (Woodrow, 1998).

Individual learners reported on their course evaluation forms that participation in courses increased their confidence and enabled them to take on new responsibilities. This was only one of the progression indicators listed on CAP's course evaluation forms (Table 3). Earlier research has demonstrated that progression for community students has a non-linear focus. Progression structures that are lateral rather than linear have implications for a higher education system which is predicated on notions of academic level and linear growth. This will be discussed again in part three. Progression here was often interpreted, for example, in terms of increased social activity. Other signs of progression included:

- attending class more regularly
- joining the library
- enrolling for a college course
- enrolling for more community courses
- increased confidence
- joining new committees
- taking up a new hobby
- improved English skills
- starting a new job
- better prepared for HE
- sense of personal achievement
- better able to help my family.

Often the changes and signs of personal progression identified by the learners were more incremental than transformational. In other words the pivotal transforming activities as a result of course participation seemed to result in small steps of civic engagement. These then facilitated their involvement in local community groups. Participation in education for those who have traditionally felt excluded from education was often only possible if the educational providers themselves were able to break down and bridge the common interpersonal barriers that inhibited effective communication with potential learners. Frequently adult learners experienced a contradiction between the rhetoric and reality they heard about higher education. McGivney (1990) believes these contradictions are the result of a perceived discrepancy between the informant (educational provider) and the potential learner. This leads to resistance or misunderstanding of information which uses inappropriate language or dialect (ibid., 39) - a common problem amongst educational providers who despite good intentions are 'outsiders' unable to make relevant connections (Cruikshank, 1994).

It was this absence of trust in educational providers that placed the community gatekeepers in a pivotal position. They were the mediators of trust between adults with limited experience of education and educational providers. They provided the bridge between the local social capital network inhabited by socially excluded adults and the more global social capital networks of the university which consisted of people with high levels of human, cultural and financial capital. Consequently, as has already been mentioned, the initial involvement with a community group was crucial. It was in these familiar and supportive learning environments that adults were encouraged to make that first step into education (Fryer, 1997; Houghton and Bokhari, 1997; Kennedy, 1997) and thus gain greater access to a global community that offered the potential for enhancing their local community. We also argue, however, that many local adults want their higher levels of study to remain geographically local.

Coleman's form of social capital also includes the notion of information channels. The diversity of activities in which CAP students involved themselves initially appears to indicate a host of potential networks for information flow from a diverse range of sources. Nevertheless access to information was not necessarily enough. It needed to be appropriate in terms of content and format (Chrisholm ,1997; Dadzie, 1990; Hillier, 1990; Imeson and Wyatt, 1996). Partial, or mis-information, relayed through conventional forms of publicity including the media or prospectuses, is designed for people with particular experiences and understanding of the system. In some cases this kind of information can be potentially more damaging than an absence of information. CAP students, through their community networks, demonstrated that they already accessed information about hobbies, local groups and activities prior to their involvement in widening provision courses. But access to information about, and knowledge of, higher education opportunities was limited, and where it existed it was often inaccurate.

Recent changes in higher education (for example increasing modularity, part time study options and different types of qualifications) satisfy supporters of widening participation by making the system more flexible and learner centred. Ironically these changes make the system more confusing and challenging in terms of supplying and opening up the information channels; hence the demand for appropriate guidance (McNair, 1998). Having access to accurate, impartial information in an appropriate format is central to good guidance, as are the skills to process and handle that information. The detailed stories discussed in later chapters highlight how involvement in the CAP courses enabled learners to dispel some of the myths associated with higher education. It appears that the link with the university widened their network of informants and thus extended the information available to them.

The third aspect of social capital is more difficult to define. It concerns the norms and sanctions that either 'encourage or constrain people to work for a common good, forgoing immediate self-interest' (Schuller and Field, 1998: 229). The questionnaire replies demonstrated a high degree of involvement in caring for family members and showed considerable willingness to embark on a variety of charitable, voluntary and community related activities. It therefore appeared that the circumstances in which they found themselves encouraged them to work for a common good. Yet from the learners' more personal stories there was a sense that for many of them charitable, voluntary and community work was the only alternative available. The sense of obligation was overwhelming; for some it was arguably social compulsion rather than social capital that was the impetus associated with any norms and sanctions. Although they recognised the personal and community benefits derived from their civic engagement, this may not have been their preferred model of active citizenship, especially if they were given an alternative lifestyle.

Another way of looking at the issue of norms and sanctions in terms of participation in education is to consider who determines the norms that influence the educational experience. The kind of mainstream higher education currently on offer is arguably not the kind of higher education adult learners with low involvement in such provision want or need. McNair (1998) outlines the NIACE position of how to meet learner needs, especially if the educational pathways and therefore type of students are to change. These principles are perhaps the most challenging to current norms and sanctions. CAP's relationship with learners was undoubtedly different as the ensuing chapters show. As yet its approach is not widespread throughout the institution. This is not unusual. Other HEFCE widening provision projects have faced similar challenges to shifting policy and practice (McNair et al., 1999). This is probably because the current mainstream student population manages to conform and adapt to the norms and sanctions inherent in higher education institutions. Adult learners, the 'Invisible Majority' (McNair, 1998), have distinctive requirements, as the questionnaire replies demonstrated. If institutions are to take seriously the challenge of widening participation then they will need to consider how norms and sanctions can become more encouraging and less of a constraining factor for participation.

The questionnaire asked for information on patterns of study, future goals and what learner support requirements institutions needed to take seriously if widening participation and lifelong learning was to become a reality. Asked if they would like to undertake a course in the future table three shows that 95 (88%) answered positively. Interestingly 21 (100%) of Asian heritage women said they wanted to study in the future. CAP students appeared to have a greater than average interest in further learning.

This compares favourably with results from the Learning Divide which show that 72% of people with recent experiences of education expect to study in the future. (Sargant et al., 1997: vii). However, the overall response rate of the CAP questionnaire needs to be taken into account in this comparison. Although the CAP students could choose more than one location there was a clear preference for local community provision. Sixty seven (63%) wanted to learn in a community context, 35 (34%) at a college (which for the majority of CAP students is the nearest educational provider), 13 (12%) at university and 29 (28%) at home. Although only 13 (12%) preferred to study at a university, the questionnaire replies also revealed that 43 (41%) were interested in studying on higher level courses with a further 33 (32%) not sure and only 29 (28%) having no interest at the moment or in the foreseeable future.

Table 3 Future Study Plans

Preferred Study Options	Total n 105	Disability n 29	Asian n 21
1. Would like to do more courses	95 (88%)	23 (79%)	21 (100%)
2. Want to study in the community	67 (63%)	12 (41%)	17 (81%)
3. Want to study at college	35 (34%)	11 (39%)	4 (21%)
4. Want to study at university	13 (12%)	3 (11%)	2 (10%)
5. Want to study from home	29 (28%)	8 (29%)	4 (21%)

It is not surprising that higher education was only one progression goal for this group of adults. Their previous participation places them in the Campaign for Learning's category of 'strugglers'. For these learners the opportunities for education are not seen as obvious and the costs are perceived as high. Furthermore they face numerous barriers to change and are disadvantaged in a number of other ways (MORI, 1996 in Sargant et al., 1997: 74). What was significant was that in response to the open question: 'Where would you like to have got with your learning five years from now?' many gave answers that related to higher level or more mainstream education. Both responses challenge the characteristics of the 'struggler'. Furthermore the majority of replies linked what might be seen as learning goals with more generic lifestyle ones. The 74 responses break down as follows: 22 (29%) mentioned employment relating to either getting a job, or improving their present position; 37 (50%) planned to study at college, 16 (22%) aimed to get a diploma or degree, and 15 (11%) had a more general career or educational goal. Five students (7%) wished to achieve their potential in respect of a personal goal, with a further six (8%) mentioning their desire to improve their computer skills. The popularity of computer skills was also singled out in the Learning Divide with 11% indicating it was a future option for study (Sargant et al. 1997). Only the two eldest replies aged 79 and 84 claimed to have no particular educational personal development goals, one stated they had no ambitions, the other hoped to 'stay alive'.

Finding time for study is never easy. The most popular length of time for 67 (64%) learners was a class each week of 2-3 hours. Given that this was the most typical duration of CAP courses, and most traditional models, this was not a particularly surprising result. From the other options Asian women indicated a willingness to study for between 4-6 hours each week. There was no obvious comparison with data collected by the Learning Divide since that survey only measured the length of time students had been learning. Sargant et al., (1997) identify the difficulties of comparison with other surveys, yet notes that this is a research and policy challenge to address if participation is to be accurately measured. CAP's student records demonstrated that many learners enrol on a series of courses. However in the course negotiation phase courses with a definite end date and within the foreseeable future were preferred. We would advocate that measuring the preferred duration of a course is potentially a useful addition to the data currently collected in large-scale surveys about adult participation.

In addition to the timing of a course there are a host of other factors that may influence an adult in terms of their decision to participate in and, once enrolled, to stay on a course. Some of these factors are predictable but nonetheless important for educational providers to remember when designing and publicising courses. Focus group discussions revealed that it was clearly important to ensure there was an opportunity to discuss all aspects of a course during the pre-entry guidance phase. The majority of tutors and community contacts noted that many adults were unaware of their entire learner and study support needs. This information indicated some of the main features that should be included in pre course discussions with prospective students (chapter six discusses this further).

If these adult learners and others like them are to realise their lifelong learning goals then the factors that relate to practical considerations, pedagogical styles and notions of citizenship need to be taken seriously. CAP attempted to cater for and take account of the practical issues that may impinge on and detract from the learning experience.

Table 4 Features Identified as Required for Future Study

Course Feature	Total n 105	Disability n 27	Asian n 21
1. Courses at right time	70 (67%)	16 (59%)	15 (72%)
2. Accessible venues and facilities	60 (57%)	19 (70%)	12 (57%)
3. Informal atmosphere	48 (46%)	16 (59%)	6 (29%)
4. A course with no exams	39 (37%)	13 (48%)	10 (48%)
5. Study support	36 (34%)	11 (41%)	5 (34%)
6. To know tutor before starting course	35 (33%)	10 (37%)	7 (33%)
7. Tutor understanding needs (cultural/disability)	34 (33%)	15 (56%)	7 (33%)
8. Course not based at college	26 (25%)	6 (22%)	11 (53%)
9. Women/men only classes	21 (20%)	4 (15%)	13 (62%)
10. Crèche facilities available	12 (12%)	2 (7%)	6 (29%)
11. Bilingual translator/sign interpreter	7 (7%)	4 (15%)	2 (10%)

(Total includes disability and Asian students plus all others).

Table four shows some of the main features of the CAP courses which participants wanted to be integrated into future provision. The percentages for the sub groups, although based on small numbers, confirmed the features tutors referred to in their interviews. A few exceptions concerned an appreciation of the informal atmosphere, which was notably greater for students with a disability 59%, compared with 29% for Asian women and 46% for the total number of replies. Similarly not studying courses at college appeared to be of considerable importance to Asian women with 53% compared to 25% of the total number of replies. The interviews and focus group discussions confirmed that this response was closely linked with their need for women only provision.

Since the questionnaire asked students to respond retrospectively it is probable that their experience of education influenced their responses. The in-depth interviews suggest that for many students their previous lack of involvement in education was not necessarily because they lacked interest, rather it was a result of their limited knowledge and awareness about the available education opportunities. Having a positive educational experience not only builds learners confidence and desire to learn it also provides them with access to communication channels associated with social capital.

Schuller and Field (1998) offer a typology that explores the potential link between educational participation and levels of social capital. They move beyond Coleman's interest in school attainment and attempt to examine if there is any correlation between levels of social capital and participation in formal continuing education or non-formal learning.

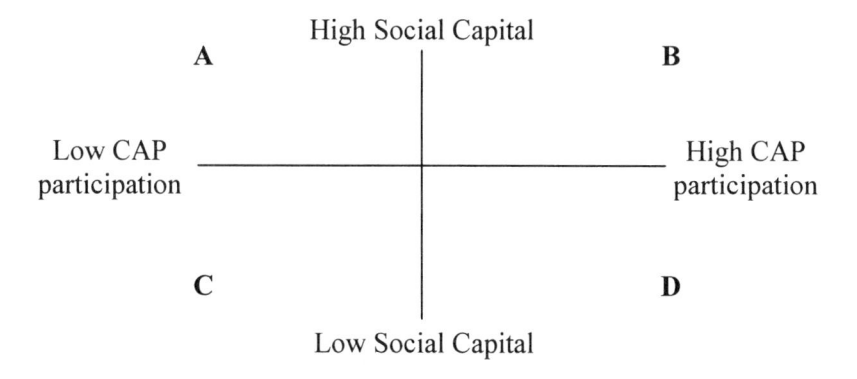

```
                      High Social Capital
            A                 |                B
                              |
Low CAP     ──────────────────┼──────────────────   High CAP
participation                 |                     participation
                              |
            C                 |                D
                      Low Social Capital
```

Adapted from Schuller and Field's (1998) typology p.232.

To some extent CAP provision is yet another form of adult education, with its close collaboration with community groups, negotiated curriculum and responsive learner and study support. It shares characteristics of formality and structure with the institutional continuing education provision, but embodies the informality and responsiveness to the learners' interests more typical of non-formal learning.

Evidence collected from CAP students via the questionnaire indicated that whilst there was access to a potentially large social network this was locally situated and therefore failed to provide information about, or personal contacts with, higher education. Like the non-formal learners described by Schuller and Field it appears that the scope of their personal contact with global, information/expertise-rich networks was small. After experiencing some education via CAP's widening provision activities learners seemed to have entered into quadrant B, (high social capital with high participation). However, given the nature of their social capital and the limited usefulness in terms of accessing a more globalised social capital network this allocation is debatable. They could arguably be positioned in quadrant D, especially if they moved away from their community group and its gatekeeper.

What appeared to be significant for CAP learners was the pivotal role of community and university co-ordinator gatekeepers who clearly bridged the interface of the two diverse communities. Gatekeepers seeking to extend communication channels often had to interpret and 'translate' the terminology and expectations of the world they inhabited. This required experience and knowledge of the other world together with considerable skill and expertise. For communication to be effective it is necessary for it to become a dialogical process that is based on establishing common goals and shared meanings (Williams, 1998). In the context of developing courses collaboratively, it was necessary for gatekeepers to acquire the viewpoint and language of the partner institution in order to behave in an acceptable manner within the other network (Brown and Duguid 1996). The challenges of operating within the norms and sanctions of a local network are different from those associated with a globalised network. Obvious differences relate to the size, scope, diversity, degree of formality and level of bureaucracy. For many CAP students the need to know tutors and other students in advance of a course was vital in terms of establishing a relationship that was based on trust and obligation. There was also a heavy investment in terms of the time taken to establish a sense of belonging, which was an essential prerequisite for the trust, and obligation associated with high levels of social capital.

The role of social capital for widening participation in education appears to have some merit. It is not however a panacea. There is a danger in attributing to it notions of correlational exchange associated with human capital. As might be expected the relationship between social capital and education is complex. The inter-relationship between education and increased active citizenship even in a local community is not automatic. The appropriate combination of factors that enabled adults to participate in education and contribute to their own and others social capital was not necessarily the same for the different learner groups. Although the results outlined in this chapter offer possible avenues for further exploration the single set of factors guaranteed to widen participation inevitably remains elusive. The learners' in-depth stories shed further light on how issues such as power relations, discourses, and dominance contribute to participation and exclusion.

PART II: EXPLORING THE KIND OF HIGHER EDUCATION DEBATES

4 Skills and Lifelong Learning in the Community

This and the following three chapters discuss the different application of learning processes which were outlined in chapter one. Their practices evolved through the action research phases described in chapter two. These chapters focus primarily on the latter phases of that evolution process. That is, course development and teaching are described in a standardised format - using the proposal form, in appendix one, and validated through one of four modules in an Access (pre-degree) level credit route, as detailed in appendix two. Whilst the practices are interdependent in terms of demonstrating 'a kind of higher education', their complexities warrant separate attention. This chapter explores some of the current literature on the relationship between skills and lifelong learning. It then looks specifically at how the tutors and students engaged with the controversial process of teaching and learning 'transferable skills'. The notion of 'skills' is usually interpreted as a form of human capital (employability), though the learners on these courses would not necessarily make this distinction, since few of them were seeking or expecting to work again. The chapter concludes that the teaching of key skills involves a complex mixture of context, process and level. Their transferability is to some extent determined by individuals but it is the educational process of making such learning explicit which helps to identify their usefulness in other settings. In this sense the skills framework adopted by CAP was partially an attempt to respond to globalisation trends for convergence - a means of accepting new boundaries for higher education across a mass system.

Chapter one highlighted two tensions in the current discourse for lifelong learning - learning for social reasons versus the vocationalist approach. Higher education's role has been described as equipping people 'with the skills and pre-requisites for lifelong learning' (Knapper and Cropley, 1995: 47). Its primary contribution is the development of 'higher order' learning skills such as analysis, synthesis, creativity and critical thinking (ibid: 81). The discourse of lifelong learning, however, as Edwards (1997) reminds us, is just that - a construction of responses to perceived economic cultural technological and demographic changes. In spite of various attempts to shift the balance of meaning for lifelong learning (for example Fryer, 1999), there is still a tendency for the language of employability to dominate (Blissand, 1999) with consequences for how existing resources are deployed. The same applies to the notion of skill. Only certain behaviour is deemed worthy of the label 'skill' and the criteria for skill are linked to certain levels of wealth creation (Coffield, 1999).

Lifelong learning in much public policy is therefore a panacea for employability and is measured for that purpose. Where there is a focus for lifelong learning social policy this is usually seen as designed for 'problem groups in the labour market' (Heinz, 1999:15) - though as Baron et al., (1999) suggest, even here, only certain problem groups count for the labour market. One way of measuring this human capital worth of learning is to identify it under categories of skills (Jarvis, 1996; Ashton, 1999). These categories are influenced by industry's conception of what will make a good employee, and incorporated in the Dearing report (1997) for translation into the HE context.

If lifelong learning is a contested concept, 'skill' is arguably even more so. Skills have been variously described, sometimes interchangeably, as core, key, transferable or simply competencies. They are presented as a way of bridging the gap between, and to avoid changing, vocational and academic qualifications. Their origin as an idea is usually linked to the vocational initiatives of the 1970s and 1980s. Hyland and Johnson (1998) suggest they were given an additional boost by the school National Curriculum concepts of common learning, but developed in their most prescriptive form during the 1990s through the National Vocational Qualifications (NVQ) system. They have become embedded in the post compulsory curriculum through two Dearing committee reports - one for the 16-19 qualifications (1996) and again in the review of Higher Education (Dearing, 1997). NVQ general key skills are broadly defined as Improving Your Own Learning, Working with Others, Learning to Learn. The Dearing report summarised these for HE purposes as Learning to Learn, along with requirements for Information Technology (IT) Communication and Numeracy skills, though there are many variations on these themes.

Discussion about their definition and applicability are almost polarised into those 'for' and those 'against' skills learning. Arguments against the idea of a core skills curriculum generally focus on criticisms of definition and slippage of the term itself, and include concern about the potential reduction of all learning to the idea of a 'skill'. Barrow (1987), for instance, points out that attributes such as maturity and disposition and caring are not 'taught' activities but: 'One cultivates the values, emotions and understanding that enable [people] to care' (p.194). Whitston (1998), Ashworth and Saxton (1990), Blass (1999) and Hyland and Johnson (1998) all question whether skills can be measured or transferred into different contexts. Whitston (1998) for instance emphasises that it is the teaching process itself and curriculum change 'more radical ... than the ... instrumental notions of skill' (p.307) which are important for learning. The emphasis in teaching should be on nurturing personal growth, development and intellectual curiosity (p.311). To this Blass adds that the supposed objectivity of skill measurement is not value neutral, as it is context-specific, and assessment relies on the interpersonal perception of evidence about skill performance. He and Barnett (1994) also question whether the proposed Dearing skills are demanding enough for higher education. Assessing people on the basis of skills is seen as oversimplifying the relationship between theory and learning, not viewing learning as complex enough and ignoring the real value of higher learning. Hyland and Johnson (1998) summarise the dilemma by suggesting that the politically motivated concept of skill which is deemed to cover life skills, reasoning and survival skills tries to do too much:

> Transferable skills hold out the promise of producing a flexible and adaptable workforce and of solving problems associated with training people for an uncertain future. Such skills are simply too good not to be true! (p.170).

It is perhaps significant that those in favour of the idea of a core (or key, or transferable) skills curriculum at higher education level enter less fervently into these philosophical arguments but concentrate on devising mechanisms for delivering a particular set of specified skills. Bradshaw (1985) identified overseas research into the facilitation of the intellectual skills of critical thinking (such as communication, quantifying, synthesis, analysis and clarification of values). In addition he specified the teaching of 'employability' skills (such as communication, teamwork, prioritising and achieving objectives). He made two observations - firstly an acknowledgement of their ambiguity but also a claim, taken from Australian studies, that 'at least some are identifiable and are developed in the process of higher education' (p. 209). He suggests the goal is primarily to make visible what is already implicit in the curriculum. In this way it is also possible to shape what is being consumed - a now well-argued trend in the tensions of globalisation pressures. Phillips (1998) adopted the NVQ performance criterion of 'improving your own learning' with a view to enabling students to gain credit for learning study skills. He argues that the mechanics of learning how to learn are not simply a matter of skills: 'It is a metacognitive skill which relates to self knowledge and is central to the notion of lifelong learning' (p.115).

The proponents of higher education skills learning seem to do so on two counts. On the one hand they argue that the 'skill' element of learning enhances the higher education curriculum, by interpreting 'skills' within the framework of personal development. This is often a means of encouraging an action learning, experiential approach to university teaching (Stephens et al., 1998; Hyland, 1994, for example). On the other hand, the experiment of actually getting students to document their broader learning under the umbrella of core skills, reveals that higher education students often have under-developed reflective skills (Harvard et al., 1998) - or strategies to record them, even at postgraduate level (Cryer, 1998). There are indications, therefore, that whilst the precise definition of core skills is problematic, the practice of attempting to achieve them facilitates new learning and new teaching, an outcome of the recasting of new relationship boundaries in the face of change or convergence. Stephens et al., (1998) for instance, introduced a range of non-traditional teaching methods including a more pastoral 'guidance' role for their tutors in order to facilitate the kind of learning which they perceived needed to be recorded within the mainstream curriculum. In this respect the 'skills' focus enabled the kind of teaching role advocated by McNair and Watson and Taylor outlined in chapter one. Whilst few of these writers denied the slipperiness of terminology for the range of skills being addressed, they all felt the process of making such learning outcomes explicit proved in itself to be a valuable exercise for all involved, requiring students to acquire new understandings and experiences en route. Indeed it might be argued that some of the criticisms directed towards the incorporation and assessment of skills in HE could be equally applied to higher education's more conventional, and equally slippery, claims for higher learning. The perceived viability of skills teaching and learning therefore is not yet resolved and perhaps depends on the amount of weight attached to their worth, along with a tolerance of the context in which they are developed.

The starting point of a 'skills' curriculum for the community access programme was addressed rather differently from those discussed so far. For one thing we were working with people who were clearly very marginalised in the labour market. Employability in itself was only a partial goal. Our students needed as broad a range of learning as possible to widen their future options in the unpredictable future. The programme did not operate with a single, existing HE curriculum and its teaching methods were generally devised around a notion of student need rather than a fixed syllabus to which students were recruited. The rationale behind developing our accreditation system was that we wanted to maximise ownership of content by the learners. This meant devising a credit-worthy framework into which a variety of course material could be poured. At the time of its inception this was a hard-won rationale, though now argued on its own merits (Wilson 1999). The scheme was developed in the 1990s, prior to the more prescriptive concepts introduced by NVQ and Dearing. To justify its rationale, the scheme looked to literature definitions of 'lifelong learning', 'capability' and 'higher'. Its teaching methods were already embedded in adult education methodology which advocates group work and the valuing of learner experience. In this respect the credit scheme adopted as its base-line the very elements which recent higher education literature supports as innovative to its existing curriculum - modularisation, flexible credit and assessment, experiential learning, group work etc. The scheme itself evolved from a mixture of our own, intuitive, understandings of learner needs and an attempt to justify this approach in the university by looking for theoretical rationales. Tutor staff development sessions to introduce the credit frameworks involved a combined strategy of encouraging tutors to articulate the learning needs of their students and ourselves as academics introducing a more formalised teaching structure which incorporated the kinds of learning we identified as appropriate for higher education.

This remainder of this chapter discusses the evolution of an accreditable skills framework and the responses of tutors and learners to the notion and value of learning 'skills' associated with HE through a subject of their choice. The programme was not designed to follow any national guidelines and, as such, is presented independently of formal literature on skills. Its research strength has been its formulation as a relatively free-floating response to learner needs, rather than the other way round.

CAP's Skills Framework

As has already been stated, the introduction of skills into higher education is a contested issue. The differences in interpretation tend to swing between notions of education for a learning society, employability or simply scholarship. The CAP approach undertook to address each of these different perspectives.

There is, for instance, the concept of 'transformative learning' with its emphasis on personal development. This approach advocates working with, and building on, knowledge gained through experience (Boud et al., 1993) and reinforced by self assessment or 'metacognition'. Metacognition is defined by Harvey and Knight (1996) as a process of self monitoring and thereby increasing our own awareness of how we think. These are aspects of self awareness and often seen as part of a learning society model (Skillbeck and Connell, 1996).

A second style of education focuses on employability or enterprise skills. As Ball (1990) suggests, employability qualities include the ability to problem solve, communicate and work co-operatively, use initiative and leadership. These are the competencies advocated by the 'Education for Capability' movement (Burgess, 1986) and were also supported through enterprise in higher education initiatives during the 1980s and early 1990s. Aspects of this philosophy have lingered in the form of much interactive project work which many undergraduates undertake as part of their mainstream studies.

Another, more scholarship-oriented way of identifying skills which have applicability in a wide range of contexts is to emphasise aspects of critical analysis and synthesis. Barnett, for example, includes the following list of 'essential conditions of HE': 'The ability to analyse and evaluate an argument, the capacity to relate what is learnt to a broad context and to make relevant connections' (Barnett, 1988: 24). They are, perhaps, the principle qualities of 'study', along with Knapper and Cropley's concerns for 'skill at locating information ... in using learning aids such as the library; ability to use and interpret materials from different subject areas' (Knapper and Cropley, 1995: 45).

A different emphasis could be described as 'investigatory' or research skills. Barnett's identification of a 'willingness to accept the rules of rational inquiry' (Barnett, 1998: 245) positions itself neatly with McNair's (1995: 5) reference to knowledge formulation as a distinctive feature of

HE: 'Gradually learning how to create new knowledge, to challenge established knowledge and test frameworks for themselves'.

Of course, these qualities are not mutually exclusive and their interdependence leads to the sum of the whole HE experience. They all, it can be argued, lead to a fifth, but real-world capacity to 'engage collectively and critically in the transformation of the world' (Freire, 1972: 14); to become independent of and stand outside, rather than a passive assimilator of information (Barnett, 1988). The ability to 'connect what is learned and apply it to the outside world' (Duke, 1992: 97) must be the ultimate test of a critical thinker able to contribute to the wider community and its goals (Coffield and Williamson, 1997). Key skills seen in these ways might be equally applicable to social as well as human capital.

Information technology is the sixth aspect of HE learning, now widely regarded as an essential medium for communication in the 21st Century. As the use of IT in the community raises a different set of issues this is discussed separately in chapter seven.

As has been shown, the development, assessment and accreditation of such a range of skills within UK HE is still under exploration, even by proponents of such a learning model. One difficulty is how to develop or accredit such capabilities for people who have disparate starting points. Of ongoing concern within this debate, of course, is the issue of 'disaffection' or social exclusion - how to engage with people most on the margins of HE. It is in this context that a loosely defined skills approach to learning might be more appropriate than a curriculum approach. To this end Merton (1997) advocates an approach to learning which centres on a notion of skills development rather than content. His focus was on young people, but the arguments might also apply to some adults:

> We need softer outcomes (intermediate qualifications) and measures of achievement (distance travelled). Alongside these we need assessment procedures and accreditation systems which are rigorous yet flexible ... programmes should focus on skills and attitudes and behaviours which will enable them to become more independent learners and better able to cope with an unpredictable labour market and with difficulties at home and in the community ... [there should be a] sharper focus on learning outcomes and teaching strategies (curriculum and pedagogy) ... [with] mentors and peer educators ... [teaching and learning should include] informal relationships ... incentives ... positive reinforcement ... effective group work ... negotiated learning ... continuous checking for understanding ... continuous individual assessment ... flexible accreditation, flexible progression routes (pp 153-4).

This holistic view of teaching and learning resonates with CAP's practices, where the idea of skill is closely intertwined with attitudes and behaviours. The programme applied this kind of teaching through a system of foundation credit courses. These were thirty hour courses to be delivered at timescales agreed with students and organisations. Content could range from the study of art or Islam to the organisation of a trip to Scotland, creation of a charity shop or investigation into fly fishing. But each outline syllabus was accompanied by a teaching pack of suggested activities and handouts. These steered an analytical teaching style and learning elements for that particular module which respectively focused on attitudes and behaviours relating to 'enterprise' 'research', 'study' or 'personal awareness'.

So how does such an approach get implemented in the community? The CAP courses did not follow a heavily prescriptive competency route in their module description or assessment guidelines. The assessment criteria outlined a generic guideline approach similar to those adopted recently for undergraduate and Masters level courses (for example University of Surrey School of Educational Studies guidelines). That is, degrees of interpretation were allowed in assessing achievement - but the guidelines followed a broad syllabus with stated learning outcomes and explanation of how grading marks were reached (appendix two). Each set of guidelines followed a particular syllabus framework of either enterprise, investigation, study or personal skills. There was a tendency for the courses to be studied in a certain order, but not always. Some groups chose only to use the study skills framework. Others would start with the more individualistic personal awareness course, which encouraged students to reflect on and explain the usefulness of their prior learning in enabling them as individuals to function in the wider world. Some would then progress through each module, finishing with a group 'enterprise' project. All students who chose to be assessed had to produce assignments. Whilst the 'study' and 'research' assignments followed academic conventions in terms of referencing and layout, the enterprise project emphasised evaluation of team effectiveness and interpersonal behaviour and the personal skills assignments required self evaluative portfolio evidence of student achievements and learning. Tutors marked the work according to the assessment guidelines and they were then quality assured in the university by CAP staff and a selected university moderator.

Empirical evidence of what skills or learning value were perceived as having been reached is drawn from individual student interviews from East

Lancs (mostly Muslim Pakistani women), the DAB Centre (people with varying disabilities) the Bridge Centre (older adults) and tutors from across these organisations. We looked for aspects of achievement or practice which the learners or tutors perceived as having re-useable value. The findings confirmed many of the arguments for and against the idea of a skills framework, though paradoxically we claim this combination of outcomes as justification for their continued use.

It was difficult to disentangle the sense of achievement or increased self worth which 'second chance' learners often express from responses that could be related more directly to the general process of learning and those that related to the outcomes of a 'skills' approach to learning. Notions of employability and ability to contribute to the wider world might well depend on simply having a good learning experience. Indeed the indications were that the transferability and developmental value of the courses depended on a combination of inter-relating factors, which broadly correlated with the concerns identified by Whitston (1998), Blass (1999) and Barnett (1994) but also resulted in the positive outcomes described earlier. Perhaps the most conclusive nature of the evidence was that the comments from tutors and students were relatively consistent across the groups, irrespective of their course content. The findings can be divided roughly into categories of Transferability, Level and Skills outcomes, with cross references to aspects of Context and Theory. Process is mentioned in terms of teaching practices.

Transferability

Most of the tutors asserted the unproblematic nature of teaching skills which are applicable in other contexts:

> I think the key is that our students are able to transfer their knowledge and skills into different situations but I don't think everybody who goes through a university degree system is able to do that (Fahana).

For Fahana her distinction was that the emphasis was different and therefore more explicit:

> There isn't so much emphasis on content, there's more emphasis on how you use that content and how you present that information ... now they feel if they

> go into another course that they can ... use what they picked up on our courses onto other courses ... so they can see the transferability.

Many students reinforced this point concerning the techniques of academic study:

> How to structure and write an essay ... it was excellent, I wish I'd done it before (Debra);

> And this book ... and I think: 'Now I really know what they mean because this man this author is very biased about it' ... well I couldn't have picked these books up and read them a few years back (Azra);

Another form of transferability was identified as making the link between theory and practice. This was exemplified within the context of the learners' interests such as a desire to put their learning of Islamic theory into practice, particularly in the way the women would argue their position in the home:

> It was always their [men's] version of Islam. I just took that in as maybe their right because they knew better. But now like I say I know more and I can contradict that (Rubina).

The Bridge Centre learners offered similar links between their increased artistic understanding from an Art and Artists course and the transferability of new insights into their own painting activities:

> Learning about the history of art has definitely helped me in the practical course ... I think it helps you understand the way that artists work and the way that perhaps methods I could use in my paintings and it's interesting to find out the reasons for them painting certain types of picture and maybe incorporating some of those things in the work I do ... it broadens the whole aspect of painting (Patricia).

Transferability was not just linked to aspects of study. The explicit process of addressing self awareness in the personal skills course helped this student develop his own insights about himself:

> My personal skills - I didn't know I knew about myself as much as I did you know, what I could achieve, what I have achieved through my school life ...

and through my working life and so forth. Yes, it's really surprised me (Kevin).

Similarly, for Susan with the enterprise course where they set up a charity shop as a team:

> Like negotiation skills - you think: 'Oh we're always negotiating and we had to negotiate to get the shop as well and we had to negotiate with one another '... cause I mean it was a real project so I think it would be handy. You could say well we did set this up (Susan).

There are two issues to consider here. Firstly these students were required to identify for themselves the range of skills they were using. This reinforced their learning in a way which Jarvis (1992) calls conscious action or reflective learning. In other words experience alone does not mean you learn. It is the reflection of that process which converts the learning (Kolb 1984). In Susan's case this included her perception of what 'negotiation' meant. Perhaps she was transferring her increased confidence into a new situation rather than a particular set of skills. The effect for Susan, however was the same. She felt better able to negotiate in similar situations in the future. This experience in isolation, of course, is not an indicator of higher learning – though the students distinguished the nature of their study from school experiences in terms of criticality and applying their understanding to the wider world. The inevitable issue is whether the learning which occurred was of university level.

Level of Learning

Earlier research (Preece, 1999a) has shown that whilst academia often conceptualises higher education level as unproblematic, the reality is more complex. Identifying depth and breadth of critical thought in teaching does not necessarily reflect the nature of critical thinking being undertaken by individual students (Preece, 1999a: 173). The traditional concept of HE level is defined as post 'A' level - as articulated by a history lecturer:

> In school history you are trying to present people with facts ... you may bring in a certain amount of debate ... at university level we are studying how you interpret the past ... it builds on school level (in Preece, 1999: 174).

The same research demonstrated, however, that 'level' is self defining in HE discourses and may not take account of thought or knowledge which lies outside of authoritative academic text.

Level also has to do with complexity of interpretation. On this basis the students' 'levels' of skills development were not consistently 'higher'. The complexity of situations was sometimes removed in order for students to make the link between theory and practice. Tutors suggested this process was a subjective concept which could be interpreted in different ways. Betty, for instance, the DAB Centre organiser acknowledged that the context for the skills being practised might be different in a university teaching situation:

> I could imagine a lot of the course concepts that are being taught would be taught in other subjects at the university - er stress management, time management, problem solving, decision making but I couldn't really imagine that the university would actually do the projects - where in our case its about the charity shop or the display board.

The issue of difference in terms of content seemed critical to how level would be interpreted. Anna for instance felt the personal skills course was academically rigorous but just required the exploration of different experiences:

> It's really getting people to look at skills they have, not particularly through work or education really, but say you've been at home and you've been bringing up children, you've got a lot of skills there and not just in sort of nurturing children and sort of coping with tantrums but also organising the family and organising the day, children's parties, taking people to sports events ... a whole lot of things, you know negotiating between your husband and the children ... you are trying to make people look at their own lives and things that have happened to them ... and see what they've actually learnt through that experience ... so although it did have a sort of academic rigour ... it was applying it to an area that people don't usually apply it to.

McNair (1998) advocated the use of lived experiences as a means of enhancing learning in HE though he did not discuss level of learning. Tutor Fahana refused to be drawn into a notion of level and suggested that university level was made up of the accumulated skills being provided through the foundation credits:

It's not the level, the academic level -its more about people being able to cope with that and having skills like investigation skills, or study skills, so I think if you have those sorts of skills you can cope with university degree level anyway.

Perhaps Fahana's comment was picking up Barrow's (1987) idea that learning attributes were also to do with maturity and disposition and these, too, are features of higher learning.

There were indications, however, from tutors and learners that 'level' also had something to do with learning processes. For instance, Jabeen a college link worker who was involved in the CAP courses, made quite clear distinctions between the kind of teaching and learning that went on at college:

They [the CAP students] were given assignments which the student had to go and research ... whereas ours [at college] we're given ... 'Well here's the book, find the relevant information' ... and [in the CAP courses] also trying to differentiate different styles of writing and from different authors, which was also university style ... and also realising which is the authentic one, which is not authentic and where to get the resources.

Mumtaz, a student, re-emphasised this distinction between being given a prescriptive piece of work and being asked to make an informed choice:

They [CAP tutors] didn't give it to us on a plate, no. They took us to library and they took us to various places to find and I didn't know all those different ways to do it. The college did take me as well but they have a different way of it, but we are only like this because they (CAP) left the choices to us. They [CAP tutors] didn't just say to us: 'Here we are you do it', they bring it to us .. they took us to the places and show us the different way, lots of other ways ... so everybody put their own bits in at the end of it ... they left the choices to us.

In her broken English Mumtaz was explaining that the college would expect students to follow a prescribed way of working and absorb the information given, whereas her experience of the CAP teaching meant that there was an expectation of independent study and drawing your own conclusions, taking responsibility for setting personal goals, gradually learning how to create new knowledge.

Hilary, one of the Bridge Centre students made reference to the same point as Duke (1992) in that higher learning would make connections to the outside world. She described her learning experience with the art history tutor:

> Looking with somebody who understood a picture .. and seeing in it things that I couldn't have found for myself ... and also linking it with the rest of what was going on in society at the time - that made me change my views a little.

Patricia, another Bridge Centre student, made similar connections in her own assignment where she had to do a comparative study of two paintings:

> I liked the Vermeer because his picture was a small, very intimate picture ... I think in a way he was kind of er glorifying domesticity ... they were so tranquil which must have been so contrasting to his own life with his large family ...

There is a sense, then, that university level is defined by process rather than content. The students' experience of learning process suggested they were receiving a higher, rather than further, education even if the content did not match conventional notions of a higher education curriculum. Similarly, when we tried to tease out what the students had learned, there were indications from the students themselves that their ultimate learning outcomes were matching the range of higher learning proposed by, for example, Skillbeck and Connell (1996), Burgess (1986), Barnett (1994), Knapper and Cropley (1995), with considerable potential for the kind of wider community needs suggested by Duke (1992) and Coffield and Williamson (1997).

Skills Outcomes

> People have been empowered to sort of take charge of their own lives ... building confidence in themselves and building up their self esteem and the confidence they get from being able to tackle and connect at this level and actually succeed (Heather, East Lancs College community courses co-ordinator).

Lawrence, the Bridge Centre tutor, tried to explain the processes behind such increased confidence. He felt the students had 'a greater degree of critical awareness'. This critical awareness manifested itself in a variety of ways amongst all the groups. Sally, a student from the DAB Centre, claimed the personal skills course:

> Made me look a lot into my past and ... its made me a better person ... I'm more aware now of disabled people and their needs than I was in the past.

A fellow student, Kevin gave a longer explanation of what the personal skills and enterprise skills courses did for him as an individual:

> It looks back at my history - what I've done and I can show it to somebody else and say: 'If I can do it, you can do it' ... I've been given the chance of trust and reliability of banking money, opening and closing the shop, taking responsibility which I couldn't have done before my accident you know - I didn't have that confidence to do it.

Similarly Sarah, a student on the DAB Centre enterprise course, identified particular activities which broadened her awareness:

> I've found that the decision making, problem solving is something that I hadn't really gone into before and I didn't really realise that there was that much to it.

Susan, another DAB Centre student, perhaps summarised the particular gains of courses which make explicit what might otherwise be implicit in a good learning experience:

> Even though I had the information it hadn't been analysed before like I analysed it so it was quite interesting to think well why has that happened and why this happened? and then to be able to look into it and find out the reasons really. It was like going into it deeper, really [and of the related assignment] ... it makes you more logical you know, planning it all and note taking ... they make you think about things that you wouldn't have thought about in the past.

The value of the courses seemed to be an increasing awareness of personal qualities as much as demonstrating achievements of certain actions or practices. The role of the reflective self - an aspect of critical learning advocated by Barnett was an element identified across all the courses. The opportunity for this to happen resulted from a mixture of teaching process and curriculum content. The latter is elaborated more specifically in chapter five but in terms of hard evidence of academic achievement their assignments perhaps also reflected some form of measurable learning. Out of a total of 54 assignments submitted between 1996 and 1998 by these participants, 45 gained a grade one or two - identified in the assessment criteria as equivalent to A level. Only one of these students had conventional academic qualifications beyond 'O' level or GCSE and most had left school with no qualifications. Of particular interest was the way the students described their assignment preparation. Catherine, from the Bridge Centre contrasted how she wrote her assignment so meticulously compared with other writing experiences:

> Writing something longer than I usually write, taking days over it and revising it, looking at books in the library, using the dictionary quite a lot ... I revised the thing and wrote bits of it and altered it over a period of weeks until I got it as near perfect as I could.

Whilst few courses used identifiable university subject matter it was perhaps the teaching process itself which most demonstrated how students used HE values of critical reflection and which led them onto their own independent learning and confidence to apply what they had learned to different situations. The potential was arguably in place to increase the complexity of these processes, as a form of progression and using the credit framework as a baseline. The process as a learning relationship with specific reference to curriculum content is discussed further in chapter five. The process described here focuses more on the mechanics of teaching.

Teaching Process

The teaching process was by no means uniform. The Bridge Centre tutor used a lecturing style with slide deliveries, the DAB Centre projects revolved round interactive group projects, the East Lancs projects were based mainly around study circles and discussion. They were all, however, interactive and demanded more independent study than school or college experiences. It was this process which struck home for the students, along with a sense that the courses taught them there could be several sides to an argument (the rules of rational inquiry).

Anna described how she would use the course material as an aid for each session:

> There was a sort of small content ... where I would present something for say ten minutes, so its like a mini lecture in a way but there is something that people have to focus and can concentrate on and pick out sort of key features of it. And they had to use that in either small groups or pairs for discussion and then when we had feedback sessions. That's really like being in a seminar in a university setting.

Claire said something similar, but used the group situation to maximise the practice of their interpersonal behaviour:

> I would put them into groups with a different group leader each week, I'd move them around. I put into the group the person that I knew would keep them, pull them together and get the information out of them.

The exchange value of this teaching process was reinforced again and again by the participants:

> When we went into small groups and worked the questions out or whatever it was together in twos or threes. That's good I like that, not just working it out myself, but getting someone else's idea as well (Debra, East Lancs);
> Being together was really good and helping each other ... whereas at school you're really only interested in your own work ... these courses you just help each other (Fazia, East Lancs).

The outcome for participants in these courses was some kind of increased self awareness and access to a range of behaviours, attitudes and understandings which were broadly described under the umbrella term 'skills':

> All the skills we set out to learn we learnt without realising - like negotiating skills and problem solving and that sort of thing, being assertive (Susan, DAB Centre).

It could be argued that these experiences were simply the outcomes of good teaching. As isolated descriptions of a process, or content or subject material or process of self awareness, that is very likely. But their combined approach to reading, writing, analysis, discussion and relating what was learned to wider contexts provided a sum of the whole which both students and tutors identified as different from school or college learning. The skills framework was an analytical tool for facilitating an engagement with 'higher' learning processes. Higher education can take place outside of the university, though the providers usually have some association with the university provider (as evidenced by the WEA, for example).

This chapter has explored some of the arguments for and against the use of a skills curriculum in HE. The CAP adopted a relatively flexible and loose interpretation of 'skills' which did not particularly slot into the more prescriptive terminology of, for example, NVQs. Rather, we chose to construct our course frameworks around theoretical concepts of higher learning, and then set up modules which explicitly highlighted certain areas of learning from that theory. No doubt the process would be open to criticism from a subject discipline perspective. We felt, however, that 'skills' was a shorthand term which tutors and students felt comfortable with. The interviews enabled us to see how they were applying that term to their own teaching and learning, resulting in evidence of reflexivity, analysis and different degrees of complexity which both students and tutors associated with university rather than college or school learning. At the same time we were responding to pressures for convergence in terms of an identifiable higher learning whilst allowing students to continue to shape what they consumed.

The combination of teaching process and emphasis on lived experiences seemed to facilitate this reflexivity as well as broaden the learners' own horizons. Whilst some activities more closely approximated to 'study', others encouraged critical thinking via material which in university disciplines would be 'off limits'. The rationale for that off-limits curriculum is explored more fully in the next chapter, particularly in terms of how it relates to social and human capital.

5 A Curriculum Off-limits: Social and Cultural Relevance

> To teach in varied communities not only our paradigms must shift but also the way we think, write, speak. The engaged voice must never be fixed and absolute but always changing, always evolving in dialogue with a world beyond itself (hooks, 1994: 11).

Introduction

A potential argument for reviewing the HE learning experience in terms of its curriculum is that we need to address the perceived relationship between educational achievement and the application of social and human capital. If educational participation strengthens the reserves of such capital we must broaden participation in learning by the population as a whole. This immediately raises the question of how to engender such participation. McNair and others advocate a more learner-centred approach to learning in the new HE. They do not explore the practicalities of this on the curriculum itself. Indeed, while 'access' strategies for getting people into the HE system are now well rehearsed, the literature is still relatively silent about what to do about the learning experiences once people are in the system. This chapter argues that educational policies need to recognise the relationship between local identity and curriculum.

There is a small body of literature which takes a particular view of the curriculum in education institutions. This literature goes beyond advocating a more generic 'skills' concept of what is taught and learned in the classroom. The *curriculum* for instance covers more than just the syllabus. The learning environment and teaching relationships also impact on the student experience. There is a tendency in such literature to theorise these issues in terms of power and knowledge. Those who argue for a new kind of curriculum suggest that current ways of constructing knowledge and therefore the teaching of knowledge are value laden and designed to privilege only certain groups in society:

> Exclusion and inclusion as well as power, are closely linked to what goes on in educational institutions; neither what is taught, nor who studies what, are neutral issues. The cultural rules surrounding education are closely linked to the organisation and resources of teaching itself (Deem, 1996: 51).

In other words, drawing on Foucault (1980), dominant power systems define who has authority to know and who determines what is valuable knowledge. Only certain kinds of knowledge count as powerful and authoritative. The education institution perpetuates the status quo of this power relationship, thus making it difficult for those already silenced to get their voice heard (Goduka, 1998; Preece, 1999;1999a). Whilst the conclusiveness of this theoretical perspective is not without its critics (Moore and Muller, 1999) it provides an explanatory rationale for claiming the need for the marginalised to be heard and made visible on their terms. Making the marginalised visible often means developing curricula which are 'off limits' from academic rules for disciplinarity and authoritative texts. This chapter looks at both the teaching relationship and curriculum content for CAP's community learners. It claims that marginalised social groups need to feel included in the whole process of developing a course at HE level as much as any other level. This argument links to the previous chapter in that the notion of a transferable skills framework is posited as meeting the demands of credit transfer, while allowing for difference within that framework - an attempt to reconcile the local with the global. To this end we discuss literature references to the teaching relationship and curriculum content for minority groups, then explore how the CAP learners and tutors perceived these issues.

The Teaching Relationship

Attempts to tinker with the curriculum for equality reasons have usually been addressed in terms of its modularisation and timing. However, some research has identified gendered curriculum and attitudes in the classroom (Cronin et al., 1999) and an experiment in the States provided evidence of the positive effects of an integrated curriculum for African American Students. Zriny Long (1997) showed that the test scores of minority students who studied English and Maths in the context of African American history or religious studies were significantly improved compared with their control group who studied Maths and English conventionally. They emphasised that this experiment also included an interactive teaching approach - a critical feature of hooks' (1994) arguments for validating the marginalised voice. Hooks also emphasises the need for more than simply the practical process of interaction between student and tutor. She calls her approach 'engaged pedagogy'. She describes it as a learning relationship where 'everyone's presence is acknowledged' (p.8). In this process teachers are regarded as mutual learners and the students' lived experiences are central to informing the academic material. The nature of the teacher-learner relationship is central to ensuring an appropriate learning environment; the relationship encourages students to challenge what has previously been taught:

> Students want us to see them as whole human beings with complex lives and experiences rather than simply as seekers after compartmentalised bits of knowledge (p.15).

To this end she actively promotes the use of 'confessional narratives' (p.21) in the classroom and advocates the teacher-learner relationship as a mutual learning process.

Aronowitz and Giroux (1991) discuss a similar teaching style which, they say: 'Makes central to its project the recovery of [those] forms of knowledge and history that characterise alternative and oppositional others' (p.119). In other words there is a need for the marginalised to link personal identities and their experiences to the teaching content and process in order to challenge how they have previously been portrayed through dominant discourses (Preece, 1999). Gore (1993) suggests this process is perhaps ideological rather than totally achievable, though the recognition of learner context within the teaching style itself is one frequently adopted by adult educators (for example, Battersby, 1990). Such a teaching style enables access to different kinds of content within the curriculum.

Curriculum Content

The idea of a curriculum 'off limits' is seldom explored in the literature, particularly in relation to HE. It is mentioned by Barnett (1998) and Cherryholmes (1988) who do so in different ways. Where Barnett still uses concepts of knowledge and discipline in order to advocate the extension of curriculum (though to a lesser extent in his later work), Cherryholmes questions the very way in which knowledge is constructed in the first place. Barnett tries to contextualise curriculum in a critical, reflexive learning experience with the goal that understanding the role of the self is critical to learning how to contribute actively to a changing world. Cherryholmes more explicitly explores this notion of curriculum as a study of issues in the here and now which are currently 'disvalued and excluded' (p.133). Both perspectives have relevance for those whose voices are seldom represented in education materials as they facilitate the opportunity to move beyond subject matter confined by the limits of existing authoritative text.

Gibbons (1999) too, drawing on earlier writers, discusses the idea of an alternative curriculum, alongside the conventional mode of disciplinarity, as a new 'mode' of knowledge - context specific, transdisciplinary and transient, 'created and transmitted largely outside of universities' (p.20). Cherryholmes (1988), however, suggests that all knowledge should be viewed as transient and that the whole rationale for curriculum design is premised on value judgements and selectivity: 'And no one asked: why not teach about sexism, labor history, minority history, social inequality or injustice' (p.139). This latter point is of particular relevance to many of the CAP students and has been the subject of earlier debates on curriculum relevance for working class communities (for example, Lovett, 1982; Jackson, 1980).

Social and Cultural Relevance

Aside from advocating a more mutual teacher-learner relationship, it is the element of curriculum distortion in the education system which particularly features amongst critics on behalf of minority groups. Much of this criticism emanates from black writers who highlight the ethnocentricity of the teaching process. This is demonstrated in several ways. On the one hand existing knowledge is described as distorting the history of people's origins and development (Torkington, 1996); on the other hand the black experience is either patronised or simply ignored (Allen, 1997). The effect is to deny the silenced person's identity and to create 'disjunction between the values and beliefs about the nature of knowledge, its transmission, assessment and constitution' (Allen, 1997: 184). These sentiments are also expressed in different contexts for 'working class ways of thinking and being' (Lynch and O'Riordan, 1998: 460), and for disability identities (Marks, 1994).

Goduka (1998) in the South African context explains in some detail why learning materials need to be sensitive to cultural orientation if active citizenship is to be realised for everyone. He, too, asks for the student's 'lived experiences' to be integrated into the teaching strategies and learning materials and sees this process as essential for giving people a sense of self: 'The process of awakening one's identity and voice is essential for the development of skills for critical engagement and participation' (p.49).

The connection between teaching style, curriculum content and a process of helping learners discover who they are is a recurring theme in literature which argues for a better representation of the minority voice (Goduka, 1998; hooks, 1994; McMahon, 1996). This process is also regarded as integral to the wider higher education goal of engaging in a more global education, bringing us back to the tension between the global and local. In order to engage with global issues, Goduka argues, you need a strong sense of place and identity within the local sphere.

As has already been argued, the structure of university disciplines and teaching styles is particularly restrictive in enabling other knowledges to be forefronted. The most common method proposed for democratising the selection and control of knowledge is through discussion and dialogue (Mayo and Thomson, 1995). In terms of engaging with those on the margins of formal participation this task can be quite challenging as educational power holders are already inscribed in the dominant value system. It may be that a compromise somewhere between the ideal of pluralism and equality and a reality goal of inclusion has to be sought. Potential interim ways of addressing these structural inequalities might be found through an outreach approach which develops different kinds of curriculum outside the system, but linking institutional education with the wider community. Apple (1993) suggests this must result in:

> The conscious building of coalitions between the school systems and the communities being served ... creating new ways of linking people outside and inside of the schools together so that school is not seen as an alien institution but something that is integrally linked to the political, cultural and economic experience of people in their daily lives (pp 40-41).

On the matter of engaging with a relevant curriculum much of the teaching would then centre round Mayo and Thomson's requirement for a critical dialogic approach to learning which recognises community experience as a contribution to knowledge and as a means of understanding their cultural relevance to the curriculum; recognising values outside the dominant perspective of the education system. There may be opportunities within this experience to address hooks' more radical, transformatory approach. Barnett and others' concerns with developing a critical being may also emerge within an environment which is privileging local space as contextualised learning. Looked at in another way community learning for specified social groups allows critical thought to be explored from an insider view (Hill Collins, 1990). That is, the academic position of neutrality is shifted so that the marginalised social or cultural viewpoint becomes the position of neutrality, against which other values are compared and critiqued. Hill Collins' stance is to call this 'situated knowledge', where the oppressed or unrecognised voices can have epistemological privilege. Experience forms the basis of such knowledge and may be used in the teaching situation to critique academic theory, rather than the other way round (Skeggs, 1997).

The point behind all these arguments is that knowledge is relative to who owns it and the dominant discourse of (way of expressing) academic knowledge is not value-free. Difference, though, must necessarily be seen as multiple, otherwise one suppressed discourse will simply claim privilege over another. Research has shown that curriculum irrelevance in HE is often embedded in the above issues (Bird, 1996; Leicester, 1993). Lack of recognition of alternative knowledge or perspectives creates a sense of exclusion for minority or under-represented groups. Learning and achievement, therefore, must address diversity. These values of difference amongst marginalised groups need, however, to be re-discovered from a starting point of trust and mutual respect if new curriculum initiatives are to grow. From this, it is argued, identities will strengthen, with consequent effects on community cohesion and social growth.

The community access programme employed a wide variety of tutors who all demonstrated different teaching styles and ways of interacting with their learners. The learners themselves came from different kinds of communities, made different demands on the curriculum and expected different levels of interaction from their tutors. A good tutor for one group would not necessarily have been regarded as a good tutor for another group. We therefore constantly talked to students, community leaders and tutors, trying to match tutors and learners who seemed compatible. We did not always get it right, of course, and some courses were more successful than others. Some of the difficulties encountered included misunderstandings between tutors and ourselves as to the kind of academic learning needed in terms of work presentation and critical appraisal. Sometimes the students objected to the tutor perspective because they seemed not to be understanding where the students were coming from. Effective learning experiences were described in very similar ways, however. They hinged on positive student-teacher and student-student relationships, where students felt their experience and starting points were valued and were they felt a greater sense of self as a result of the opportunity to engage critically with their own values from perspectives which were supportive to their social or cultural identities.

We looked for examples in the tutor and student interviews, of off limits curricula and aspects of 'engaged pedagogy'. We wanted to see how people's identities were being validated to give the students a stronger sense of self and place. We looked for the promotion of insider views in the teaching relationship and examples of mutual learning. This meant finding ways in which the student voice and lived experiences contributed to the construction of knowledge and the development of critical being.

Teaching as Engaged Pedagogy

Whilst hooks and others discuss teaching styles primarily in terms of student-teacher relationships, the learners indicated that this was also somehow entwined with where they learned. Every student interviewed made reference to their local learning environment as a contributory factor to their positive experience. The comments were consistent across all three community groups. The environment gave them a sense of place in their locality, contributing to their identity and motivation to learn. Local space helps validate the fragmented identities of communities who are increasingly under pressure to respond to global definitions of themselves as homogeneous members of the wider (in the UK's case) European community. Local courses have a symbolic as well as practical value. Fahana described this environment specifically in terms of her East Lancs students' religion, gender and practical needs:

> They walk into the community centre, at that time there are no male classes, there is a crèche facility, they are all women crèche workers, they are all women tutors and its a real sense of community and belonging and sisterhood and they feel comfortable, they feel that they own that place and they belong there.

For that time at least the women were able to dominate the public space and localise it with their own shared identities. Whilst each group had practical needs for nearby teaching locations, such as access or crèche facilities, they also valued the atmosphere created in their learning environment. All said at different times: 'It was very informal, it was very open'. The opportunity to have a say in where the learning should take place also meant they felt valued particularly in its organisation: 'We feel as though we are part of the consultation'.

Alongside a desire for locally constructed learning environments, many also appreciated how the whole teaching approach catered for a range of learning abilities: 'You could work at your own pace'. Such comments are frequently cited indicators of learning value amongst community learners (see Preece, 1999; McGivney, 1999, for example). The consistency with which people articulated their satisfaction with both teaching location and atmosphere (sometimes in spite of the location's inadequate facilities) related directly to the way they were taught and learnt. If learners are to engage with the demands of global changes and their contingent unpredictability, their experiences must first be grounded in familiar locales, where difference is given its own sense of certainty, pace and place. This experience included the type of tutor input, the way class discussion was managed and a sense that their own input was valued equally by tutor and students.

Tutor Input

Those students who felt most marginalised in terms of their identity and culture were most appreciative of tutors who visibly shared something in the way of culture or physical appearance. For the Muslim students this was the starting point for building trust and engendering a sense of empathy. Tutor and course co-ordinator Fahana, for instance, said:

> If I were to walk in ... as a person who isn't an adherent to their religion or even from their cultural background it would set up barriers. ... so [it is important] to develop this relationship of trust ... [because] the women are still concerned about who has actually written this course ... I can understand their background and where they come from.

Though not all the students from the DAB Centre felt they needed to be taught by someone with a disability the presence of successful role models had a certain influence over the motivation of some students, as Tony indicated to his interviewer: You're in a chair ... and I am in a chair and [so I think] look what she's done ... so if you can do it, I can do it'.

The Bridge Centre participants did not appear to need the same tutor identity affiliations. This was perhaps influenced by their unanimous appreciation of the young, clearly spoken tutor who simply made them feel worthy students. Their sense of place was not threatened. Indeed, of consistent influence across all three groups was the way they felt they were being treated as equals by their tutor and fellow students. Here hooks (1994) and Mayo and Thomson's (1995) references to mutual learning and dialogue were paramount. The students' positive experiences hinged on being seen as whole beings and valued on their terms:

> She wanted to know our opinion as well, she wanted to know what we thought (Rubina, East Lancs);

> The tutor was actually coming round and asking us what ideas we'd come up with ... so the tutor actually became like another member of the class itself (William, DAB Centre);

> The way in which he could pick up something somebody said and sometimes say 'Oh I hadn't thought of that' - so that made you feel that things that you were saying were of equal value (Hilary, Bridge Centre).

In addition, the opportunity to share within the class produced a sense of togetherness:

> Empathy ... amongst the students as well.. a lot of empathy because you know, we've all got the same childcare thing going on and family responsibilities, so its good you know (Debra, East Lancs).

These comments were validated by the tutors as well: 'Hopefully we all learn from each other' (Betty, DAB Centre); 'It's the feeling that they are in control and that they are actually being genuinely listened to, they have a voice and their views aren't being policed' (Fahana). For some students the sense that the tutor was interested in your opinion and the opportunity to discuss issues with other students was something they had not felt was a part of more formal teaching situations. This latter kind of sharing is argued as a feminist, consciousness raising way of teaching:

> Connected knowers see personality as adding to an individual's ideas and feel that the personality of each group member enriches a group's understanding (Hill Collins, 1990: 217).

Its applicability to marginality, or even just good teaching is demonstrated here.

These exchanges in themselves, of course would not have been worthy of the label higher education. This came about from a combination of subject matter which was meaningful to each student as individuals and as members of a group - and a teaching strategy which encouraged student confessional narratives to become part of the tutor's educational tool. Fazia said for instance:

> Fahana she taught us how to learn, think about history of Islam really - we know these things but we don't think its history, how to put ourselves in the history, then pretend we're there and think about issues, why they were done and everything.

Similarly, Sally made connections with the opportunity to input herself and her particular disability experiences into the personal skills course and study skills courses and her own development in the way she thought and contributed to those around her:

> Because its a subject very close to my heart and something that affects me very badly and ... you see doing that, putting bits on paper about feelings and soon it did encourage me to get out there and help, to reach other people who have the same problem.

For hooks, this is part of a process which she calls 'coming to voice':

> Coming to voice is not just the act of telling one's experience. It is using that telling strategically - to come to voice so that you can also speak freely about other subjects (hooks, 1994: 148).

It is also another means of reconciling the re-fragmentation process of difference within converging systems of cultural homogenisation so that people had an opportunity to shape what they consumed.

Devising a culturally or socially relevant curriculum which simultaneously engaged with critical analysis, the student voice and reflexivity seemed innovative but potentially insular. The trick was to build on people's lived experiences as a knowledge base to construct new knowledge which was validated by and within their shared social or cultural heritage. Whilst all three groups achieved this strategy to varying degrees, again the East Lancs and DAB Centre groups demonstrated the process most clearly. Their 'differences' and choice of curricula were more off limits in relation to conventional UK university disciplines than the Bridge Centre's art courses. It was not their relationship to vocationalism, however, which counted - it was the way critical thought came from within the students' self identification and position of being different from the norm.

Curriculum off Limits

In different ways tutors and students demonstrated how they explored knowledge which was specific to their 'social situatedness'. Fahana saw curriculum relevance as validating the student voice and working outwards from a black perspective, using the learner's insider standpoint as a position against which other views could be critiqued with rigour. In her case 'black perspective' was a Muslim perspective, though the premise of her arguments held true for any marginalised group:

I walk in and teach as a Muslim. I challenge things as Muslim. I look at Muslim beliefs ... and I don't go in dogmatically with one set of beliefs, we look at the whole flexibility and universality of Islam. We look at non-Muslim views so these views are still stemming from me as an insider ... it doesn't reduce the academic level or the level of intellectual discussion in class.

Fahana explained how courses on this basis could apply the same principles across a range of issues:

A course which starts from the preset that you are looking at a particular group's norms, beliefs, values, way of life, way of thinking from an insider view and you are developing a course with particular people in mind ... it could be about the impact of unemployment on unemployed people and you are looking at it from the view of unemployed people. It could be about women in Islam so you are looking at it from the point of view not as an outsider whose looking in.

It was also about the value and status of such situated knowledge:

You are not saying that these are marginal views ... you are elevating those views to an important level ... by giving value to their beliefs and their way of life.

For hooks (1994) this process is critical to distinguishing between simply listening to those on the margins and according 'their work the same respect and consideration given to other work' (p.38). This insider perspective was referred to by Hegel as the Phenomenology of the Spirit (in Gosden, 1994). This standpoint argues that the growth of consciousness can come from one's position of being 'other' in opposition to and in relation to the normative dominant viewpoint. This gives the position of otherness a vantage point of being able to see things from a broader range of perspectives than the more constraining dominant view. Put another way, it enables the localised identity to re-group so it is better able to interface with the recasting of new relationships and interfacing systems.

This kind of curriculum operated on several layers. On the one hand it simply connected with otherwise unrecognised life experiences, motivating students to participate: 'I know this has got something to do with my everyday living as well and that's why I'm more interested in it' (Farida, East Lancs). On the other hand it validated personal knowledge in a way which encouraged people to make that knowledge public:

I thought well deafness is part of a disability anyway and I want to do something on disability ... that's because I'm disabled myself and thought well with the points that I put into this essay it may help other people who read it (Kevin).

In a later assignment he used his insider knowledge to critique from a unique perspective how non insiders might view another form of disability:

> I chose epilepsy because I'm an epileptic myself, I know what er types of epilepsy there are - how people react to them and I know when people go into [a fit] - the colour of their faces changes ... I tried to find out inside people [their thoughts] who do not have epilepsy, how would they react if they saw somebody in one, would they know what to do.

From these base lines, the students talked about how they critiqued and analysed issues, topics and perspectives which had little or no academic subject base but nevertheless were placed in a critical framework which meant that their analysis of situations was generating new knowledge. Susan, a DAB Centre student talked about how she developed her investigation into the local Age Concern organisation's activities:

> Even though I had the information it hadn't been analysed before like I analysed it, so it was quite interesting to think well, why has that happened and why has this happened and then to be able to look into it and find out the reasons ... it was like going into it deeper really.

Farida made a similar connection about her interest in women's issues and Islam:

> I found writing on the first Caliph ... I found it really interesting to compare it in my own mind when I wrote about it. I kind of compared it to now, nowadays and everything, so I found that really interesting.

So, drawing on Skeggs (1997), experience informs our take up and production of positions but it does not fix us in time and place. All these examples demonstrated a high degree of reflexivity. They also showed increasing application of the citizenship concept of self responsibility in civic society, articulated by Jordan (1996), in that they were putting their own learning into wider social contexts beyond their immediate circumstances.

A crucial aspect of using curricula off limits or subjects which are based around some sort of social or cultural relevance to the learners was the relationship between the curriculum and the student's sense of self. This meant their learning was inextricably linked to how individuals reconstructed their own identity as a result of their participation on the course.

The Reflexive, Critical Being

Being reflexive meant moving people beyond simply feeling more confident, though as DAB Centre tutor Claire said, this was also part of making themselves aware of their citizenship rights as well as responsibilities: 'Giving students a perception in life that they had rights, that they weren't to be put in a corner and dictated to and forgotten, that they were able to speak up'. Fahana developed this argument along phenomenological lines (Preece and Bokhari, 1996) which claim that her Muslim women's sense of difference should also be celebrated:

> They see themselves now as a different way of life but a very valued way of life ... its knowing your own history that empowers you ... they are exploring (Islam) and analysing it and they are repositioning themselves as Muslims in Britain.

This view was confirmed by the students themselves: 'I put my scarf on now when I go out - that's personal' (Rubina);

> I'm 43 and I didn't know all these things. And it makes you wonder where you are, what you are, so at least it really made us think that we've found something, the history ... that's what you want to know, don't you? Where you come from, who you are and what you are (Mumtaz);
>
> You gain a lot of knowledge, its helped me change you know in my home and family life, towards my children ... that knowledge it gives you a real life and how to go about it (Farida).

The consequences of a globalising world in terms of time and space were particularly significant for the Asian women - whose personal boundaries had been reconstructed through a Diaspora (the experience of living in a country twice removed from whence you originated). In a world where our identities develop from the discourses and images and attitudes of those around us the courses were a transformatory experience for women whose Islamic identity was marginalised by their social context in the UK but whose gender relations were also constituted differentially through 'contingent relations of power' within their own families and communities (Brah, 1996). In this way the women would both benefit from and struggle against the recasting of time-space boundaries of their experience in the UK. The course content was both a reflection of the changing world and an opportunity for these women to regroup and regain some stability through a shared identity which they could link with their homeland through the global concept of Islam.

The DAB Centre students, too, offered similar processes of reconstruction. Adult returners often reveal stories of identity transformation. They usually do so, however, in relation to their ability to conform to dominant values. Clearly there were aspects of this going on too in these courses as the students learnt to use academic conventions in their writings and gain grades approved from within the university. But they were at the same time validating their own insider knowledge and giving public credence to their own sense of difference, often radically different from the position they were used to:

> I mean we are not outcasts from society because of disability, there is room for people with disability to go on and do this sort of thing. I think that has come over quite strongly (Tony);

> It did make me look in a different light at what I thought I was ... it helped me so that I was helping other people as well in their personal life (Kevin).

Part three looks in more detail at how identities interface with citizenship and notions of social capital. Perhaps the conclusion to be drawn from these snapshots of the students and tutors' comments is this. A curriculum off limits needs a teaching style which validates the learner's experience as contributing to the creation of new knowledge. It can be explored in a critical framework through systematic inquiry and rigorous examination. But for marginalised adults this needs to be achieved in a context which allows people to be grounded in issues which directly connect with their own selves. This often means privileging the space of the local in order to contribute to more global concerns for social justice, civic awareness and shared values. Higher education tutors which use a curriculum off limits must also engage in mutual learning and see students as whole beings - allowing their individual narratives to be part of the syllabus. For Hill Collins (1990) this kind of knowledge construction was particularly pertinent to the African American student. We are suggesting that it also has applicability in the discourses for Barnett's new kind of higher education student as a critical, reflexive being. As the following chapter shows, however, there are implications for guidance and student support strategies if those most on the margins of higher education are to maximise their ability to create new knowledge which can be more widely disseminated.

6 Educational Guidance: Customer or Citizen?

Educational guidance and learner support, in common with notions of key/core skills and culturally/socially relevant curriculum, is open to multiple interpretations and consequently the subject of considerable debate amongst practitioners and policy makers. The need for a coherent framework of guidance and support is notable in the recent policy documents concerning further, higher education and lifelong learning (DfEE, 1998; Dearing, 1997; Fryer, 1997; Kennedy, 1997). The Fryer report states for instance that: 'The provision of up-to-date, accessible and impartial information and advice will be essential if a strategy of lifelong learning for all is to be successful' (Fryer, 1997: 8). It is not easy to address questions about the scope of this information and advice, or how it might be delivered effectively in diverse learning locations to a range of existing and potential learners.

The Community Access Programme's (CAP) approach to educational guidance and learner support was a holistic one. It was developed for the learners and contexts in which we worked. It included activities designed to enable adults with different educational and life experiences to find out about, enrol on and successfully complete a course. Throughout the learning experience they would be supported in collecting and processing information about educational opportunities that might form part of an individual progression route. CAP worked collaboratively with local communities in seeking to ensure guidance work addressed factors such as the learner's home circumstances, their previous educational experiences and current study support requirements, together with future life and study plans. This grassroots approach to guidance was intended to meet the needs of adults who lacked recent positive experiences of education. Many of them fell within the Campaign for Learning's category of 'strugglers' (Sargant et al., 1997). For these adults, educational opportunities are not obvious; they face multiple barriers towards change, experience multiple disadvantages, lack information about education and perceive costs associated with education as high. Yet, given the chance to participate in tailor made courses that took account of their needs they began to acquire additional knowledge and skills appropriate for lifelong learning and citizenship.

In this chapter we outline common guidance activities, underpinning principles and recent developments relating to guidance and learner support. Those selected provide a context for examining the rhetoric and realities of the community tutors' beliefs about educational guidance. We use tutors' accounts of their practice to discuss how guidance was incorporated within the teaching and learning process and consider the benefits of this holistic approach as a strategy for tackling educational exclusion and engendering independent learners and citizens. The findings conclude that many adults, especially those without recent positive experiences of education, often benefit from a more informal learner-centred approach. This kind of guidance potentially contributes to their development as autonomous learners and active citizens.

Educational Guidance and Learner Support - in Policy and Theory

One of the difficulties when writing about educational guidance is that there is no single definition or agreement about what activities it encompasses, what it is intended to achieve, who it is designed to assist and who is best equipped to deliver the activities. Bailey (1993) describes it as a family of practices that share something in common, whilst remaining distinctive, if only to the practitioners. The family of practices typically includes educational, vocational and personal guidance, counselling, career advice, learner and study support and possibly others. The National Educational Guidance Initiative (NEGI) final report (Further Education Unit, 1994) outlines the origins of the adult guidance movement in the UK. It places the initial recommendations of bodies like the Advisory Council for Adult Continuing Education (ACACE), the National Association of Educational Guidance Services (NAEGS), the Unit of Development for Adult Continuing Education (UDACE) and National Institute for Careers Education and Counselling (NICEC) in a wider political, social and economic context. Adult guidance gained wider recognition in the mid-eighties when UDACE (1986) built on previous work by NICEC and the Open University devised a list of core activities which formed the basis of subsequent discussions about educational guidance. These activities include processes such as informing, advising, counselling, advocating, assessing, enabling and feedback.

To underpin the delivery of these activities and enhance the delivery of guidance practitioners a series of underpinning 'values' (Brown, 1991), key principles or features' (Further Education Unit, 1994) or 'guiding principles' (HEQC, 1995) were developed. Given the overlap and collaboration between key personnel working on these frameworks at the time the overlap is not surprising. In essence these values and principles were all versions on a theme. The Higher Education Quality Council was clearly influenced by the rise of quality audits and offered their 'guiding principles' as a means of enhancing the quality of 'guidance and support arrangements for all learners, full and part-time, pursuing varied programmes of study both on and off-campus' (HEQC, 1995: 6). HEQC's guiding principles include a focus on learner centredness, confidentiality, impartiality, accessibility, and equality of opportunity. In their review of the guidance and learner support requirements of students in higher education the HEQC (1995) divide the multiplicity of guidance activities into four phases:

- pre-entry phase including information and advice about the course, and application process;
- entry and induction phase, focusing on the enrolment and familiarisation of institutional support available;
- on course phase, covering support services such as library, counselling, careers, and learning support via tutorials, effective learning programmes;
- and end of course phase assisting students in preparing for transition and progression to another course or a job.

These artificial divisions highlight the inherent problem of listing activities, principles and guidance phases. All tend to assume that it is possible to place aspects of the learning experience in separate boxes for sequencing into a linear and logical order through which the learner passes. Unfortunately, real life is not like that. HEQC and some institutional providers recognise the dilemma of adopting a model that makes assumptions about potential learners. Nevertheless there is a tendency for guidance services to fail to take account of the needs of adults operating at a pre, pre entry phase, the initial stage for most community learners (Oglesby and Houghton, 1997). The neat distinction between phases and associated activities inevitably becomes blurred especially within a lifelong learning context where learners arrive with an ever-increasing diversity of life and educational experiences. Furthermore it is not only learner diversity that contributes to the complexity of the guidance process. Courses delivered in semesters and available on a part time basis all add to the complexity of the challenge facing the potential learner as well as the guidance practitioner (Edwards, 1998). Basically the rise in the number of qualifications, plus the diversity of course titles and acronyms, is overwhelming. HEQC (1996) advocate greater explicitness about courses, arguing that: 'Clearer and more explicit articulation will also enable providers to explain to external stakeholders (including potential students) the purpose and value of education' (ibid., 42).

Whilst greater clarity of information and increased diversity in the educational opportunities available are to be welcomed they do exacerbate the confusion faced by prospective adult learners. Technology is potentially a revolutionary source of support for the guidance provider who faces the task of storing, processing and retrieving the ever-increasing mountain of information about educational opportunities. Yet despite the enthusiasm with which advocates refer to technological aids it is not that simple (Hillier, 1990). Their contribution to the guidance process encompasses information retrieval, information processing and matching systems, decision aids, work simulations and games, self-presentation aids and psychometric tests and checklists (Hunt, 1998: 129). There is a vast array of packages each designed for specialist markets and relating to education, training and careers. Yvonne Hillier (1990) at the beginning of the nineties asked: 'How do adult students learn about educational opportunities?' Her paper reviews the rise of technological support systems for processing information about courses. Her list includes the Training Access Points (TAPS); the Educational Counselling and Credit Transfer System (ECCTIS); Materials and Resources Information Service (MARIS); the Further Education Curriculum Information System (FECIS) and the National Educational Resources Information System (NERIS), together with guidance computer packages like CASCAID and Career Builder. To this list we might add a host of web sites developed by individual institutions as well as those devised by the University Admissions Service (UCAS), the National Union of Students (NUS) and regional initiatives like LAWTEC's current Adapt project developing a CD-ROM and online web service the 'Learning Experience'. The rapid rise of web sites provides further opportunities for individuals to undertake independent searches for information. This is a bewildering and overwhelming number of services and acronyms, even for those with some knowledge of the education system. The UfI through Learndirect, a DfEE national freephone help line, is designed to ensure adults have access to a service that will help anyone and redirect them to more specialised or local help as required. To complement this, and in response to government consultation on adult information, advice and guidance investment for local services is being established. Whilst technology enables guidance advisors to overcome some of the challenges associated with information overload this is only one of the many arenas in which it is making a contribution.

Chapter seven explores in more detail the problems and possibilities technology offers in terms of guidance, key skills and teaching and learning for a kind of higher education in community settings.

Despite the changes to education arising from globalisation and the increased numbers participating the evidence still highlights that those who have participated in education before are more likely to participate in the future (Beinart and Smith, 1998; Kennedy, 1997; Sargant et al., 1997). If educational providers are to redress this situation then the adoption and development of a coherent support framework that takes account of changes within higher education, as well as the diversity of potential learners, is essential.

People and Places

Delivering guidance activities depends on many factors - guidance providers, potential learners and the environment or context for delivering guidance. Firstly there are factors influencing the person who is giving guidance. These include their training, professional qualifications, allegiance to codes of practices, own educational and life experiences and the context in which they work (Blair et al., 1998; Sadler and Atkinson, 1998; Williams, 1998). The second influence on how guidance is delivered is the potential learner who is either seeking, or, who might benefit from guidance. There is a clear distinction between adults who are in a position to frame and ask questions to enable them to pursue a particular goal and adults who for a host of reasons are not ready, willing or able to seek advice. Blair et al (1998) studied learning in different learning contexts in Scotland. They found it was uncommon for adults to seek out information since many believed that they should cope or find out for themselves. The majority of the CAP adults (and young people) had not yet reached the autonomous pre-entry phase (Oglesby and Houghton, 1997). Consequently, they rarely sought, of their own accord, information about educational courses. If educational providers want to address the needs of this group of learners we argue that they need to adopt alternative strategies to communicate with and inform them about the educational opportunities available. The need to adapt guidance to the learner is therefore particularly important for black students, disabled students and people who are unemployed or have specific requirements and obstacles to overcome in returning to education (Clare, 1990; Dadzie, 1990; Houghton, 1998b).

The third factor affecting the guidance process is the environment, context or place. Fryer (1999) notes that there is 'no 'one best way' or universally applicable learning culture. Learning cultures will work effectively when they properly reflect the circumstances and needs of the people involved ... and suit their own practical priorities and desires (p.9). The dynamics of the guidance process clearly change according to where and when guidance is given (Watts et al., 1997). The conventional mode of guidance is a face to face interview, prior to a course. A recent alternative for pre-entry information and advice is the DfEE's free phone Learndirect service (DfEE, 2000). In both cases guidance occurs outside the learning environment on the 'boundary' (Watts and Young, 1998). This is usually in a rather formal context with the interaction focusing on the individual's decisions about course selection and often with little regard to the wider learner support issues. There is however, increasing interest in delivering guidance in more informal settings within a group context, as an integral part of a course which is more akin to a 'systemic' approach (Watts and Young, 1998). One of the benefits of this integrated approach is that it creates an opportunity to extend the localised networks, linking them to the global networks of the educational provider, thus enhancing the social capital available to the individual learner and their community.

Earlier work with long-term unemployed adults identified four guidance continua that enable providers to review their guidance strategy. The continua related to the degree of formality, spontaneity and choice given to the learner as well as the number of people involved in the guidance process (Houghton, 1998b). As with most aspects of teaching and learning the process of identifying a suitable environment, context and guidance worker to ensure guidance is learner centred, accessible and takes account of equal opportunities is not straightforward.

According to Watts et al. (1997) decisions about who is an appropriate person to provide guidance, as well as where, and how that guidance is best delivered, need to be made within a lifelong learning guidance strategy. Watts et al. proffer three reasons to support the need for a lifelong learning guidance strategy: to ensure that the best use is made of existing resources; to encourage continuity and progression and to identify gaps in provision and ways of filling them. Whilst supporting the rationale for guidance to take a central position in the lifelong learning agenda, we argue the strategy is incomplete if it does not also explore gaps in the links between providers. Whilst Watts et al. (1997) acknowledge the importance of establishing links they concentrate on mainstream transitional routes from school and adulthood. This approach is likely to continue to disadvantage people who drop out of the educational system. Beinart (1998) reports that these individuals have limited access to information about educational opportunities (Sargant et al., 1997: 74). For a host of practical and real life reasons there is always going to be a sizeable proportion of adults that need a grass roots pathway back to the mainstream, if that is where they want to go. Community contacts and tutors play a vital role by encouraging and inviting adults currently not involved in education to restart their lifelong learning journey. Chrisholm (1997) confirms the importance of 'grass root initiated and non institutionalised services' for women as a means of filling a gap in mainstream provision (p. 68). Arguably this approach is highly relevant and appropriate for other groups who have either been excluded or are seeking to return to education.

Learner Autonomy and Active Citizenship

CAP's proactive approach is designed to deliver guidance to adults currently failing to access other services. In addition to providing a complementary service it is equally important for anyone providing guidance to build links with existing services that have expertise in other areas. It is through these networks that issues of transition and impartiality are addressed. CAP learners belong to groups in society whose status and role as active citizens are often dismissed. As Fryer (1997) states:

> Developing a culture of lifelong learning for all will both recognise the forms and varieties of active inequalities and exclusion, wherever it occurs. Active citizenship will take many forms, and manifest itself in a great variety of ways (paragraph 11.13).

Arguably the attributes of an active citizen are similar to those of an autonomous adult learner. If true, then opportunities to enable adults to become autonomous lifelong learners are important, not just for the individuals, but also for their communities. The personal stories described in part three of this book highlight how learning brings with it feelings of self-confidence and self-esteem leading to a greater ability and willingness to contribute to society. Perhaps more significantly these learners acquire a belief that they have a right to participate. As Lister (1997) states:

> To act as a citizen requires first a sense of agency, the belief that one can act; acting as a citizen, especially collectively in turn fosters that sense of agency (p. 38).

The same sense of agency is necessary for adults who have previously felt excluded from, or who have not been involved in the education system for some time. The strategies for enabling them to restart their lifelong learning journey are not automatically the same as those provided by the mainstream. The conventional college, university, and even Learndirect guidance services assume that potential learners have questions to ask, have the confidence to ask their questions and have a belief that education is for them, or rather they are for education.

Unfortunately the majority of the learners with whom CAP work do not, at least initially, have this sense of agency. In addition to their own lack of belief about themselves as potential learners the messages they perceive from educational providers reinforce feelings of exclusion. For instance, depending on an individual's circumstances, issues such as inaccessible buildings, the timing of courses, or mixed classes, emerge as practical reasons to prevent people from pursuing education. Rather than belonging to communities of choice, with the luxury of choosing appropriate lifestyles, they belong to communities of fate (Jordan, 1997). In order to extend the choices open to their members organisations have to work towards reducing the disadvantages, in this case relating to educational opportunity.

Tutor Accounts - an Holistic Approach

In terms of widening provision, one of the issues CAP sought to understand concerned the community leaders' and tutors' strategies for extending learning opportunities. This meant identifying and tackling obstacles that hinder educational, personal and often economic advancement. The educational guidance action research cycle involved focus groups at the end of each course to gather feedback from students about barriers to learning. This information supplemented the personal explanations shared during the learner interviews. (Only brief references to student views feature in this chapter as these are incorporated within personal stories in part three.) There were three major strands in the guidance action research cycle involving tutors and community contacts. These related to personal interpretations of guidance terminology, practical implementation of guidance activities and participation in staff development activities aimed at developing educational guidance record sheets. This third strand was primarily a practical activity. Nevertheless, during the process of developing record sheets the use of terminology and alternative perspectives about issues such as translation support and accessibility emerged as potential areas for misunderstanding between policy makers and practitioners. The danger of assuming that all participants in the guidance process use language in the same way is a real one that educational providers would do well not to ignore.

The rest of this chapter compares tutors' and community leaders' discourses about guidance with their actual practice. It incorporates commentary on the guidance strategies used with a variety of adult learners. Groups included adults who are unemployed, in prison, have family responsibilities, have limited mobility and/or chronic health conditions, communicate using languages other than English, celebrate festivals that don't coincide with the Christian calendar, have concerns about travel, have acquired a variety of educational qualifications. Common features identified by tutors included:

- the quantity, format and timing of information and advice given to students;
- the importance of the tutor-student relationship and supportive learning environment in creating an effective learning culture;
- the assessment and counselling strategies for combating students' lack of awareness of their guidance needs;
- the positive contribution and role of peer or group guidance;
- and the diverse strategies for integrating guidance into the teaching and learning process.

The chapter concludes with an exploration of the possible benefits of adopting a holistic and 'educative' approach to guidance in terms of nurturing citizenship.

Asking tutors to explain what the key terms, educational guidance, learner support and study support meant to them, allowed us to gain an insight into what grass roots practitioners think. Whilst official definitions of educational guidance activities and principles exist, there is a dearth of research and evidence about what these terms mean in practice to those who provide guidance. In recent years, only impartiality is singled out for examination in any depth (Payne and Edwards, 1997). Other discussions focus on generic policy or provision for specific student groups such as women (Bailey, 1993; Chrisholm, 1997) black students (Dadzie, 1990; Hunjan and Kent, 1997) and disabled undergraduates (Manning and O'Hanlon, 1995).

Although the majority of CAP tutors did not have a specific guidance qualification they provided definitions that encompass many, if not all of the conventional guidance activities. This was reassuring. Some tutors described educational guidance, learner and study support as separate and distinctive. For instance Najma explained:

> Guiding somebody would be to guide them to make their own decisions, informed decisions. ... And learning support, now that you've mentioned it, puts it (the guidance) into context, it would be childcare facilities, travel

arrangements. And study support is actually assisting them to learn, it would be more academic.

Tutor descriptions tended to take account of the circumstances in which the tutor worked and the needs of the learners they sought to help. Overall, tutors adopted an holistic approach that tended to merge the activities. For example, Melissa, a tutor with considerable experience of working in a college environment described her approach to delivering guidance in a community context as one where she:

> Tried to weave this (guidance) in, to make it part of the process; because I think with a small group like this people who are coming from very different levels, different stages, different expectations. It is important to try and get some sort of understanding for everybody, of where they are educationally and where they want to be and what they want to concentrate on.

The desire to enable learners to achieve their goals and make informed decisions was something Carol stressed in her definition of guidance, which she explained was an activity that focused on:

> Enabling people to look at what they've done or what they can do in a positive light and then giving them information so that they can choose which way they would like to go, which direction.

A common strategy among tutors was to integrate guidance from the outset, focusing on helping and enabling individuals to realise their potential, and in many cases develop skills that contributed to the local community.

The tutor-learner relationship and learner centred approach was paramount. For adults feeling excluded from the education system the choice of guidance provider was crucial. According to Watts (1999) there are three categories of non formal guidance agents: those with existing relationships as family members, friends or personal contacts; those acting in a voluntary capacity; and professionals who have incorporated or been assigned guidance activities into their responsibilities. Community contacts and CAP tutors fell predominately within the third category and therefore shared features with other 'non-formal guidance agents who were more likely to have the contacts, the credibility, and the 'street-knowledge' (ibid: 21). CAP tutors explained what these attributes meant in the context of their learners. John one of the few male tutors stressed the importance of encouragement:

Sometimes (people) are a little apprehensive of going into what is seen as a learning zone and academic zone, it may be completely alien to them and they need that, they need encouragement.

For another tutor, guidance and student support was about 'unique sensitivity, communication and helping people' (Betty, DAB Centre). Likewise Kerry, who taught at Ash Centre, highlighted the supportive nature of her pre entry guidance encounters by explaining how: 'We kind of chat to them, and demystify the whole thing, saying its going to be relaxed, friendly and that we'll give any help that you need'. Silma, who worked with the women in East Lancs, was typical of those tutors who linked their personal and professional roles: 'Whether it's learning or their personal lives and basically giving educational guidance, me as a tutor and for me as a Muslim sister to them'.

Ultimately the meanings learners and tutors brought with them influenced the guidance process (Bailey, 1993). In recognising the importance of this claim, CAP appointed tutors who shared something in common with the learners they worked with. This allowed them to act as role models. This was a deliberate and important strategy as it enabled tutors to demonstrate, by what they said and the experiences they talked about, that they understood the learners' perspective. As Hannah (Poplar tutor) explained: 'I know exactly how they feel because I went to college when I was 35 and I thought I'm going to be alone as Methuselah's mother'. Furthermore this approach allowed tutors to anticipate learner needs.

The conventional guidance services assume that, if asked, learners know what their learning and study support needs are. Significantly the majority of CAP tutors reported that students were oblivious of the reality of their personal, practical and academic support needs until they started the course. Often this gave them the opportunity to think about their needs and begin to address earlier negative experiences that were preventing effective learning. Tutors responded to students by using their knowledge of the learner, and drawing on their own experience of studying. Perhaps more importantly they anticipated the issues that students didn't ask about, but which they needed to consider in order to complete a course successfully. As Najma, who worked with women of Asian heritage, explained: 'In a sense you mentally ticked off a number of issues'.

Working out what a course involved and what was required of them, as a learner, was very important. It was also a very individual and therefore complex process. Learners understandably based their assumptions about learning and what would happen in a session on their previous experience. For one disabled learner they assumed that the experience would be like school and therefore involve them listening to the expert teacher. When given an opportunity to comment, express their opinion and share their views they did not feel ready to participate. It was not until they experienced the course that they realised what they as learners wanted and needed. For other students, the opposite was true. Their concern related to a fear that they wouldn't be able to understand the tutor, or be able to ask questions, or share their experiences. Lucy a tutor working with adults with a disability pointed out:

> People have very different needs ... poor educational opportunities in the past, but their needs as individual people are very varied and include emotional needs to be able to get to the point of being able to learn and face a class situation.

Providing appropriate information and advice was not a straightforward or routine activity. It was not enough to supply details about the time, place, cost and a summary of the course. In making decisions about how to inform potential students about a course there was always a careful balance between supplying too much or too little information. As Fazey observes, 'we (guidance providers) are often guilty of presenting students with too much information and advice without helping them to unravel its complexities' (1996: 38). Tensions relate to the choice of language, visual imagery and format of information produced. Ultimately CAP publicity was designed to encourage a potential learner to enrol. It sought to counter the view that learning is 'unnecessary, unappealing, uninteresting or unavailable' for them (Fryer, 1999: para 3.9). Course information therefore presented the positive aspects of the proposed learning opportunity. Since many of the CAP students appeared to have a limited knowledge and experience of the education system the process of extracting enough information from publicity material was a further challenge. This was exacerbated by the fact that many did not believe they could cope with, or were the right sort of person to undertake an educational course. Carol, who worked with single parents, explained that information needed to be:

> Accessible so that they can realise that its for them and they can do it, and being encouraged and enthusiastic about things, so that they feel confident in order to move on to a course.

The community contacts stressed the importance of informal interaction with potential students as a key strategy for counteracting the multitude of challenges associated with the guidance activities of informing and advising. Invariably the most effective strategy for transmitting information and enabling adults to decide if they would join a course was personal contact. The learners needed informal but informative conversations with people they trusted and respected. Tutors gave a number of reasons to explain this approach. These often contrast with the centralised mainstream student services approach adopted by many colleges. Many tutors reported that a personal invitation to a student to join a group was significant. Students confirmed the usefulness of this approach, reporting that they wouldn't have thought about studying before the invitation.

The dialogue between community contact and potential student seemed to work, possibly because trying to translate the jargon and information in a prospectus does not have the same sense of immediacy or reassurance as a personal chat with someone they know and trust. Even when students tried to make personal contact with a mainstream provider to find out more information: 'Its not always easy to get hold of people. You need a fair amount of tenacity to be able to keep phoning' (Hannah, Poplar tutor).

Once the courses started tutors played a pivotal role in enabling students to evaluate their ongoing needs and identify possible solutions for themselves. Guidance activities were on-going. Paul (Poplar tutor) commented:

> They (the students) seldom know their learner support needs. Its difficult to give an example, (their awareness) evolves, you can sit down with a form and say 'tell me what your disability is, and if something happens in the course who do we contact?' ... You can start formally like that, but really its only as they become confident that little bits and pieces come out and you may not be consciously aware you are solving a problem, because they may not be consciously aware that they have a problem. It's the ethos that's important.

Whilst raising students' self-awareness was very important; it was only part of the challenge. Tutors described how it was also essential for them to ensure that the group learned about the tacit rules associated with a learning experience. For example, attending each session, especially for new learners seemed to be very important. It was not automatically obvious how best to catch up after missing a session; nor was it that easy, if the reason for your absence was a family commitment. The challenges of learning to become a student were exacerbated if the student made an unrealistic assessment of their learner support and study needs. Tutors suggested that in reality there was frequently a mismatch between what learners thought they could do and what they actually could do. This also applied to what they thought their learner support needs were and what they really were and perhaps more importantly what needs they were in a position to articulate. For instance, getting to the sessions wasn't a problem until the student had the reality of juggling various tasks. Similarly, finding somewhere quiet to study at a time when they had the energy to study was not necessarily straightforward. One of the benefits of having short courses, and integrating guidance activities into the courses, was that it was helpful in: 'Getting back into the rigmarole of learning, producing work, producing assignments and being involved in a learning setting' (Najma). At the same time Najma's women only courses provided opportunities for the women to build their confidence and self-esteem.

Students also provided their own source of guidance and learner support. Sometimes tutors facilitated this activity, at other times it happened naturally. Kerry offered several reasons to explain why and how students assisted one another:

> I think they probably support each other because we're seen as experts, whereas other people doing the course are more inspiring because they've done it. (Saying things like): 'Oh yeah, I remember how I felt, but don't worry, if you go to such and such a place you can find this out' - so I think they've probably supported each other, because they can see its achievable (Kerry, Ash Tutor).

Group and Peer Guidance

Group guidance and peer support is frequently neglected as a source of support, yet it is perhaps one of the richest resources available (Tallantyre, 1996: 82). When discussing their approach to group work, tutors referred to many of the factors associated with small group work identified by Yalom (1980) in Llewelyn and Haslett (1986). The beneficial factors tutors spoke about (not always using this terminology) included universality, cohesiveness, guidance, interpersonal learning arising from their individual input and output, often leading to an increased self understanding and engendering feelings of hope for the future (Llewelyn and Haslett, 1986).

Not all CAP courses were taught to self designated groups. Despite this the groups usually consisted of learners who shared a number of factors in common - such as physical, social, cultural and educational experiences. Furthermore the process of coming together to find out more about a common interest appeared to evoke many of the same benefits. Perhaps the most common benefit for individual learners was the sense of belonging to a group (cohesiveness) and a sense that they were not alone (universality). It was important not to underestimate the significant contribution of cohesiveness and universality when working with adults with low self-confidence, especially relating to their learning. Feelings of isolation varied from group to group and learner to learner. Sometimes they related to a learner's uncertainty and lack of confidence concerning a specific study task, such as their ability to write, or use the reference library. Alternatively the feelings of isolation connected to a learner support issue. For example, the challenge of trying to manage their time to cope with the demands of, or lack of support from, children and family; or a fear that the distance from the car was too great, or that the toilet facilities were inadequate for their needs.

The realisation amongst the learners that they were not alone was often an important breakthrough. Najma reported that after attending a community course women would say: '"God I can do this" and so just getting out and meeting other women who are in the same situation has been good enough to start them off'. As with the information, advice and other support mechanisms students provided for each other, group learning tended to relate to what some might describe as peripheral and unexpected issues that emerged during the course. In many respects the issues were located on the spontaneous end of the 'planned – spontaneous' continuum (Houghton, 1998b). Hannah (tutor) explained: 'People will come up with problems and they just get solved by the group, by us and by themselves'. A flexible approach from the tutor ensured that the opportunities for students to help one another became part of the learning process.

It is possible and often desirable to 'integrate' guidance into the curriculum (Watts and Young, 1998). CAP's foundation credit frameworks adopted this approach. The personal skill framework was particularly useful for dealing with personal learner support issues. As tutors became aware of issues of concern to students they endeavoured to build in opportunities for interpersonal learning, which Yalom (1980, in Llewelyn and Haslett, 1986) artificially divides into 'input' and 'output'. Many CAP tutors spoke about strategies they used to facilitate learning. In essence they described activities which supported the notion that educational guidance is an 'educative process' (Killeen, 1986). Consequently tutors sought to include opportunities for learners to learn from others within the group (input). To ensure that the process was an educative one they also encouraged learners to be critical and evaluate the possible learner support solutions generated by the group. For instance learners might share how they resolved a practical problem, or how they tackled a piece of work. Encouraging learners to respond to the needs of others in the group on study matters was sometimes more difficult than the more personal problems. Often this was because students underestimated what they had to offer. One tutor described explicitly how she integrated opportunities for 'output' interpersonal learning.

> We'll have a discussion about the learning, which has come from (an earlier activity) and actually encourage them to talk, not just about the subject matter, but how they did it, how they got there, what techniques did they use. And we've done quite a bit in the group and I have had them sharing their individual reading techniques, highlighting and note taking, ... letting students share their methodology as well as the content of their learning has been very useful (Melissa, DAB Centre tutor).

As well as providing study support this group approach was usefully applied to the often forgotten guidance activity of feedback. In respect of course facilities, one group identified that having a room closer to the lift would pose fewer physical obstacles for some of their group. They discussed the possibility of a room change for the next course with course organisers. A comparable issue for a group of mothers related to the starting time of a course. Taking and dropping children off at school took longer in reality and so after discussion the group agreed that the course would start slightly later, in order to minimise the disruption at the start of the session.

Of course, not all educational providers are in a position to change the location or starting time of the course to comply with the needs of individual learners. Transition is difficult for any learner whether they are moving from community provision to further education, from school or further education to university. The educational journey individuals want and are expected to follow is complicated. It was therefore essential for learners to think carefully about their needs and evaluate the range of options available to them. The approach employed by CAP tutors was similar to the 1970's DOTS career model (Decision-making, Opportunity awareness, Transition Skills, Self-awareness - Sadler and Atkinson, 1998). Although these activities permeated each of the foundation credit frameworks they were particularly important in the personal development and enterprise courses.

Conclusion

Although recent changes in higher education have opened up opportunities for adults who have previously not participated some of those changes have meant higher education is an increasingly complex arena for adults to negotiate. The status of a citizen, moreover, is defined as: 'The ability of all to share in the use of public institutions and facilities as full members of society entitled to equal respect' (Hoatson et al., 1996: 128). Learners' lack of confidence alongside their marginal socio cultural status diminishes their role as active citizens. Most of the CAP students were not confident as learners. They did not have a sense of their rights or obligations. Guidance delivered in a multiplicity of ways during the learning process can arguably help combat the problems faced by adult learners currently experiencing social and educational exclusion. Through the guidance process adults can be enabled to formulate an understanding of their needs and then be better able to vocalise those needs to the relevant person or agency. By incorporating these skills into the curriculum and making them more explicit the likelihood that they will be transferred to other areas of their life is increased. Reflecting on alternative ideas and facts, formulating an opinion and then being able to articulate it in different forums is a constituent activity of what it means to be an active citizen. Whilst guidance is not directly concerned with developing active citizens it can contribute to a learner's autonomy to <u>act</u> as well as <u>be</u> both a student and a citizen (Lister, 1997).

The integration of guidance activities within CAP provision offered the opportunity to develop awareness and decision making skills. This enabled individuals to think initially about their own needs, then identify and evaluate the available options in order to make realistic progression plans. Acquiring these and other higher education skills via a curriculum that was socially and culturally relevant empowered individuals to become more autonomous learners with a better sense of their status as social citizens. It also prepared them to access formal guidance services with a greater confidence.

Alongside these discussions about skills, guidance and curriculum is the question of IT as an integrated part of learning. An overriding aspect of globalisation has been the impact of information technology on all aspects of our lives. It would be remiss, in talking about a kind of higher education for adults if we did not explore in what way information technology interfaced with the CAP community learners. The next chapter discusses some issues and challenges around this aspect of the educational process.

7 Technology in the Community

The development of ICT skills is identified as a key requirement of learning for the twenty first century (Dearing, 1997; Fryer, 1997; 1999; Kennedy, 1997). Key skills are seen as 'essential features of government plans for education and training' (QCA, 1999). In essence:

> Digital (ICT) skills are seen as essential for the future prosperity of the nation as well as having the potential to remove barriers which exclude and disadvantage many people (Clarke, 1999: 16).

Unfortunately there is an increasing divide between those with and those without technological skills. Even though it is a government priority to place ICT equipment within easy reach of local communities, there are few explorations as to the impact of such strategies on new learners.

This chapter reviews how technology might enhance the educational experience of adult learners on the margins of higher education. In exploring relevant literature it highlights some of the obstacles and opportunities faced by higher education institutions and individuals seeking to integrate technology into the teaching and learning process. Finally it assesses the practicalities of CAP's engagement with technology in its goal to help bridge global demands and local identities, contribute to human and social capital and extend opportunities for active citizenship.

European Union policy suggests that technology is important in terms of developing competitiveness, combating social exclusion and enhancing social and regional cohesion (Field, 1997a). In acknowledging that technology is an extremely important feature of globalisation, bringing many benefits to students and tutors, it should be recognised that these gains are not automatic and need careful consideration if implementation is to be successful. Although the theme of technology was not a key feature of CAP's research, comments from tutors and students alerted us to the possible discrepancies between the rhetoric of policy and the possible reality of practice. We argue that whilst technology can enhance community learning it must interface with cultural and social relevance and appropriate learning support strategies.

As non-specialists, perhaps one of our greatest difficulties when considering the role of technology in education was our own unfamiliarity with the language. It is true that having explored the literature and considered the issues for this chapter our knowledge base is now considerably extended! However there is clearly a language barrier which influences the extent to which people can access technology (Mansell and When, 1998). We are very conscious that there remains a bewildering array of jargon that can exclude potential learners (and tutors) from engaging in this apparently inclusive globalising phenomenon. For instance, telematics, information communication technology (ICT), multi-media, hypermedia, digital, information or interactive technology, distance or open learning strategies are just some of the umbrella terms used in the literature. These and similar terms are often used interchangeably and this in itself can lead to serious problems, of understanding and engagement with the rhetoric, especially for the uninitiated. Although many working in this area recognise the problem of terminology (Field, 1997a; O'Rourke, 1999; Roberts and Keough, 1995; Tait and Mills, 1999) and attempt to offer explanations and a rationale for their particular stance, the possibility of a communication gap remains. Arguably this continues to perpetuate exclusivity and limit the use of technology within education. Significantly it is not only learners who may be deterred by the terminology. Boddy (1997) reported on a small-scale study that looked at the perceptions and attitudes of staff operating within a single faculty toward a sample of terms relating to new technology. His study suggests that tutors need to become familiar with the language, aware of what technological resources are available and build up a useful knowledge base about the capability of those resources. These pre-requisites, of familiarity, awareness and knowledge, are necessary in order to distinguish between the host of new technologies that may sound similar but may offer a diverse range of alternative ways to enhance the teaching and learning experience.

Staff concerns regarding the use of ICT are similar to those associated with any change process experienced by their learners. Thompson (1999) divides staff into 'enthusiasts' and 'adopters' whose willingness and capacity to use technology differs. Inevitably tutor attitude towards computers influences the learning experience they provide and their response to learners whose interest and ability to use computers does not match their own. The challenge of enabling learners to communicate effectively in the twenty first century using appropriate ICT equipment is not solely the responsibility of tutors. We would argue that policy makers within further and higher education have a crucial role to play in providing the structure and resources to support tutors in acquiring the necessary skills and confidence to adopt technologically based teaching strategies.

Appropriate staff development is crucial if tutors, who themselves are often learners in this field, are to have a positive attitude and the confidence and competence to integrate technology into their practice (Clarke, 1999; Thompson, 1999).

Care and attention are necessary when exploring how, and in what way, a particular piece of technology might be used. For instance, the amount of time required by staff to answer e-mails, or the disruption to other work caused by participation in more regular video-conferences should not be underestimated. Although tutorial support via e-mail can provide a valuable link for isolated students, educational decisions to address their needs should not only be paramount they should also be explicit and realistic.

Jane Field (1997b) provides a useful checklist of good practice for anyone wanting to incorporate the use of technology into their provision. She identifies a series of pitfalls as well as opportunities and benefits that may be experienced by those embarking on this venture. Pitfalls include student and staff attitudes, access to hardware and software, time and cost factors, the potential isolation of students, and lack of tutor expertise or competence to integrate technology into their teaching. Ironically the benefits derived from its use are often the antithesis of the above pitfalls. Many of these issues emerged during interviews with students and tutors and will be discussed later.

For students (or tutors) who fall within the 'techno phobe' category (Field, 1997b) an initial fear of the actual technology can seriously inhibit the likelihood of learning (Robinson, 1997). Many learners, especially those, who are unfamiliar with computers, need to have a positive introductory experience to establish a baseline level of confidence in their ability to use the equipment. If this grounding is missing the technology itself can become one more obstacle that they have to overcome. This is particularly true for learners engaged in adult basic education: 'Learners need a system where they feel self-confident and self-reliant as they use the technology to help them achieve their educational goals' (Buck, 1997: 25).

For learners and educational providers obtaining access to suitable equipment can be a hurdle. This was an obstacle we encountered whilst exploring the possibility of using specialist ICT equipment to enhance provision for students with a disability. There are a host of hidden costs that need to be taken into account when providing ICT equipment. These include maintenance, upgrading, and compatibility with other equipment, together with the cost of software and consumables. From experience we add a note of caution when concurring with Jane Field's (1997b) advice to research thoroughly before investing in equipment.

Although IT maintenance for the educational provider may be cost effective, unfortunately the reverse is often true for the student. A cutting edge university may seek to reinforce this message by presenting an image that it only uses the latest technology. Regrettably this can inadvertently reduce the access of its community learners who may be using last year's, or even last century's model. Not all learners in the community have access to up to date resources, which can result in them spending an inordinate amount of time on-line trying to down load complex large files. Alternatively they may have to bear the brunt of printing costs because material is sent via e-mail, or is accessible off the web. If money is a concern this may reduce learner motivation, or force them to try to work from the screen, making the learning task more difficult and potentially less effective. John Daniels of the Open University reminds us:

> Individual access to new technologies will vary in a way that has the potential to make the rich educationally richer and the poor, poorer (*Preface*, Daniels, 1995: vi in Roberts and Keough, 1995).

As well as real or imagined cost, there are clearly differences in learning alone at home and learning in the company of others or having ICT equipment as an optional rather than a compulsory component of a course. According to Brindley (1995) guidance and learner services should:

> Take into consideration the unique and changing needs of the students being served and the institutional context, and should be revised as appropriate, to accommodate changes in student population, the institution and the environment (p. 109).

As new technology is introduced the limitations, as well as the advantages, need to be understood by tutors and students alike. The complexity of using IT to create opportunities for interactive teaching and learning experiences and the importance of providing quality learning materials are confirmed by Quentin Whitlock's (1999) article, 'Author! Author!'. Simply making conventional teaching material available on the World Wide Web (WWW) is unlikely to connect with the local identities of many learners, especially those adults learning in a community context. It is all too easy to be lured by the possibility of using ICT to bridge the global time and space divide between learner and provider. Whilst community provision might be enhanced, Jill Mannion Brunt (1997) in her chapter entitled 'can you put your arm around a student on the internet?' cautions against the loss of features such as personal contact that cannot simply be substituted by the new systems.

Different learners need different learning opportunities and support to enable them to achieve their goals. As Tait and Mills (1999) point out, the normative expectation that all learners will be able to operate independently is an inherent danger associated with the increased use of technology. The chapters on key skills and guidance have already highlighted how for many CAP adult learners the learning process is a communal activity. Considerable thought needs to be given by providers to the process of integrating technology into the learning experience if they are to avoid excluding students who are presently not ready, or whose circumstances makes independent learning difficult or unsuitable: 'No matter how "virtual" an institution can be made by new technology, the need to establish local identity remains' (Challis, 1997: 123).

The role of guidance in helping people to choose the right course alongside appropriate learner support throughout the course is also important, perhaps more so in courses using ICT. Cost and access to equipment are two of the practical factors that might be discussed during the guidance process. They have been identified as influencing the participation rates and adoption of technology, particularly for women (O'Rourke, 1999) and adult learners falling into the categories of 'other' (Tait and Mills, 1999). The creation of a network of locally based learning centres like those developed in Sheffield through their CITINET initiative (Wynne, 1999) are an attempt to address learner support needs and concerns about access to equipment by making technology more readily available. Creating the necessary infrastructure is a major, but crucial task (Kirkpatrick and Jakupec, 1999). Learning centres with hardware and trained staff available to support students are commendable and necessary. They are, however, only part of the overall equation. Students also need access to appropriate learning materials. Technology offers the technologically confident tutor the possibility of adapting teaching material for specific groups. Currently there are many tutors who lack the necessary expertise or time to be able to maximise the benefits of this new technology. The challenge of moving it from the margins to the mainstream of our educational provision:

> Requires new synergies in working relations and much rethinking as they are integrated into the fabric of tertiary (and community) life, impacting on teaching, research and administration (Thompson, 1999: 150).

In terms of the organisation of the learning experience these new technologies offer opportunities to provide greater flexibility - a feature valued by the majority of adult learners, including CAP students. The flexibility of new technology means that students can, at least in theory, have the opportunity to learn asynchronously using materials that have already been adapted to their needs. This addresses their diverse time and space learning requirements.

One example of this flexibility is the role of the Internet. Giving students access to the Internet and enabling them to explore for themselves the range of material available might increase their access to a diverse range of culturally relevant information. Simon Cooke, physics student and a BBC competition winner, described the Net as:

> Possibly the largest store of information on this planet. Everybody can be part of it; it is one of the few places where race, creed, colour, gender or sexual preferences do not prejudice people against others. All through the magic of modern technology. Communication is the key. People talking to people. The Net isn't computers. That's just the way we access it. The net is people helping each other in a worldwide community (Cited by Buck, 1997: 23).

Accessing culturally relevant information via the Net can increase learner motivation and provide them with an opportunity to develop the critical qualities required of higher education using material that is relevant to them. At least, this would be the case if all marginalised social groups had equal opportunity to present information on the web.

In spite of these messages of concern community based education which uses IT can provide some adult learners with an opportunity to gain the skills and confidence to use technology in other aspects of their life including employment, community capacity building, leisure interests relevant to themselves, and their families or local communities. Further Education colleges and continuing education departments offer a myriad of courses with 'computing for the terrified' or basic computer courses proving to be a popular pathway for adults to recommence their lifelong learning journey (Gain and De Cicco, 1999). This provision is to be complemented by the University for Industry (UfI) which is a central component of the Government's vision for tackling the digital divide and maximising the uptake of the lifelong learning agenda (Wills, 1999).

Once acquired, ICT skills can be used to provide access to education in the home or workplace, as well as bringing geographically separated groups together to share information. So for example, specialised self-help groups, like those with whom CAP worked, might be assisted in supporting, at a distance, learners with similar needs to their own. At present the potential for this type of networking and the opportunity to use this global medium to support the transfer of local knowledge is greater than the reality which can be restricted by cost and compatibility of equipment (Robinson, 1997).

The literature confirms that within certain boundaries the contribution of technology is potentially great (Buck, 1997). There are clearly issues that need to be addressed if it is going to be used effectively for marginalised adult learners studying in the community context described in chapter two. The factors already identified relate to terminology, staff and student attitudes, confidence to acquire and extend existing ICT expertise, staff and equipment costs, management, production and access to suitable materials, quality control and the appropriate integration of ICT opportunities within conventional teaching and learning. Although not a primary focus, ICT featured in CAP provision in a variety of ways that responded and extended the learning opportunities available for adults learning in the community.

IT in the CAP Community

The CAP interpreted IT, or ICT, broadly. It included TV, video, audio cassettes, telephone, computers, CD Rom and the world wide web. Some equipment was purchased specifically to provide a mobile service of laptops as well as more low tech facilities such as tape recorders. Ways in which CAP used ICT included:

- a community focused information technology foundation credit course;
- optional activities within other foundation credit courses to use ICT equipment to find information, complete assignments;
- encouragement of students to complement learning in class by watching suitable television programmes, using a tape recorder to undertake their own interviews;
- response to student requests for additional equipment, for example laptops;
- opportunities to use organisational resources to improve the presentation of assignments;
- advice and guidance to aid progression on to ICT courses available from other educational providers.

We looked at how this provision operated in terms of the curriculum, assessment, learner support, and changing attitudes.

Curriculum

ICT featured both directly as the main focus of a course, and indirectly in the form of additional facilities, depending on availability of equipment, individual confidence and interest. In addition to the four foundation credit courses – personal development, study, investigation and enterprise - described in chapter four, CAP designed an 'information technology in the community' course. This focused on the application of technology within a community context. Students were encouraged to make explicit the relevance of technology in their studies and in their everyday lives. The assignment consisted of the practical application of word processing, database and spreadsheets for specific community or individual goals. This opportunity was responded to across the whole range of student groups.

The introduction of laptops and CD-ROMs was a novel experience for a group of older adults attending the Bridge Centre. Lawrence, their tutor recalled:

> They smiled about [the computers] today, because I said next week we'll probably get someone to show us how to use the computers to track down books and they all laughed as if to say I'm never going near a computer but I think with the CD-ROM it'll be good for them.

The introduction of technology into this study skill course on art history was a notable success increasing the active participation and interest of the learners and other people attending the centre. The art history course was designed to include an introduction to the use of CD-ROMs. Laptops were located in the Bridge Centre and a National Art Gallery CD-ROM was provided for the students to use in between sessions. This addition to the course allowed members of the Centre who couldn't get to museums and galleries to complete their assignment by visiting a virtual museum.

> I think the fact that we've got the CD-ROM is a benefit from that point of view. ... There are just so many images on the CD-ROM and often they'll say, I'd like to know more about a particular image. I've got 2000 slides and I can't know everything about every single slide, so often its been useful for them to get another view of that image. I think this is what [the CD-ROM] does, and especially for students that haven't got physical access to galleries or libraries, its terrific that they can come here [to their local centre] and there's a library that they can press a button and get access to (Lawrence, Tutor).

For Lawrence the laptop and CD-ROM addressed some of the time and space difficulties faced by learners studying at a distance from the main university base. It was an opportunity to bring learners to the main library and introduce them to what was available.

From this first introduction learners at the Bridge Centre, in common with other 'silver surfers', began to understand new links between global events and local needs. On a practical level one woman used a spreadsheet to monitor the expenditure for her mother's nursing home, another lady found that a database was the answer to her problem of cataloguing a vast collection of cigarette cards.

For IT provision to be appreciated, however, it still had to be delivered on the learners' terms. A group of Asian women attending the Unity centre welcomed the opportunity to have a women only introductory course, 'technology in society'. Women attending this course varied enormously in their levels of ICT experience. Through group work they discussed current terminology, their children's IT curriculum at school, the opportunities they had to use computers for personal and community goals such as writing letters to school or future employers, producing CV's, or preparing publicity material for the centre. The importance of access to women only provision was highlighted by Farida, one of the women from East Lancs, who explained how she had attended a basic IT college course. Although this course had been delivered in the community the tutor had been a male which made her feel uncomfortable. Subsequent attempts to develop her IT skills to help with assignments were quashed because they were only available at the college, which was an option her husband did not support. The way IT is introduced to individuals and groups, therefore, must still address issues of identity, cultural and other personal needs.

Attempts to participate in IT courses at college were not always a smooth process. Farida's need for women only provision has already been discussed. Melanie faced a different obstacle when she tried to enrol on a college computer course. Unfortunately she was not able to attend as the class was held on the first floor and there was no lift, which made it inaccessible for her as a wheelchair user. The importance of supported community learning proved an essential bridge for overcoming this problem. The obstacle was discussed during a personal skills course with other members of the group offering suggestions and support for how she might offer constructive feedback to the college. The education officer at DAB Centre, Betty reported:

> The positive outcome from that (personal development course), is that she is actually going along to [the local] College to do computer studies, she's coping with that now, ... at least by coming to the group it gives me the

opportunity to say, you're on the course, how is it going, so that can boost her confidence and get admiration and support from her fellow students.

The above example demonstrates how CAP tended not to focus on developing computer skills per se. Rather the goal was to enhance other learning by drawing on ITC as and when appropriate. Instead of competing with the colleges, we provided tangential opportunities for students to recognise the importance of ICT in their study, voluntary activities, for future employment or as a resource for their family or local community. Computers provided a useful focus for engendering peer support, with students gaining confidence from working alongside other members of their group who had more experience. Several enterprise courses made good use of ICT equipment and provided students with real life opportunities to develop their communication skills. Two such projects were undertaken at the DAB Centre; the first involved the development of promotional and informative material about the centre and the second involved setting up a charity shop to serve the local community and raise funds for the organisation. The promotional group used computers to design leaflets about the centre's activities, and produce a portable display with clear and professional signs. This has since been used to promote the services of the disability centre throughout the local area. Prior to their own involvement in the organisation, many students reported feelings of isolation and loneliness. In their assignments they reflected on the importance of reaching out and helping other people and believed that their professional display would send out the right messages to others in their local community and beyond. The second enterprise project, the charity shop, also involved a computer to produce leaflets to request 'good as new' items for the shop and to remind local residents about collection days. This group created a database for keeping details of volunteers and organising the timetable. In this respect the equipment became a further tool for enhancing and extending social networking opportunities for active citizenship and as a reinforcer of social capital.

The skills gained were also viewed as potential human capital by some. The enterprise activities allowed groups to share their existing expertise with their peers and through a process of critical reflection and evaluation of the group's strengths and weaknesses, they identified skills, including ICT skills that they needed to acquire in the future. Several of the DAB centre students have since progressed to other computer courses. William, for instance, felt he would like to develop his computer skills and use them in a future career:

> I hope to have a career later on in life in management, and I hope to be learn computer accounts, because I actually do a lot of dealings with the money, book keeping (at the centre and the shop). I hope to learn how to computerise those and hopefully ... in turn ... September/October I hope to be learn to do computerised accounts which will help me later on in life.

The role of IT in contributing to social or human capital had to be nurtured and contextualised, however. Whereas computer skill courses focus on the technicalities of how to align text, insert a picture, CAP courses encouraged the learners to consider critically the end product, its purpose, and its audience. Another enterprise course involved a group of Muslim women living in East Lancs. Their course, entitled 'Voices in the Community', involved them using a computer to produce a questionnaire, which they used as the basis of their consultation with the local community about future educational interests. Some of the group spent many hours designing a guidance leaflet to answer questions about returning to education. There was probably as much time spent by the whole group talking about the layout, presentation and content of the leaflet as on the IT skills themselves. The leaflet was designed to complement a presentation that the women gave at a dissemination event also entitled 'Voices in the Community' (Houghton and Ali, 1999). In this way the use of a global phenomenon was appropriated for local ends, but re-invested for wider, regional purposes – again enabling the women to extend their social capital networks, whilst retaining their own cultural identities.

Similar experiences could be identified across the different projects. A third enterprise course involved adults attending Riverside Resource Centre, who wanted to produce a magazine. Whilst some became computer experts, others assumed greater responsibility for editorial decisions. This course and the work undertaken by learners outside the session made considerable use of computers. Competition for using the centre's computers for 'work' rather than games increased, with some members not previously involved in the magazine offering to type up articles, or design the front cover. This enterprise also involved the use of other communication technology, including the phone and audio-tape. Since some of the members attending Riverside Resource Centre have visual impairments or limited literacy the magazine group recognised the importance of producing their publication in different formats including tape. Learning to use an audio-tape effectively and produce the taped version provided some of the group with a regular commitment to the needs of others in their wider community and gave them a clear role and responsibility as active citizens beyond the centre itself. It moved them from being recipients to contributors and thus increased their citizenship activities (Barnes, 1997). Within the centre skills and confidence gained by learners in one group on one course were sometimes used to benefit other learners. A group of older learners at Riverside had been studying local history. Listening to the taped magazine contribution of their group broke down some of their fears about using and listening to audio-tapes. After several practice sessions, learners began to interview other centre members about their memories of the past. This brought to life the history and documentary evidence that they had discussed in class. A booklet of their memories is currently being produced.

The adoption of better known technology for educational purposes can build learner confidence in modern systems (Mansell and When, 1998). As an educational tool the benefits of television have, according to Field (1997b) been proven. Certainly CAP learners reported watching television programmes to extend their knowledge of a particular subject. Elsie, an older adult attending the art history course at the Bridge Centre said:

> I've recorded on video, television programmes on artists, you see, ... because if the subject interests you, you do, you just do want to see it again. ... so, with listening to Lawrence [the tutor], I'm having the video as well, and the books I've got - I've got a lovely enclave of learning in my little bungalow which I return to, you see.

The importance of visual images brought into the living room, or classroom is clearly recognised by the television companies who are actively seeking to maximise the links between their programmes and the Internet, with many programmes now having their own web sites. In response to external agendas for lifelong learning and widening participation the BBC commissioned a small-scale inquiry 'BBC broadcasting as a means by which viewers may access higher education learning opportunities' (Storan, 1999: 13). The partnership between education and television is likely to grow as global channels like the BBC offer quality stimulus that is familiar and non threatening to the majority of adults.

Obviously television alone would provide a learner with an impoverished diet. Putnam (1995) expresses concern about the impact of television on everyday lives. He believes it is partly responsible for the demise of civic engagement and a decline in social capital, resulting from time spent alone at home watching television and an increased passivity when watching. Although there may be some truth in Putnam's claim it perhaps depends on how and for what reasons people watch television. Several CAP learners moved from simply watching television as a source of entertainment to watching for a specific purpose. Television for them became part of their education extending their knowledge and supplementing topics covered in their courses. Arguably they became more discerning viewers, who asked questions and thought more critically about what they watched.

Assessment

The stimulus to learn basic computer skills often originated in the students' desire to submit professionally finished assignments. Some centres like Ash, Riverside and DAB were able to provide access to computers. Kerry from Ash highlighted the benefits:

> It is so much easier for them to put their work on and then revise, not revise change it round, slot it in, because if they are constantly having to rewrite everything they would just lose interest and its too time consuming.

Nicola from Ash, was typical of many students; she found the opportunity to enhance the overall presentation of her assignment a significant source of motivation. This was not, however, a universal response and the usefulness of a computer was not surprisingly influenced by other factors including confidence in the technology as well as reasons for study. Student Tony explained:

> I started doing it (the assignment) and I got a lot of it done, I actually did it on an Amstrad laptop and then when we came down here to try and transport it, we couldn't do it. And then the tutor at the time managed to do it, managed to get the bit, and then it went all hey wire in the end, so it didn't get done.

In spite of this non-universal acceptance, computers did provide a focus for learning together and sharing of expertise. Diane, a tutor working with the young adults, described how students would attend the centre for additional study support:

> So that they can use the computer facilities and they can use the adults around to help them [with their assignments]. There have been adults doing other courses for the University of Lancaster in the past, so they know the sort of [presentation] criteria they should be working towards.

Several groups, especially those with students who had a physical, sensory or learning disability, arranged for the results of group brainstorming activities to be word-processed. This enabled individuals to help their peers, practise their IT skills and 'produce a neatly presented finished piece of work which provided a permanent record of the group's ideas' (Diane).

Learner Support

Time-space constraints do not always require high-tech solutions. Tutors encouraged students to support one another and talk about their work via the telephone as a conscious effort in developing support networks:

> We made sure at the beginning that everybody was happy that their telephone numbers were circulated among them, so everybody has each other's telephone number, and everybody has my telephone number. I know that some of them ring each other, nobody has phoned me. Now, I've told them they're quite welcome to do so. If anybody had, if people had got into the way of phoning me and saying "I've just been doing this piece of work, I'm a bit stuck, can you help me?" I suppose that would be an example of direct learning support (Claire, DAB Centre Tutor).

The mutual support and opportunity to discuss ideas outside the session was something some students felt hadn't happened with other courses that they had attended at school or college. As William explained:

> When we were doing the Lancaster University course, after the session had finished you could come away and be working, and you could phone your colleagues up of an evening and see them the next day and discuss it with them. Whereas with the college, you don't, once the whistle goes you are out, and you don't see them till like the next week. I think [the tutors] were definitely approachable. I mean they let us phone them outside the course of an evening if anyone has a problem.

Even telephones were not an attractive feature for everyone, however. Not all students felt comfortable or confident when asked to use the telephone to find out information, make arrangements for their enterprise. These concerns often emerged during personal development courses and were particularly prevalent among students who did not have a phone at home, or who had a physical disability that made using the phone difficult. Several tutors explained how they would support students in using the telephone to talk to official people. The DfEE Learn-direct free phone (DfEE, 2000) is a national service designed to provide information and advice to adults about educational opportunities. In addition to issues about the terminology and prior knowledge learners are presumed to have, this service should not automatically be deemed suitable for all people.

Attitudes Towards Technology

As one might expect the attitudes of CAP students towards technologies included enthusiastic converts, hesitant beginners and disinterested luddites. In many ways ICT was a leveller. Some adults like Mumtaz obtained support from their family, 'I've got to be grateful to my son, he's done all the work on computer for me'. Others found the computer aided communication between the generations. Bernadette spoke about her friend Rose, who also attended the Bridge Centre: 'She was 70 this year and she's got a computer she uses with her grandchildren [and] they have got those weird and wonderful [game] things'.

Increased confidence gained from a personal development course enabled Debra to participate more in her child's education indirectly. This contributed to breaking down her fears about the equipment:

> I'm not as frightened of computers as I was before ... they've got them at [my child's] Nursery - they've got two computers - and my three year old is now I think probably better than me - setting the game up - she can actually do that and I can't.

Asked about the impact of the CAP courses Debra went on to explain how they gave her:

> More confidence to go on to do another course. I think I wouldn't be scared of going down to the College and doing something. I would have the confidence to enquire about any course I wanted to do.

The interface between various forms of technology and community learning extended the content of the curriculum and equipped learners with skills to access information that was relevant to them, their family and local community. As we evaluate the impact of ICT on the lives of these adult learners there are indications that lives and family relationships have been transformed by their involvement with new technologies. Skill acquisition and technical competency may be better developed by attendance at further education courses. However alongside the development of critical skills associated with higher education it is clear that community learners have the potential to be more discerning as they interact with more global communities via the Internet. For some learners, ICT provides a means whereby they can develop their confidence to participate and take an active role in a wider, more diverse social capital network that utilises new technology. There are many advantages, but as highlighted at the start of this chapter there are pitfalls. It is therefore vital that:

Distance educators [and those using ICT] must respond to learners and their learning preferences, organise both human and technical infrastructures based on what is already in place, and envision all future possibilities and challenges from the perspective of the community (Paquette-Frenette and Larocque, 1995: 178).

In particular it is important the ICT becomes a supportive facilitator rather than replacement for face to face learning and allows participants to shape what they consume.

PART III:
THE LEARNERS' STORIES

Introduction

Chapter one introduced some of the tensions between globalisation trends and the reaction of local and regional communities to the convergences of time, space and new communication cultures. The perceived tendency is that communities re-fragment or re-group in order to retain their distinctiveness so they may shape, rather than be shaped by, the new world they are consuming. These tensions between the local and global are particularly pertinent for higher education in its trans-situational relationship between these two opposites. A kind of higher education necessarily plays a part in both worlds. Brah (1996) points out, however, that the fragmentation of communities and assertions of difference do not guarantee a place for the minority voice as difference also represents a vehicle for legitimation of dominance (p.90). Marginalised differences therefore may need a helping hand to redress the imbalance of power.

Global education discourses currently promote human capital as the desired transportable commodity. The literature also suggests there may be causal links between acquired social capital and the ability to achieve or generate human capital in communities. UK government desires to secure non economic or indirect economic, arguments for education, which do not carry immediate human capital benefits, are fuelling an interest in this perspective.

These ideas bear some relationship to notions of citizenship where citizens of a given country have both rights and responsibilities to that nation, manifested in public and civic actions. Both these terms have implications for lifestyles and status of some social groups, particularly in relation to class, dis/ability, race and gender. The concept of citizenship, for instance, has been criticised for its lack of acknowledgement of the private rights and obligations of women and the undermining of minority community differences. Those 'differences' are often the very characteristics of distinctiveness through which minorities construct their subjective selves. There is a relationship between the discourses of social capital, citizenship and identity which can define and exclude the local in the interests of the global. This is evidenced in the way some individuals choose to participate in or support education through the dominant culture.

The next three chapters offer a close-up exploration of some of the complexities of these interfaces for individuals from three different social groups. They look at what social capital and citizenship might mean in practice for these groups and analyse some of the intersections between localised and globalised identities. Within their separate contexts, the chapters explore the relationship between a kind of localised HE and the indirect economic benefits of responding to new contexts for building social capital.

As the majority of participants interviewed were women we look in particular at the gender status of social capital and citizenship with its implications for economic accountability. In chapter eight we also look at the additional complexities of Diaspora - how Muslim women of Pakistan and Indian heritage have formed identities and roots in locations which have resulted from multiple generational journeys.

Social Capital

As chapter one outlined, social capital is generally defined as a form of social behaviour which is found amongst cohesive families and communities where reciprocity and mutuality form the basis of informal communication networks. Collective interests and mutual trust create a kind of interdependence where each informal member absorbs and understands the unwritten rules of behaviour of that social entity.

Wann (1995) suggests that social capital is a form of social wealth which provides what the market cannot. In this sense social capital has economic value. It is a non market driven means of exchanging 'knowledge skills and power' (p.103). It is a means of creating the ability to manage unpredictability by relying on spontaneous responses to local situations generated through an ethos of self help. Etzioni (1995) suggests this comes about by communities' 'interpersonal bonds to encourage members to abide by shared values' (p.ix). The difficulty with Etzioni's model of community is the implicit assumption that communities are homogeneous and that one community's concept of 'civil and moral order' is the same as another's. Similarly his emphasis on family values as an indicator of social capital (p.135) presupposes that all members have an equal power relationship within that family.

Fukuyama (1995) also suggests that the trust which emanates from shared values has 'measurable economic value' (p.10). Fukuyama evades the problem of differential values between social groups by suggesting that there are some core societal values which individuals with high social capital can draw on which enable them to 'form new associations and operate in several different groups' (p.27). To this end he advocates that family trust alone is not a sufficient resource for social capital if there are no links to wider social bonds. Fukuyama's version of social capital is strongly economic and links to wealth creation. He identifies highly capitalist communities like Japan as having high levels of social capital. As with Etzioni such a definition would suggest that only certain forms of gender, cultural and context specific activities have any discursive value - leaving minority social groups without equal rights to share in that wealth creation. Chapter one discussed how Putnam, Coleman and others are looking to wider definitions of social capital which have a broader social welfare, as well as economic, role - linked to educational achievement. The extent to which social capital in adults feeds into, or is led by, educational participation is inconclusive. However, high initial social capital, it is argued, provides the foundations for initial educational achievement and therefore the resources for sustaining good citizenship values which in turn build strong economic communities.

Citizenship

Citizenship is defined in terms of status, rights and obligations. Status is defined by membership of a country or nation state as 'participating in the political, economic, cultural and social arenas' (Oommen, 1997: 10). This assumes a homogeneity of membership alongside its civil, social and political rights without reference to notions of identity or equality. Alfonsi (1997) points out the ambiguity of these terms for different ethnic groups and Rosenau (1997) emphasises the increasing instability of a citizenship based on national identity and culture in the light of increased mobility between countries. Indeed many nation state activities transcend political citizenship boundaries. The influence of globalisation therefore means that citizenship is not a stable reality, though its discourses give an appearance of making it so.

Another feature of citizenship, as many feminists have articulated (Brine, 1999; Ackers, 1998; Lister, 1997), is the lack of a legal and therefore political or social definition of citizenship which takes account of the private or family role played by women. In terms of rights or participation in society, these activities are largely ignored, both as a contribution to the economy and for their social capital values:

> The family constitutes a system of welfare provision largely operating outside of the formal labour marked based on relationships of 'mutual obligations' and 'compulsory altruism' (Ackers, 1998: 30).

Ackers emphasises the informal care role played by many women as well as their shifting forms of dependency over the life course - affecting their social status and rights. If such women are also migrant women, their legal status as citizens is further diminished (Ackers, 1998; Lister, 1997).

Lister (1997) discusses further how citizenship discourses assume an obligation to support and uphold the common standards of the dominant community, thus diminishing the rights of disadvantaged groups to react against their own status or treatment:

> To refuse to apply the label of citizenship to ... the struggles of poor women, or black or disabled women for justice, is to reinforce the very exclusion against which these groups are fighting in the name of a common good (p.30).

Similarly voluntary work and care work or being active in the private sphere are not seen as part of the public or work world of the assumed citizen.

In spite of these ambiguous distinctions between legal citizenship status and public discourses about 'active citizenship' Green (1997) points out the limited attention in UK schools to citizenship as a subject. This both delimits the chance of challenging what is simply an internalised concept imbued with everyday behaviour and opens up possibilities for exploring what an alternative, gender, disability and age or culture sensitive citizenship might look like. Lister suggests we need a multi-layered analysis of citizenship which takes account of globalisation influences and the dynamic position of the modern nation state. Such an analysis would have to take in the private and public world of rights and responsibilities and one which also takes account of identity and difference.

Identity

Whilst identity and culture are never fixed, Woodward points to the paradoxically increased tensions for identity, brought about by a transient and converging world. Nation states and communities are breaking up and re-forming and economic and cultural life is increasingly becoming transnationalised. This has resulted in changing consumption and production patterns with a convergence of global consumer identities alongside new identity positions or resistances to convergence. This and resultant migration, she says, has impacted on the pluralisation of identities and also helped create contested identities (Woodward, 1997: 16). For those migrants whose ethnic and cultural selves are significantly different from the host society the word 'Diaspora' has been coined. Diaspora represents the experience of identities which are not located in one home and cannot be traced back to one source. Hall (1990) describes Diasporic identities as 'those which are constantly producing and reproducing themselves anew, through transformation and difference' (p.235). Individuals from diasporic communities find their identities are shaped and located in and by different places. For some there is a tendency to re-group and re-assert the identity of the country of origin. Multiple identities constitute our 'subjectivities' - our sense of self in relation to how we perceive others see us in a particular social context. The conceptualisation of these selves is constrained by the discourses available to us at any period in time. The sense of self, however, is a critical influence on individual decisions to participate in education (West, 1997; Preece, 1999a).

Giddens (1991) claims that self identity today is necessarily a reflexive process where individuals have to negotiate their way through a variety of experiences, making sense of the present in relation to the past - both in its social context and in relation to personal histories. Subjectivities constitute our multiple selves which evolve as a consequence of how we position ourselves in relation to others. Whilst our identities and subjectivities are a product of, and constrained by, the discourses to which we have been exposed, they are also sustained by power relations (Code, 1991; 1995; Skeggs, 1997). Power is contingent at least in part on how individuals interpret those discourses and respond to influences around them. Individuals therefore always have the possibility of agency or self determination (Code, 1991). As identities are not fixed they are open to reconstruction (West, 1997). The relationship between personal biographies and their collective historical contexts is complex and contradictory (Brah, 1996). Feminists would add that issues of race, gender and disability are also subject to contingent relations of power, manifested through those discourses (Brine, 1999; Brah, 1996). From their various positions dominated groups may create political identities, appealing to 'bonds of common cultural experience in order to mobilise their constituency' (Brah, 1996: 127). But in order to analyse the practice of culture for such groups at any point in time it is necessary to remember that culture too is a process rather than a fixed entity: 'Our gender is constituted and represented differently according to our differential location within the global relations of power' (ibid: 102).

It was within this theoretical framework that we tried to understand the citizenship and social capital values of each community of learners by listening to the personal stories of individuals who had chosen to do several courses through the community programme (CAP). The rationale for understanding the social capital outcomes of their reflexive interface with a critical higher education environment was precisely because many of them had limited human capital value - due to age, physical condition or social circumstances. Yet we wanted to find out whether such a programme could be justified for reasons beyond quantifiable employability outcomes.

The following chapters attempt to find examples of citizenship and social capital which are based around the identities of those least entitled to conventional citizenship rights or status. We also explore how aspects of social capital identified in the literature might enhance the learner's individual and social potential. We look at how the learners' sense of self interfaced with their learning experiences on the CAP. This sense of self would contribute to underlying social networks and activities which might form the foundation for future learning and economic development within their communities.

The categories through which we sought to explore these issues are:

- evidence of *human capital* - through qualifications and training or choice of learning programmes;
- indicators of *citizenship* - especially socially or culturally bound examples of citizenship as duties or obligations;
- influences of *globalisation*, such as diaspora, space-time constrictions, communications which impinged on or were appropriated by the local communities;
- forms of *social capital* - as an existing experience, acquired through course participation or influenced by disability, culture, race, gender or class;
- *subjectivity* - discussed as the contextualised sense of self, informed by culture, family, location, friends, school and connected power relations and manifested in different identity formations.

'Discourse' is used throughout to denote the way meaning is given to words or behaviours. Discourses are usually context bound by culture, time and dominant values.

8 Nurturing Social Capital in Communities: Women in East Lancs

> Identity is simultaneously subjective and social and is constituted in and through culture (Brah, 1996: 21).

Of the ten students we interviewed in East Lancs, two were white and English, one was a Kenyan Muslim Asian and the remaining seven were all Muslims who were born in Pakistan but came to England at varying stages during their childhoods. These experiences were vastly different from each other. Mumtaz, for instance had never been to school in Pakistan, due to a mobility disability. By the time she arrived in England at the age of thirteen most of her remaining school years were spent in hospital. All spent their final school years in England but few had qualifications beyond O level or GCSE. Their ages ranged from 25 to 50 in 1997. All had children. Naomi, aged 48, was a grandmother. Azra was a single parent.

Although coming from vastly different backgrounds the women shared two constraints - a general sense that education was not 'pushed' at home for them and a more recent struggle of ongoing commitments towards young children throughout their participation in the courses. The Asian women's stories of when they arrived in England and all the women's stories of their school experience and family relationships contributed to how people saw themselves. These self images were mediated by their particular interchange with other discourses as well as how they used their own personal agency in response to those discourses. The most disadvantaged sometimes appeared to travel the furthest, while those apparently on the road to wider opportunities would find themselves following a life path in which they felt powerless to intervene. Sometimes the CAP courses gave the women access to new discourses which could be used on their behalf to re-negotiate their identities within their family. As the women's subjectivities were constituted by their experiences as citizens within a globalised world and in relation to social and human capital, these features are discussed separately in order to put their identities into context.

Human Capital

Only three women indicated they had never taken up paid work. Debra, one of the most qualified had been a graphic designer though her most recent job was a playgroup assistant. Naomi had been a district nurse, though she was now arthritic. Azra and Rubina were sewing machinists. Shazia worked in factories and shops while Nasreen had taken an office job and at one time helped with her father's business. Their human capital in terms of skills and qualifications were generally unguided. Early qualifications were often incoherently packaged and simply taken up because someone suggested that course or because they thought they would try something at the FE college after leaving school. In this way their memories replicated many stories told by working class women in the UK - particularly of an older generation (Preece, 1999). Debra, for instance, aged 41 and with three children, lived with her Libyan husband. She obtained three O levels at grammar school, a diploma in design at art college and had done a number of pre-school playgroup courses, plus an IT and first aid course. Farida, age 32 lived with her husband and five children. Although she taught Urdu at home she had not worked officially. She had some CSEs from school, started a BTEC course at college but eventually did a YTS nursery assistant course till marriage at the age of 19. She too had done an IT course and was in the middle of a correspondence course with an Islamic Society.

Human capital, it appeared, was not linked to any strategic plan for these women. Many used their own initiative to study an IT course and / or crèche course in the interests of helping their children, though at least five were hoping to gain employment related qualifications - either to teach or do nursing. In this respect their ambitions were already different from earlier generations (Yuval Davis, 1994; Preece, 1999). Their human capital value was, nevertheless, in most cases both untapped and under-developed - by school, family and careers advisors. The courses they had taken were usually ones which had been made available at the local community centre and which accommodated their family circumstances. Perhaps more significantly most women indicated they were attending courses at the community centre for as many as five or six sessions per week. The apparent incoherence of the programmes on offer had their own rationale for the women who adopted their own definition of human capital in terms of their multiple roles within the family and community. Fazia, for instance, did a crèche, computer, sewing and the CAP Islamic and Studies Skills courses:

> The crèche course, um I wanted it for career value, but also to understand my children's needs and what they needed at certain times of their life. Cause I think even though motherhood might come to you naturally you don't always know what they need at which stage. The Islam course, to gain further knowledge about different areas of Islam. Studies skills course because at school they never teach you how to do essays, you know, it doesn't come naturally. Now I feel that I can do essays better. And my sewing course because I can sew but I've forgotten everything about sewing. .. My computer course because computers is something that you need today.

Human capital for Fazia intersected with her unwaged role as a mother, as a carrier of cultural values (Yuval Davis, 1992), as a resource for future ambitions and a recognition of the modern technological world in which she inevitably lived. The concept of employability was multifaceted, with an eye on many fronts. Fazia's own efforts to re-skill herself with human capital was already interfacing with her multiple relationships with globalisation, citizenship and social capital.

The Global/Local Interface

Although, as Giddens states, no-one can opt out of world changes, both global and local events influence each other. Furthermore the diasporic nature of the Asian women (and indeed Debra was married to a Libyan) produced an intriguing kaleidoscope of interactions between countries where the women had lived and sometimes worked. Some examples of the rooting and shifting of ideas and values and use of constricting time-space mechanisms seemed to simultaneously reinforce old values and hurry the pace of change and communication between individuals and communities. This manifested itself at college and in everyday life. Sometimes the diasporic space created tensions such as Farida's experience when she tried to attend the local college: 'In Islamic ways ... we had strictness and everything in the home ... but in college ... the girls that went ... their home atmosphere must have been different'. At other times it enabled the women to re-negotiate their needs, such as Mumtaz's disability facilities: 'I don't think that I could have done what I've done if I was in my country ... you haven't got any help in Pakistan, have you?'

In other ways the global concept of Islam became a focus for broadening local perspectives and raising local awareness about wider global debates which affected local issues. Farida, after attending the

Islamic studies courses was keen to draw on this knowledge for the benefit of other women: 'I want to write on the plight of women. I don't know, something Islamically and yet also in society today for women'. In this way she was capitalising on old, but global knowledge to maximise its value in the modern, local context. Giddens calls this making sense of the past in the present (1991).

The most obvious influences on old, local values were the use of technology and the new discourse of qualifications. The women took on board both these issues. Forty eight year old Naomi identified a need to learn about computers in order to link with the world of her grandson: 'They have computers at school ... but I wanted a bit of an idea how they worked and everything'. Similarly, she internalised the new world of qualifications - not necessarily for herself but in the education discourses she used with her family: 'A lot of my friends they wanted to leave school and go into a job ... but now the jobs aren't there ... so people are looking at other things like further education'.

Perhaps the most striking effect of globalisation, however, was the opportunity to physically slip between the countries of Pakistan and the UK. For the women of Asian origin their families were often split across Pakistan and England during childhood within families and across generations. Going back to Pakistan, even after long absences was essential for two reasons. On the one hand it was necessary to recapture cultural links. After eleven years of absence, Shazada returned at the age of 16: 'I wanted to see Pakistan and see what its like and you know, all the family was back there'. But it was also necessary to reconcile intergenerational changes. Otherwise parents of one generation would stay rooted in one set of traditions which had already shifted during their absence. So, for instance, local attitudes to study were perceived to be caught up in the global discourses for skills, and convergence of gender opportunities. Rubina observed:

> When we went to Pakistan I'd see more girls studying than boys. The attitude has changed over there, has changed so much, girls are doing better at school and getting jobs ... but my parents, like when they came, my father came in the early 60s and from what he saw back then children, their parents didn't send girls to school ... they kept that attitude you know.

Sometimes attitudes for new generations would change, though Rubina pointed out that somehow the old gender power relations for her generation were harder to let go of: 'My husband ... he is eager for both my daughter and son ... I ask him - well you didn't let me go and he'll say well it was different then, education is important [now]'. This generational connection of changing values towards education is not confined to Asian cultures (Brah, 1996) and is found particularly in research with working class communities in England (Purvis, 1991; Roberts, 1995). Indeed Naomi and Debra in these interviews discussed similar parental attitudes to their education.

This rooting of cultural positions and shifting of new values is identified by Yuval Davis (in Lister, 1997) as an example of how culture is constantly in progress. These stories of rooting and shifting from a Pakistan perspective were also mirrored in perceived attitudes about England towards the Pakistani culture, as Mumtaz, one of the longest residents noted: 'It has changed a lot in thirty years, its working towards our community (now) and only if they know how to get things in the right way, I think they still try (to do this)'.

There was evidence then of globalisation influences in terms of convergence across and within communities irrespective of distance and timescales. These samenesses were also matched by strong efforts to retain a sense of personal, religious and cultural values which would give the women a sense of belonging and sharing within their immediate locality. The location of the CAP courses contributed to this desire as chapter five showed. The women's own roles and responsibilities within their community, however, showed how dominant globalisation discourses also silence and make invisible whole lives and communities. These lives and communities would function almost subliminally through their own social networks, performing particularly gendered acts of citizenship and building particularly gendered forms of social capital.

Citizenship

Citizenship in terms of responsibilities was demonstrated in two ways by the women. On the one hand women performed particular 'compulsory altruism' family roles expected of them: 'Once the girls were married they were supposed to do the home, cooking, cleaning, bringing the children up' (Farida). As Ackers (1998) states citizenship for women was about following expected norms through a sense of obligation about their role. Their citizenship membership was first and foremost to their cultural ties and to their status as women, rather than the UK. Citizenship, then, was a power relationship, held in place by dominant discourses both from UK immigration discourses and from within the culture of their local communities.

Within that power relationship the women would appropriate their family duties and obligations by extending them sometimes to the wider women's community and at other times specifically in relation to their own religious or cultural members. So Debra described how she worked part time with children: 'I worked in the playgroup two days a week. Apart from that I've been to children's parties here, we have our staff meetings here'. Farida spoke of her desire to teach about Islam as a form of social responsibility: 'Islamic teaching, I would like to head in that direction, not as a career but as benefit to my family and to other Muslims'. Fazia extended the idea of such unpaid versions of work to the business world, suggesting that courses could be provided to facilitate this: 'Some of our husbands have got businesses, we could help them by doing their accounts or knowing how to run a business'. Citizenship as an obligation and duty to others was instilled at an early age for many women:

> We were eight brothers and sisters and I used to look after them - I was only seven years old and I used to help my mum changing nappies and picking my youngest brothers and sisters up and feeding them as well. I was ten and I could make chapattis and do the cooking (Azra).

Azra also extended this role as young adult to preparing her younger Pakistani cousins for school in England:

> I made up flash cards ... I learned them how to ... read one word each, first the alphabet, then the words, and then make sentences, sort of progress from there. I helped my cousins out and they can speak English, sort of not very good but sort of broken English.

Such activities were not always confined to family relationships. Mumtaz, for instance cited how such acts of caring would be extended to wider global concerns, usually around membership of the global Muslim community: 'I've always been active with Sister Shazia and we did all the what you call this money raising things for Bosnia'. Indeed it is interesting to note that the majority of Muslim women would refer to fellow Muslims, particularly teachers, as 'sister' - denoting the discursive, universal bond of one Muslim family.

This level of gendered responsibility was not confined to the Pakistani women. Naomi, a grandmother, who had in the past shared the upbringing of her own daughter with her grandmother, explained her responsibilities for her grandson:

> Taking him to school and picking him up from school, amusing him in the holidays ... I have to take him for hearing tests and things like that ... [he is] diagnosed with dysphlexia .. so I'm taking him here, there and everywhere ... because you're on the phone you know, [to chase appointments] to see if they've forgotten his name and everything.

Also, echoing Mumtaz's religious family connections, Naomi talked about her work for Oxfam: 'I'm in Oxfam, I contribute to Oxfam'; as well as attempts to do other voluntary work: 'I did a little bit of voluntary probation work which at the time ... but with me working in the hospital working shifts, I couldn't do it ... whenever they wanted or needed you'.

The other women would report similar 'care' activities either within their immediate extended family or in relation to wider 'care' roles. Their citizenship activities were controlled only by their economic and political status. Responsibilities and duties to care superseded rights to paid work and any employment laws against exploitation. Civic duties were largely private and behind the scenes and built in to their daily lives. Where efforts were made to go more public, as Farida hoped to do: 'I would like to write something that would fit in with society today ... you know nowadays, facing the problems and everything, Islamically how it should be'; these were often unwelcome by the men. Farida's husband told her she should not do any writing, (though Farida was ambivalent as to whether he was going to succeed in preventing her).

Many of the women were trapped in a set of discourses which produced a gendered state of citizenship which might at first appear passive. In spite of this they often showed signs of an active mutuality which gave them an opportunity to trust each other and reciprocate as well as validate their activities separately from the men.

Social Capital

The focal point for almost everything the women belonged to was the community centre where the playgroup, CAP and other adult classes were held. Here the women formed friendships, exchanged information, tried out new activities and built up support networks for themselves. Debra, for instance, said: 'Through the toddler group, I met Lesley (employed by the college as a playgroup leader) and then found out about the classes'. If the women did not obtain their information direct from attending the community centre then they would from links via people who did. Such people usually held some known position of authority for the women:

> I used to see sister Jabeen (college and community centre outreach worker) going to school and she's a governor at school, so I used to talk to her and she gave me some information about the courses (Azra).

The mutuality of needs would spill over and intersect with all the centre's activities, as Farida commented when discussing one of the CAP courses: 'And we might have sorted a few problems out, you know each others' problems by just talking, cause you've got different views'. Social capital is understood as an arena for generating trust, establishing expectations and in creating and enforcing norms (Coleman, 1994). For the Muslim women this meant interfacing with their wider family and community, building on their own sense of agency derived from the shared social experiences of being a Muslim:

> It has affected my life, I've changed myself and I'm now applying it (Islam) to myself ... my children ... my husband, to the family members .. so everything is just changing (Farida).

In this sense their experiences of the CAP courses reinforced Wann's (1995) claim that social capital is also a form of social wealth which would help the women to manage the unpredictability of their changing identities and circumstances. The courses tapped into existing social capital but the courses themselves extended that social capital so it could be used as social wealth.

Putnam (1995) claims that social capital consists of a series of different relations between people, which are interactive and productive, making possible the achievement of certain ends that in its absence would not be possible. For Mumtaz this meant engaging the support and practical help of her children to achieve the qualifications she had always been denied through lack of schooling. Unable to write in English, or use a computer, Mumtaz would dictate what she wanted to say to her children and together they constructed her assignment: 'And the enjoyable thing was that my children did it with me and they helped me a lot. If it wasn't for them I'm telling you I wouldn't have done it'. The ripple effect of this behaviour did not stop there, of course. Her children gained new knowledge about Islam which they then passed on to their school teachers and friends.

Coleman (1988) emphasises that where human capital is brought about by changes in the level of skills in people to enable them to act in new ways, social capital is about changes in the 'relations among persons' (s100) which enable new action. For the women in East Lancs social capital was about changes in power relations. Their interactions, strengthened by shared Islamic discourses for the Asian women, meant that people felt more informed for themselves and better positioned to help other family members, particularly their children. By using discourses within culturally acceptable boundaries the women could temporarily change the balance of power between themselves and their husbands. As Fazia said: 'He knows I go for a purpose ... I go for the benefit of my daughter'. So the women became active negotiators within their own cultural values (Bhachu, 1993). Within these networks women could move relatively freely, even crossing into economic spheres. Mumtaz managed to obtain a bilingual assistant job through this same cellular network:

> I got the job in my lap ... Somebody else suggested it. My son's friend's mum used to come to see Ahmad (her child) here and the lady who works there, Jane, she became friendly with me and when they needed the job ... they said that they applied some people and they didn't get the right (applicants), so she suggested I go.

The women's social capital was a well developed and sophisticated web of social networks that were founded on mutual activity, communication strategies, collective interests and mutual trust. Their economic value, however, was constrained by the dominant discourses which gave no status to women's networks or activities and which set boundaries on the women's spaces - geographical and social. In the end these women were constrained by racial and gender relationships which created tensions in different ways for all of them as they struggled to make sense of their own identities in a world of conflicting and changing discourses and meanings.

There are implications, of course, in terms of how educational achievement can be gained. If the women's own social capital networks are ignored or marginalised it is difficult to capitalise on the richness of these support systems. Consequently it is difficult to develop the wider social bonds which Etzioni (1995) and Fukuyama (1995) identify as necessary for Schuller and Field's (1998) high educational achievement and high social capital matrix.

Subjectivities

Subjectivity is influenced by context and culture, family, location, friends, school, power relations of gender, age, race or disability. Trust in others stems from the strength of one's subjectivity or sense of self (Giddens, 1991). As Giddens points out, however, identity formulation is a reflexive process. It is mediated by ongoing experiences and changes around each individual and the constant internal aim of trying to make sense of the whole subject within whatever discourses are at our disposal. Brah (1996) talks about multiple axes on which identities are formed and reformed. For Diasporic women, even the notion of 'home' is a contested discourse. Although Mumtaz had lived in the UK for thirty years she still talked of Pakistan as 'home'.

For the two white women and the Asian women there were some similar experiences. There was a tendency, for instance, for older generations to have received less schooling than their children. So Debra stated her parents were 'a bit distanced' from her school and 'just left me to get on with it I suppose'. Yet as regards her own children: 'I want to keep up with them and encourage them'. The CAP course achievements had built up Debra's confidence to consider going to college and she was even challenging her previous role as a playgroup worker: 'I'm at a bit of a crossroads really ... I don't particularly want to stay in childcare'.

Farida also saw that the meaning her parents had attached to education for her had been partly an outcome of their own experiences:

> My parents weren't educated ... they didn't really guide me, they did their best ...they taught me Islam ... they taught me Urdu at home ... they sent me to the M. Mosque ... I don't think my mum was educated at all.

Traditionally girls would receive Islamic rather than academic education, so on that basis Farida's upbringing would have been regarded as conscientiously carried out (Yuval Davis, 1992). But Farida was determined to give all her children different opportunities: 'I can't let them make the same mistakes - and I try and encourage them and help them'.

At least three of the women identified themselves as being mentally unwell - either nervous or depressed. The CAP courses and in most cases the association with a university course, had a significant impact on their psyche. Here was a new context with new discursive arguments which could radically shift how they felt about themselves:

> I've had bouts of depression before ... because it was a university course I was really pleased with myself that I did well ... think it brought something from inside, something that I had that I didn't realise that I had it (Farida).

Azra, the eldest and 'second mother' to seven brothers and sisters described herself as 'a very lonely child and I had no friends'. Her school concentration had been poor and she received little expectation that, as a girl, she should be particularly educated. These sentiments echo the comments made by the older Bridge centre women and other literature on girls in England a generation earlier (Roberts, 1995; Purvis, 1991). Azra was a single parent but nevertheless attended classes at the community centre almost everyday, plus a counselling group, in defiance of family opposition - until she received her foundation credit for the CAP course: 'When they heard that I'd passed ... they were very happy and they kept telling everybody about it ... they were proud of me'. Again this apparent contradiction was a similar story for the women. It was as if their earlier identity had been constructed before they were born by discourses which had been formed without reference to the internal psyche of the women as individuals. Once their personal agency was verified by a new authoritative identity then their position was accepted within that new framework. But each new piece of identity was often hard won, as it broke into the coherence of old, and safer, discourses. For these women the convergence tendencies of globalisation brought both tensions and resistances, resulting in plural and contested identities. The courses gave the women space to re-group and build up their own sense of self.

Azra's self esteem had been knocked in several ways. She arrived in England half way through her schooling and was sent to a special needs school, where she received a restricted curriculum 'just to learn English'. Her progress at school was further hampered by a problem of short sightedness ('I couldn't see the blackboard'), which was not rectified till a school medical examination. Her reasons for choosing the Islamic and Personal Skills courses were predicated on a need to know her own Islamic subjectivity: 'I had to understand why I was doing this ... I've learnt a lot about Islam'; and to help her make sense of herself: 'The personal skills I did to gain more confidence and assertiveness ... because I had very low self-esteem'. Her sense of self was now constructed round a self realisation and ability to reconcile the different axes of her diasporic life: 'I've come a long way ... all this bitterness and resentment its finally gone and that's from going to the classes'. She was now ready to look for new identities:

> I wanted to teach young children and then I thought well in order to teach young children I need to learn myself ... I'd still like to teach, maybe one day in the future, when my children have grown up ... combine English literature and teach Islamic Studies ... sort of learn them all the ways of life in Islam.

She even felt able to use her own agency in the face of ongoing power relations with other discourses around her, recognising her skills but making choices within that as to how she would use them: 'I love sewing ... I sew my own dresses and everyone likes my dresses and they keep harassing me to sew but I want to stick with my studying now'.

Fazia was struggling with an even more complex subjectivity. She was born of mixed parentage and brought up by white foster parents. She ultimately made contact with her birth mother who proved to be an alcoholic, adding further to Fazia's problematic identity. Fazia started life with very low self esteem fuelled by her own peers: ' I was bullied at lot at school because I was the only girl of Asian origin'; and within the school context: 'The teachers said I wouldn't get any 'O' levels at all'. She eventually married into a Muslim Asian family, almost as part of her search for self: 'I was mixed race so I sort of wanted to know about the Asian side of everything'. She didn't have the confidence to go to college and was glad of the women only classes where power relations would feel more reciprocal.

For the East Lancs women the CAP courses had a multiple role. First and foremost the programme enabled them to broaden existing social capital and reconstruct the power relations which influenced their sense of self and ability to trust others. The women only classes were a critical feature of this process. They had been able to re-group as women, re-assert old Muslim identities but within the context of their diasporic world. The convergence of educational expectations brought about by changing dimensions of time and space meant the women became more conscious of their denied place as citizens with rights. But participation in the courses helped them to start re-shaping their lives. They did this by seeing their minority religious status in its global context and at the same time constructing a local citizenship where they were members of a local, social and cultural community.

These are only a few of the ways in which the women would make connections with the past and reconstruct themselves in the present throughout the interviews. Whilst their stories were all different there were some common patterns. Their choice of subject matter and learning environment were connected to their sense of self in relation to their life experiences and the attitudes of those around them. The courses offered opportunity for interfacing with new discourses and new relationships. Invariably this was enough to trigger their own agency so they could move forward as individuals but re-position themselves to renegotiate a new power base within their own social and cultural environment. Sometimes that power balance shifted only slightly but it had to be understood in the context of complex and multiple pressures on who they were and how they understood their place in the world at that particular time. The courses were both sources of a power-knowledge intersection (Foucault, 1980) and a platform from which to look at themselves as critical beings.

9 Nurturing Social Capital in Communities: The DAB Centre

> Thriving communities are an essential counterbalance to globalism, giving relevance to the actions and aspirations of individuals. ... In the end, it is this 'community capacity' - the skills, experience and know-how within the community itself – which will secure the long term sustainable improvements we are seeking to achieve (Blunkett, 1999: 12).

Whether Blunkett's recognition that empowering local communities is an important factor in tackling social exclusion is simply rhetoric or a reality has yet to be decided. As far as the disabled adults whose stories we recall in this chapter are concerned, there exists a real disjuncture between how society responds to them, how their families and friends react to them and how they regard themselves as disabled but potentially active citizens. The challenge facing these learners, like the women from East Lancs and older adults from the Bridge Centre, is to disentangle their life aspirations from those externally imposed on them by people with authority to know. Their opportunity to acquire qualifications, a sign of human capital, and interact in a global society that will value their individual contribution to society as active citizens is often determined by others' perceptions of them. In their case the disability label oppresses them because it ascribes notions of helplessness (Finkelstein, 1993) that must be dispelled if they are to be recognised as valuable members of society whose skills, knowledge and insights can transform the local and global communities to which they belong.

As learners with a disability they belong to a group in society whose participation rate in higher education has been poor (Robertson and Hillman, 1997). Inevitably the dominant models influencing how disabled people are defined and perceived in society have shaped institutional and individual attitudes towards education generally. Michael Oliver, amongst others, provides further discussion of how different medical, social, pluralistic and radical models influence educational provision and participation (Oliver, 1990; Oliver, 1996). On a more practical level the National Bureau for Students with Disabilities (renamed SKILL) plays a crucial role in seeking to redress low participation rates. They support individual students and have campaigned for the introduction of the disabled student grant that can be used for equipment, personal support or additional costs. Providing individuals with information, advice and money to tackle some of the personal and practical obstacles associated with disability is not simple. There remain many institutional factors that need to be tackled across the system if unequal participation rates are to be redressed.

Throughout the nineties there have been a number of HEFCE funded special initiatives designed to address these institutional factors. The HEFCE special initiative grant supported CAP's provision for disabled adults who were not eligible for the full time disabled student grant. This provided extra funding for locally based accessible venues, transport, additional guidance support at the points of transition, and equipment for assistance with assignments.

This chapter explores the stories of eight adult learners who belonged to a locally based self-help group, the DAB Centre, which was formed by and for people with a physical and sensory disability. It was located in a remote, Northern industrial town with a higher than average proportion of blue collar jobs. In this respect, to have a physical disability would place many people at a disadvantage in terms of accessing conventional working class occupations. Although 17 learners participated in four CAP courses within this centre, the stories belong to four men and four women aged between 18 and 56. They are supplemented with commentary from tutors who worked closely with them. Four of the learners have had their disability since birth and three acquired a disability during their life time. Two of the tutors also have a disability that was visible or known to the students. The students all left school by the age of sixteen. With the exception of Melanie, who was the only learner to attend a special school, they have all worked at some point in their lives. Their employment history was influenced to varying degrees by their education and the attitudes of family and employers towards their disability, gender and class. For some learners their disability limited their choice of employment, for others it meant they needed to work part time, or finish paid work earlier than expected. Although two of them studied since leaving school, this was some years ago. Returning to learning was therefore a new and challenging experience, which they were actively encouraged to undertake by Betty the DAB Centre's education co-ordinator.

The DAB centre collaborated with CAP to deliver all the foundation credit courses. Sometimes the courses enabled students to develop individual interests. A study skill course resulted in assignment topics ranging from epilepsy to fly-fishing to shorthand. Other study skill courses were delivered around a common theme that was relevant to the learners, such as disabled people in society. The enterprise course was probably the most instrumental. This focused on activities that would foster individual skill acquisition as well as contribute to building the capacity of the organisation itself. The enterprises included the creation of a charity shop and a promotional display that was used to publicise the services and facilities available at the Centre to members of their local community. The use of ICT in these enterprises is described in chapter seven.

The learner biographies inevitably shaped their response to the experiences emanating from the local DAB - CAP partnership. Their previous educational opportunities to acquire human capital and the impact of their disability and working class backgrounds on employment opportunities were interconnected.

Human Capital

Human capital was often hard won, even though the students' accounts of school itself were often favourable. Their stories reflect a mixture of common working class issues with the additional constraint that their disability would socially and practically impede educational progress. Family circumstances, or their own health conditions, influenced when they left school and consequently their acquisition of qualifications. Sally, for example, said: 'I enjoyed school very much ... But I lost a lot of schooling due to asthma and bronchitis and being the oldest in my family and having to help, I missed a lot of school and I do regret that part of it'. Aside from health issues, Sally's career plans were quashed because of her family's expectations and the need for her to contribute to the family finances: 'I had to get out and earn and bring some money in the house. There was so many of us in the house we needed the cash'.

There were other constraints beyond family circumstances. Sarah felt her opportunity to return to education (and add to her human capital resources) was limited by the college, in terms of course combinations, timing and pace of sessions. She was not alone in experiencing difficulties in accessing mainstream college provision. Melanie, a wheelchair user, had difficulty accessing a first floor teaching room, though this was later redressed.

The disability label therefore often limited personal progression opportunities both practically and environmentally. In some cases, subsequent education initiatives were simply thwarted by local issues. Although Kevin had wanted to be a printer in his uncle's business, his disability meant he 'ended up' doing shop work. His compassionate dismissal from this job, because he suffered from epileptic fits, re-routed his career out of the mainstream and into sheltered employment with the town's major employer, where he worked until he, like many people in the town, was made redundant. An accident shortly after this stimulated Kevin to retrain as a bookkeeper. His attempts to enrol on a college course were thwarted when it was cancelled due to lack of numbers. It was only a chance encounter that brought Kevin into contact with Betty at the DAB Centre. The role of the centre in enabling people to re-build their lives will be discussed later, particularly in relation to issues of social capital and citizenship.

A feature that differentiates some learners with a disability from conventional working class exit points from education was their school leaving age. Some members of the group actually stayed on at school after their peers left at fifteen. This was made possible through parental support. Brown (1997) suggests that parentocracy, measured by the wealth and wishes of parents, is replacing post war notions of meritocracy which is dependent on ability and effort. It seemed there was a recognition amongst parents of these individuals that disabled people would need more, rather than fewer qualifications in order to compete on a level playing field in the job market. Parental encouragement and financial assistance meant some would continue with their education beyond the minimum school leaving age. As Brian explained: 'Well me father, he sort of said you've got to get some qualifications. He were right, although it were me friends who'd left school and were earning wages – he sort of subsidised me by extra pocket money'.

The pace of change meant that individuals took different perspectives about the value of learning and qualifications. On the one hand Tony still felt this was part of a new generation of needs and consequence of changing times. Having already taken early retirement he was prepared to relinquish his place on the course if it would benefit someone younger:

> I felt I'd give someone else the opportunity (of doing this course), a younger person, 'cause they have got to find work, got to find jobs and things like that, and anything that they've got behind them helps, any little thing like that is going to help them in their future life.

On the other hand, Susan who worked part time at a local Age Concern Centre, and was under threat of redundancy, believed that: 'It will help …

having these qualifications. I'm sure they will help because they look quite impressive on paper'. Sarah, however, saw that credit not only added to her human capital, it also enhanced her knowledge and understanding about educational opportunities generally: 'I find that I know quite a lot about starting courses now, actually that is only because I've started these courses. Betty's helped me an awful lot. ... Obviously its going to do me in good stead for later, whether I get a job or not'. In particular students realised that their potential to participate in the future world of learning was in part being transformed by the pervasive impact of ICT.

The Global/Local Interface

ICT in one sense brought the remoteness of their isolated, social and geographical, existence into a form of convergence with other learners. Access to, and interaction with, computers could be a leveller, though there were other issues around this as chapter seven shows. Inevitably, however, the imposition of new world orders onto familiar territory was sometimes perceived as impinging on individual identities (Bauman, 1998). Susan, one of the more confident computer users, was also proud of her shorthand and typing skills. She wrote about the benefits of shorthand in her study skill assignment and commented somewhat regretfully that: 'Computer training was the only sort of course (her) employers would support'. Whilst Susan recognised the benefits derived from computer literacy, she felt that with the demise of shorthand in the workplace there was an inevitable loss of the more personal interaction she had with her bosses.

In other cases the technology created new interfaces between generations. Kevin's new ability to use computers provided him with an opportunity to interact with his sons and offered a focus for mutual support. It gave him a better understanding of a communication medium that his children were comfortable with, and which he recognised was part of a larger global movement.

> Well it's helped me, I helped my lad my eldest boy whose just left school er three days ago er I've helped my eldest lad on several of his courses and course work for his GCSE's. ... At the moment he wants to be a computer analyst, ... I'll be honest with you he helps me he helps me on the computers and that because he knows things which I don't know so we work each way on that score. ... and of course my youngest lad's learning off the two of us so he's coming up to the stage and that so he wants to be something to do with computers when he leaves school.

Interaction with the CAP as a member of the university also created new perceptions about how people placed themselves within time and space. For many participants the university, with its global connections, was identified as a point of contact for knowledge, resources and people, who belonged and operated in a world beyond their locality. Although the university as a globalised institution had seemed distant the DAB - CAP partnership helped to bridge some academic, social and geographical barriers. For instance, the academic activities in which the students engaged during their study and investigation skill courses allowed some of them to see their disability as more than an individual condition. Some students (though not all of them) began to appreciate that they shared something in common with those involved in national disability movements. In response to reading material and other course stimuli learners reflected on their own experiences and were able to take a more critical stance in terms of their health care, access to education and employment. Sally, who was no longer in employment, appreciated the opportunity to acquire basic computer skills recognising how they could be used to promote her voluntary self-help incontinence group in a professional manner. In common with the women from East Lancs and older adults from the Bridge Centre, these learners were using their personal experiences (the local) to make a connection with wider global and societal debates about issues that were of personal importance. Kevin, for example, chose his topic because:

> I thought well deafness is part of a disability anyway and I want to do something on disability because I'm disabled my self and I thought well er with my maybe with my points that I put into this essay it may help other people who read it.

It was particularly important for the local organisation to be seen as worthy of involvement by something as remote as a university. The status of the university, with its global connections but still wanting to partner with a local group gave the students a sense of place and value:

> The input from you [CAP] being a university, coming down here, the fact that there was the support there, the material was coming down from Lancaster University. I'm not being detrimental when I say this, had it been a course coming down from [a local] College ... they might not have the same kind of get up and go for the course. ... It was because it was a university putting on a course and the university people thought that they could achieve something on that course and they did (Claire, DAB tutor).

The exchange value of this partnership was heavily dependent on the university making the first move. This indicates that for global-local interfaces to achieve maximum benefit, it is the larger, more powerful institution which must make efforts to link with the local. But in doing so the institution must validate local identities and concerns. The role of the voluntary organisation in developing individuals within this process should not be underestimated.

Citizenship

Elsdon et al. (1995) claim that all voluntary organisations:

> Encourage individual members that they own, have ultimate responsibility for, and are personally involved in the organisation. [Consequently, they] are potentially, and ought to become, training grounds for active citizens (p. 148).

The Dearing report reiterates many of the features outlined by the school focused National Curriculum Council's framework for citizenship education (NCC, 1990). It recommends that higher education should provide opportunities for individuals so that: 'They grow intellectually, are well equipped for work, can contribute effectively to society and achieve personal fulfilment' (Dearing, 1997: 5.11). For adults participating in all CAP foundation credits the same goals as those advocated by Dearing apply. However, the underlying assumptions that work means paid work, and contribution to society means a financial contribution, are not taken for granted by CAP. A number of writers (Barnes, 1997; Lister, 1997; Meekosha and Dowse, 1997) suggest that there are alternative ways of acting as a citizen, and of using the knowledge, skills and attitudes acquired through education. Lister (1997) cites Ray Pahl's (1990) alternative definition of citizenship which involves: 'Local people working together to improve their own quality of life and to provide conditions for others to enjoy' (in Lister, 1997: 22).

This definition resonates with the rationale of the enterprise course. There were two enterprise groups at the DAB Centre. Both enabled students to fulfil their obligations to their local community in a tangible way as well as developing and improving their skills of negotiation, problem solving, decision making, being assertive. The first worked on establishing a charity shop. This project required students and others involved in the centre to generate funds and embark on regular voluntary work that demonstrated very visibly their contribution to their local community. The second enterprise was a promotional display about the agency and about disability related issues. For Sarah it enabled her to share some of her newly acquired knowledge with others in her local community: 'So the public can find out more about them (the DAB Centre) and also help them (the public) with any disabilities that they have. It's surprising how much people don't know'.

Both enterprise projects afforded the students the chance to participate in 'a very worthwhile project, [which] means that I'm [doing] something and not wasting my time' (Brian). The sense of self was and is important for adults with a disability, who may feel that their lack of opportunity to contribute as wage earners to their local community diminishes their status as a citizen (Finkelstein, 1993). Participation in the courses helped people reconstruct their social status as active citizens. For Kevin the charity shop gave him an opportunity to be seen as an integral member of society alongside other local people: 'It's run by disabled people and able-bodied people as well, so we've got a variety of people working together'.

The partnership arrangement often provided the impetus for people to become more involved in the disability agency or other local voluntary groups. In different ways these students contributed to the overall quality of life for the wider community of people living in their locality. So for instance, Tony described how the courses gave him the incentive and motivation to get involved in other DAB Centre activities: 'I'm Vice Chairman now. ... And we've got the charity shop [so] I have a sense of purpose, going in the shop, trying to keep that going, ... and I've got commitments outside the (DAB Centre) as well'. According to definitions of citizenship which have an economic and political focus, Tony's contribution as an active citizen would diminish when he retired. Meekosha and Dowse (1997) confirm the additional paradox surrounding the concept of active citizenship for people with a disability, who are presumed not to be in a position to undertake voluntary work irrespective of age. The DAB Centre students challenged these notions of helplessness. They used the enterprise course to create their own space in the town and opportunities for voluntary work.

According to Barnes the opportunity for disabled people to contribute within the wider society is an important one since there is a danger that people who need support and assistance are frequently consigned to a category of 'ex-citizen' (Barnes, 1997). It was important, therefore, for the students to have an opportunity to articulate an alternative image on behalf of other people with disabilities: 'We are not outcasts from society because of disabilities. There is room for people with disabilities to go on and do this sort of thing' (i.e. studying at university - Tony). As with the East Lancs women the courses helped the students carve out a citizenship space and identity which included helping friends and family. It also provided routes into the wider community through public displays and charity shop activities.

Participating in the democratic process and processing information in order to make an informed decision is an important aspect of the political dimension of citizenship. It was this feature of learning to respect and accept that people have different viewpoints which many students highlighted:

> The idea where they say your opinions count, your opinions aren't wrong. There might be set answers that are given but if you disagree with them, you can disagree with them, ... because you are allowed your own opinions and ideas (Susan).

In part, the opportunity to formulate their own opinion, by weighing up the evidence before deciding what they thought, was in direct contrast to their recollection of school. That was where: 'What the teacher said, went' (Tony). It is also a necessary pre-requisite to taking an active involvement in democratic processes whether they relate to micro matters associated with the democratic organisation of their disability agency, local, national or party politics, or the increasingly common phenomenon of issue based politics: 'You've got to learn to respect other people's points of view and getting feedback from other students, ... I think that was a good way of learning' (William).

Greater participation in activities that served the local community extended the range of networks learners were able to access. In common with other CAP learners these were initially channelled through family and local community centre contacts. Although links between learners were strengthened as a result of their involvement in education, it was their disability networks that provided the initial impetus for further learning.

Social Capital

Betty, the education co-ordinator, had two very distinct reasons for embarking on the CAP (and university) partnership and promoting participation in education. The first was to aid individual development and the second to build the capacity of those associated with the DAB Centre:

> And we felt that they had problems that they needed to address, look at themselves, analyse themselves and see themselves as being useful members of society and not just a disability. ... We are not an education provider we are just providing a means of helping students access education. They

learned [things] that helped them to study in a more effective way and give them a thirst for knowledge which was very useful. ... we chose all these four modules [personal development, study, investigation and enterprise] because each complements the other, and whatever they want to do in life, whether its education, or employment or if its just for some quality they need all these skills. From the students' point of view they [have now] become more positive about life and they believe in themselves and understand that they do have skills and they do have disabilities but they also have abilities. Those are the things that I personally wanted for the students. ... Yes, we feel that after they've gone through these four modules they will be excellent committee members, which is very important to us. Being a charity the organisation is actually run by members of the committee but now some members of the committee do a lot and some do little but after they've had this education and training [opportunity] we feel they will all be very useful [to the DAB Centre].

The Centre was a central hub for both defining and extending individual networks. Through their contact with the disability agency students had access to an established framework of support that formed the bulk of their social capital. Our contacts at the organisation were already trusted members of the community. They introduced and vouched for the CAP team who, in turn, provided the link with networks in the university. Using this situated and localised information structure that was built on mutual trust, students gained access to enriched information channels and increased the possibility of reciprocal arrangements with an enlarged network. Admittedly this group's existing range of contacts makes it difficult to isolate the direct contribution of the CAP courses to their developing social capital. Despite this the interviews, and focus group discussions with additional students, suggest that the camaraderie and peer support encouraged within the courses were valued by all the students: 'Learning together helped a lot' (Tony). According to Susan this was probably a result of: 'All [the] different experiences. We've all got different experiences of life and I suppose you are all bringing them in aren't you?'.

The courses became a medium for students to test out and articulate aspects of mutuality, trust and obligations which would then feed back into the centre's own social fabric. In turn the security of the centre as a base from which to test out new skills and relationships would nurture individuals' confidence to move beyond familiar ground and into different activities.

Initial contact with the DAB Centre was originally related to issues associated with their disability. This was a starting point for learners to extend their personal, social and information networks. For instance, Betty (education co-ordinator) and Claire (tutor) played a valuable support role and were pivotal players in the students' socialising activities. Betty in particular would answer students' questions and reassure them in respect of concerns they had about returning to study. As Susan explained:

> Betty came up to my house originally because she wanted me to come on it [the course], ... it's nice because she explained how it would be and what it would entail and everything so I knew exactly, and chose to sort of embark on it.

Once participating in this kind of higher education, the students became part of a peer support network which enabled them to study and tackle obstacles that in the past had caused them to drop out, or not consider education courses. People phoned one another for advice, support, or to talk through their assignments and share references. Additionally they started to work together to negotiate, solve problems, or organise themselves and others in terms of duties and responsibilities associated with the charity shop.

The increased human capital obtained via the course qualifications was not only a personal resource that enhanced employability, it was regarded as a contribution to the family resource base. Susan described how her sons and family:

> Are always wanting to know how I'm doing ... and they are quite impressed and it's nice that they are feeling that way, because I feel as if it might be helping them at school. I mean the younger one keeps saying: 'Well I'm going to university as well'.

Kevin reported how assembling his personal skill portfolio enabled him to recognise the skills he had acquired throughout his life: 'I'm getting a copy [of the portfolio] done so my children can look back on it and say my dad did that, ... its like a family heirloom'. The contact with the disability agency as well as the CAP courses appeared to provide Kevin with an opportunity to enrich his personal power base in the family and become a resource for his sons: 'My eldest, he's been asking me questions and it makes a change for me to say that I can answer him with pride and joy to say that I know what he's talking about now'. Breaking down intergenerational barriers and encouraging learning between family members is identified as a key to creating a learning culture (Fryer, 1999) and increasing the participation of those who have previously been excluded from the education system. The CAP role was distinctive in making connections because it was part of a university. The value was in the partnership between university and a local organisation where the power of HE as a resource was appropriated for community ends. The CAP co-ordinators and agency staff operated together as educational resource agents providing a link between the global university and local self-help disability group. This was not simply a matter of information flowing from the global to the local community. What was valued by all involved in this process was the two way communication exchange, the local information being seen as valuable in its own context but given university credibility (Houghton, 1999).

The recognition that local knowledge can contribute to understanding within the university and through its networks to other educational providers and policy makers was important. By sharing their experiences, concerns and insights into the possible obstacles associated with learning, these adults were also having the opportunity to influence future educational provision in locales beyond their own community:

> You've been like a link which has been good. And to be able to take things back and then bring things back again, ... I mean action's been taken. Often you get these things where people sort of ask for it [feedback] and nothing happens, but because it [change] has happened this time you know, it's been good to do it that way (Susan, student).

The positive experience of being heard would also have its effect on individual identities.

Subjectivities

Many disabled people internalise the labels that describe them as passive recipients of a welfare system. According to Peters this:

> Cultural invasion leads many disabled people to a silent world of passive acceptance where they adapt to the status quo of a governmental system devoted to their 'welfare' rather than achieve an integrated positive identity from their own lived experience (Peters, 1999: 103).

The learners studying at the DAB Centre had acquired their disability label in two ways. Firstly, through the disability itself (although in the case of a hidden disability this was something they could hide or try to ignore). Secondly, through their membership of this self-help association which made their disability more public. Joining the association was therefore significant in terms of how they labelled themselves and how they wanted others to see them. Becoming a member of DAB was often a pivotal moment: 'It changed my life' (Sally); 'Since I joined [DAB Centre] I never looked back' (Kevin). Joining signalled to themselves and others that they had either accepted or were coming to terms with their disability. The realisation that they were not alone, together with the information, advice, learning and social experiences provided by the DAB Centre, frequently empowered them to challenge the negative aspects of the disability label and become informed about their benefits and rights as a citizen. Betty, DAB's education co-ordinator, felt the courses contributed to the process of personal growth enabling the learners to continue to reconstruct their perceptions of themselves in the light of new insights.

Identity is not a fixed commodity; rather it is shaped by the interaction of a multitude of external and internal factors. Kevin for example, was influenced by a perception of himself that originated from childhood. Although he had enjoyed the majority of his schooling, he still had no sense that he was an achiever: 'When it was time to leave school I thought I didn't have a brain behind me to take on qualifications, so I left and did shop work'. The enterprise project brought personal gains which made Kevin re-construe his sense of self:

> I've been given the chance of trust and reliability of banking money, opening and closing the shop, taking responsibility, which I couldn't have done before my accident, I didn't have the confidence in me to do it. So this [course] has helped me a lot.

As is often the case with adult learners students would see themselves differently after the course experience: 'I'm more confident, I know more about my abilities that I perhaps didn't realise before. It's good to see it all on paper, you know, you've learnt all that and what you are capable of' (Susan).

Part of this sense of self came from working alongside others. The collaborative approach to learning enabled each person to contribute and thus find him or herself in a position where their efforts could be recognised and valued by others. For Tony, it was a passing comment from one of his peers that enabled him to recognise and then value that he was assertive: 'I wouldn't have known that, if I'd not gone on the course, ... I learnt my lessons through experience probably, but I hadn't realised I was learning'. If higher education is about encouraging critical awareness and reflexivity then the courses provided an opportunity for students to reflect on their experiences and see themselves differently. This process enabled them to create an identity that took account of their whole selves, not simply their disability, gender or working class background. Recording on paper their skills and how they achieved them provided a contrasting piece of evidence to the forms that they were required to complete in order to claim their disability living allowance. The study, investigation and enterprise courses all provided opportunities for interacting with others that focused on what they were achieving. This was a dramatic contrast to the focus of their interactions with health and social care professionals who concentrate on what they can't do because of their disability.

For those students who had acquired their disability this had the effect of redressing the power of earlier discourses. It enabled them to reposition their current selves as members of society. For the students in this group who had been born with a disability it was friends, family and people they came into contact with who usually influenced their sense of self. The course was an external means of giving the participants access to another mirror, which reflected other aspects of their identity. Participating in learning provided a definite sense of purpose and achievement that they felt enhanced their quality of life. Not all the students were operating at an advanced 'academic' level. But all sensed or gained something from the critical analytic framework in which the courses were operating. Tutor Claire talked about the benefits derived by Melanie one of the students who had attended the personal development course. She described Melanie's personal life which had lacked involvement in anything outside the home:

> I look at Melanie, who some would say has done nothing, a young women who sits indoors seven nights a week, who is ignored I believe even by her family... They don't think she has anything to input into the family; they don't defer to her in any way to ask her opinion about anything. Since this course she has become, she realises that she has a right to state her case, she has a right to make a decision for herself and choose what she wants to do, she's actually stating those rights, she's becoming positive and she's gained a lot of confidence, and she's joining in, ... talking to people, asking for help, it's a big change.

The fact that the courses were provided by a university was very significant for some learners: 'It made them feel good about themselves' (Betty). The university connection, the sense of achievement and subsequent motivation that the students felt when they successfully completed their foundation credits was evident: 'Once you got the results and the next major report, you thought, 'well I've done all right on this so I can go and do the next one' (William). However the outcome did not necessarily result in participation in more courses. For some, new interests arose which re-directed how they saw their role in society. For Sally this led to the formation of her self-help incontinence group. This brought her into a different relationship with health professionals who she now invited as speakers to her group, thus shifting the balance of power from her identity as a patient to provider. Similarly, Kevin and Brian increased their voluntary work activities associated with the shop. Arguably the courses were important in allowing students to gain the confidence that would allow them to shift their subjective selves beyond immediate family or other identities. Even when perceived new identities could not be realised immediately, some participants felt more able to control how decisions would be made. Susan's new sense of self manifested itself in the way she made her own informed choices about future study. Torn between her personal desire to enrol on a degree course and family responsibilities of being a wife and mother she used her new, extended social capital network to seek out and make sense of educational information. She opted to pursue a counselling course, which could either act as a stepping stone to other things, or become an end goal in itself. It allowed her to fulfil a personal study interest and still put her children first.

Conclusion

Like the older adults and the women of East Lancs, DAB learners shared a common set of experiences that influenced their own and others perceptions of them as learners and citizens. They talked about having to come to terms with, and then enable others to see beyond, their disability. Their experience of being undervalued, dismissed and excluded is not restricted to their locality but is a challenge they share with other disabled adults who were described in a report presented to the European Parliament and Commission on the European Day of Disabled persons (1995) entitled the 'Invisible Citizen'. This report revealed the extent to which disabled people are ignored and discriminated against in community law and policy. Although this sense of invisibility is one that resonates with aspects of these students' stories it is clear that a kind of higher education which encourages a reinvestment of self can help people to acquire the confidence and skills to fulfil their role as active rather than invisible citizens.

10 Nurturing Social Capital in Communities: The Bridge Centre

Introduction

Age stereotyping has meant that adults beyond the age of 55 or more are often banded together as a homogeneous group; their increasing years proportionately associated with decreasing mental and physical capacities along with poverty and isolation (Bradley, 1996). In terms of educational policy the post retirement ages have been largely ignored (Carlton and Soulsby, 1998). Furthermore, initial educational achievement for present day older adults is not easily distinguishable by social class. Most people, irrespective of social background did not go to university during the 1940s, particularly if they were women.

This chapter looks at the life history contexts of nine women between the ages of 63 and 77. It looks at how they acquired skills and training in terms of human/employability capital. It discusses the influences of different global situations on their local circumstances throughout their lives, followed by an analysis of citizenship activities in relation to their gender, education and social backgrounds.

The way the women positioned themselves with regard to the CAP and other learning opportunities suggests that these older adults had a similar range of needs and motivations for supported and accredited learning to other age groups. The interface between social capital and educational achievement proved multi-layered and dependent on context. Higher education suited them if it was local and provided on their terms. It also stimulated further social involvement in the same way that it did for the other groups. The way the women had attempted to exploit learning opportunities throughout their lives depended on a variety of factors - indicating that learning choices are unpredictable. People's decisions to attend formal education are contingent on a mixture of power relations, internalised discourses, and past experiences, plus a subjective sense of who they were. The personal circumstances surrounding this particular group of women were significant in influencing their educational participation.

The Bridge Centre interviewees were all women, (though men did attend the course as well). They left school between 1936 and 1949 - a whole generational difference in experience and educational policy. Their schooling was significantly affected by the war years and the 1944 education act, depending on which year they were born. Their entitlement to work and education depended on their status as women. It was only the most professionalised of women who received anything more than initial education. In this group of nine, Hilary, whose father was a schoolmaster, managed a university education at the start of the war. She became a missionary teacher and spent most of her adult years in West Africa. Of the remaining eight, three took up grammar school scholarship places and achieved School Certificate exams. Two of those schools had been Catholic convents. None of the other five left school with qualifications, though three studied for 'O' levels in their adult years. As with other stories of this age group (Preece, 1999) access to a grammar school education would determine what and how they were taught and whether qualifications were part of the school curriculum. The war produced a further set of learning obstacles. Catherine and Liz, aged seven and five when war broke out, both reported disrupted teaching or schooling as a result of evacuation policies. Surprisingly for this age group five of the women never married though Roberts (1984) notes that 80% of women in Preston were married in 1931. Of the four that did marry only Nora and Liz were still living with their first husbands. Elsie had been widowed then divorced, Patricia was divorced and remarried at the age of 50. Of those who had married, Liz had adopted children and Patricia had no children. The absence of children or conventional wife roles for some of the women created opportunities which might not otherwise have been available to them as adults.

Their human capital reflected the accumulated efforts of a working life span of some 45 years contextualised by the limited range of opportunities for women already revealed in similar studies (Bourke, 1994; Preece, 1999).

Human Capital

All the women had worked, but with the exception of Hilary, reported comparable tales of thwarted study ambitions to the younger, mostly Asian women in East Lancs. Apart from Hilary, five women recalled learning shorthand and typing for some form of office career. Catherine and Bernadette started with shopwork, though Bernadette then took up a hairdressing apprenticeship with her father, taking over the business when he died. Liz started working in the local mill but eventually progressed to a civil service job, in spite of no qualifications, because she managed to pass their internal test. Whilst most of the women tried to capture some of the lost opportunities for academic study as adults, only Nora went as far as taking an Open University degree after completing teacher training at the age of 47. Hilary, already in possession of a university degree, went on to do an MA whilst in-between jobs. Nora and Mary were conscripted and received a spell of army training. Their employment records suggest these women were a product of the war years where women's employment was encouraged. Their marriage status may well be a reflection of that short era where women's independence had a brief fling thanks to the necessities of the time and where marriageable men were in short supply. Their eagerness to participate in the relatively academic nature of an art appreciation course may also be indicative of people who were upwardly mobile in social class terms. Certainly shorthand and typing skills were generally regarded as a passport to a 'good job' for young women during the 1940s and 1950s. Nevertheless the women's achievements were largely due to their own perseverance as adults, sometimes in spite of children or other family responsibilities. Patricia, for instance, studied for 6 'O' levels over a period of years in her 30s and claimed she was the oldest person in the class during that time. Liz too, who started life in the local mill, took five Open College courses in her late 40s and early 50s. The complexities of their interface with a sense of self and changing discourses of the time would ultimately determine who tried formal education and who didn't.

A significant influence was globalisation. In many respects the women's stories indicated that the effect of changing education systems and more technologically advanced communications were already beginning a generation ago. This suggests some verification of Waters' (1995) position that globalisation has been an ongoing process for some time. The opportunity to study out of hours, for instance, was one indicator that 'night school' and gender power struggles for learning were already under way.

The Global/Local Interface

Perhaps stimulated by the war, the effects of globalisation in terms of time, space and distance were already a part of these women's lives. Unlike the stories of many working class women of the early half of the twentieth century, nearly everyone in this interview group had travelled away from their home town as adults. In this respect they may have been atypical of their working class generation. They were relatively independent women with some opportunity to capitalise on their personal agency and develop a sense of self to consume the evolving educational products which had been denied them in their younger years. This included use of distance learning techniques and access to early information technology. Seventy seven year old Nora had been an early Open University student and 77 year old Mary talked about working with the first computers, along with the frustrations of training youngsters:

> I did learn to operate a VDU ... I retired about six months early ... it was getting a bit big and they were bringing in new youngsters who would put in a comma wrong instead of a full stop, which would send the whole thing up the spout.

Even Bernadette, the hairdresser, talked about the effect of women's new economic power relationship on her hairdressing business: 'The war came and the girls were put into munitions ... and they had money so of course they had their hair done'.

She, too, benefited from increased travel opportunities as a young hairdresser and attended several different training courses on new hairdressing techniques. She also spoke, with some wonderment, of modern day communications:

> When I think of the computers and all the things I think they are absolutely wonderful. Internet I didn't know what that was ... (a librarian) she was doing you know the computer ... and I said: 'What is Internet?' So she said: 'Oh well that brings everything'. 'Oh', I said: 'I couldn't cope'. She says: 'You could', she says: 'I've done it'. ... Rose ... was 70 this year and she's got a computer and she's taken that course.

The effect of distance and time bound events were being felt then, across several generations and locations, creating an intensified consciousness of learning and the opportunities that they both missed and were now taking advantage of. Most were two generations away from a university education ('The grandchild of some of my workmates goes to university' - Catherine); but few had sat back and made no effort to 'catch up'. Indeed only Catherine had done no previous adult education study. Her evacuation experiences meant she attended 12 schools, leaving her with a different sense of sustained learning or achievement. She gained a grade two (A level standard) on both her foundation credit submissions, an indicator of the provider's responsibility for keeping learning options open in order to pick up late survivors.

The Bridge Centre's power relationship with the university and its participants was slightly different from that of the other two organisations. Whilst the centre itself engaged with local working class activities, the discourse of 'university' was adopted less for working class curriculum purposes than for its resource as a disseminator of conventional academic material. The course itself therefore attracted a new set of centre members. Many (though not all) were at an intermediate stage in their learning. Whilst Nora and Hilary had undertaken higher level study prior to the Art courses, the other women had dabbled with GCSE, O level or Open College courses. The opportunity to study locally at a higher level had not been placed within their grasp before. When it was, these women did appropriate that learning to their own ends. Some did the foundation credit assignment and all of them saw the courses as a development of their existing interests. Their more limited family commitments, moreover, seemed to place them in an unusually available role for adult learning. When one considers how the East Lancs women were starting out on their struggle for learning and qualifications it is interesting to consider the potential outcome for women at the other end of their life cycle. Both sets of women were constantly adapting to new economic cultures brought about by different facets of globalisation. The extent of their mobility and ability to capitalise on its opportunities depended on immediate family power relations as well as wider gender specific discourses. Global infrastructure changes alone would not automatically be accessible to women.

In keeping with their more public engagement with education, some of the women's involvement in citizenship activities was also more public. Others were more aligned to the feminised citizenship roles identified by Ackers (1998) and others.

Citizenship

Both married and unmarried did not escape their private citizenship obligations as carers. Nora and Mary both took on caring responsibilities of a similar nature to those mentioned by the East Lancs women. Nora was looking after her husband who had Alzheimer's disease and Mary had cared for her parents till they died. Those who remained single did manage to avoid the convention of diminished legal and social status of married women, though their overall gender status was circumscribed by the discourses of the time. Five women talked of a range of more public volunteering activities. Liz was originally a volunteer for age concern before becoming a member, Frances was a member of the WEA committee and Bernadette worked at a charity shop for the hospice. Hilary's activities were much more elaborate and perhaps indicative of the kind of public role more commonly associated with citizenship:

> I was in the missionary society ... for 15 years. When I returned I still did a lot of work for the missionary society and the church ... I do quite a lot of public speaking... I'm concerned with justice and peace and world developments ... I'm also involved in Homeless Action.

Patricia's citizenship activities were directly linked to her interest in art and stemmed from her personal experiences when she was a novice artist struggling to learn how to paint:

> I'm heavily involved in the art group ... I was the secretary ... I ran a luncheon club in T for three years and a bit. We (she and her husband) were involved in starting up the MB Art Association and we've always tried to encourage the members ... we always say don't be afraid to come because we all began somewhere ... we like to encourage them.

There are a number of things to consider here. Firstly, Patricia's activities seemed to reflect Glover's (1998) position that successful ageing is characterised by the ability to accommodate the ageing process by keeping mentally, physically and socially active - with a tendency by some at least to re-cycle their combined wisdom of earlier experiences. Secondly the women were also an indicator of a new demographic reality - that more older people are healthier and active (Walker, 1998) and that there is a need for local community politics to enable older people to participate within their locality. The third point is that it would seem that the art course was also reflecting the findings of Benn and Fieldhouse (1997) who suggested that courses attract 'those students who are already socially active' (in Thorne, 1998: 24). It may be, however, that it is the definition of citizenship itself which decides whether people are socially active or not. In one sense, only Hilary's activities were overtly civic in nature. Both she and Nora, the two most educated, said that they now gave talks on Art as a result of attending the CAP course.

The strength of the Bridge Centre seemed to be its ability to straddle the most and least educated, with unanimous appreciation of the course content by all participants. As has already been mentioned, the participant mix in terms of educational background was also more varied - a feature of the Art course, rather than the Centre's membership:

> The people who've come to the lectures, you know they're not bothered with the trivial things that perhaps some of our long standing members ... you know, niggle about .. well, these, these people who we'll call students, they're a little bit above that ... they are very erm easy going people in a way ... and they're quite different to some of our members (Doris, Bridge Centre secretary).

Doris's comments suggest that the discourse of learning somehow intersects with a different sense of self - people who were already able to see themselves as citizens of a different nature from their peers. There is a sense that those who attended the art course had already acquired a different understanding of their place in society. This sense was not always class based, but it perhaps linked with a combination of axes relating to previous educational achievement, a different sense of womanhood as single women (where relevant) and the accumulation of different discourses over many years.

In this way the course echoed the philosophy of traditional liberal adult education classes run by extra mural classes of the 1980s (Fieldhouse, 1996). Some saw the course as building their own art skills which could be passed onto others - either as a lecture or as practical art clubs, others simply enjoyed the opportunity to attend an accessible and stimulating event. In either case there were indications that the assignments and the teaching stimulated further activity between the participants and occasionally further activity in the Bridge Centre itself. Citizenship roles for this group were shaped by an intergenerational combination of factors. On the one hand the women were born in an era where citizen values derived from a moral and political order which was about duty and loyalty to one's country. The women were secure in their membership as UK citizens. Their gender status had been defined by education, marriage and work legalities and cultural expectations. Their participation in public life was constrained by the gender values attached to women where civic duties were usually behind the scenes - helping in a shop or looking after others. The fluidity of circumstances over time meant they would dip into and out of citizenship according to their marital or age status and their experience of self sufficiency. Few had taken up totally economically dependent roles as women. This meant they participated in worlds so far denied to the other two groups. Perhaps because of these factors their social networks were also more extensive and established beyond the Bridge Centre than was the case for East Lancs and the DAB Centre.

Social Capital

Social capital for this group was multifarious, accumulated over several years and used for different purposes. Like identity, social capital was constantly in flux and contingent upon power relations with others. Social networks would be built around family and work at different times and with different degrees of intensity. Their interconnectedness was broader and less enclosed than for the other two groups. It may be that, as Fukuyama (1995) suggests, this was a bonus for the Bridge Centre participants. After all this would imply the greater transferability of their social wealth. Even so, the communication boundaries were relatively self contained by gender or class boundaries. Most of the women talked about their family and working class social connections regarding early employment days. They learned the value of networking, maintaining communication links and reciprocal arrangements that provided mutual benefits in the market. Liz, for instance described how job opportunities would circulate amongst her peers:

> Everybody started off in the mill but as soon as you got older you kind of met a friend who said oh there's a job going at my place and a job somewhere else and you kind of drifted ... some landed up in shops ... and got to know people, and mixing.

This kind of reciprocity also took place within the workplace. Nora talked about her first job in an insurance company. Here she and other colleagues would utilise their own school achievements to help others seeking to get theirs:

> Some of the women who were in classes used to ask my friends and I if we'd do their writing for them and I remember doing essays on leisure and my favourite city and all that for people who took them back to the class and read them as their own. We didn't mind, because we just liked doing it you know.

Whilst the precise motives for these exchanges were rather unexplored in the interview, it nevertheless provided a basis for understanding how mutuality and exchange was valued. The use of such non competitive communication links regarding education proved valuable for Nora herself in later years. She learnt about her teaching course for mature students through the mother of one of her children's friends: 'A friend of mine, Catherine ... our children were playing ... and she said to me: ... "I've got a place and start in September ... you ought to do something about it"'. The way education was shared in these interviews suggests there are implications for the way education is marketed. It may be that the very discourse of learning as a competitive individualistic goal excludes those who wish to contextualise learning amid other values. Equally the way social capital and learning gain intermeshed would influence how the women could develop a sense of personal agency to further their education successfully. Nora, for instance, made good use of her social networks to further her own education. Where Nasreen from East Lancs was exploited by such arrangements, Nora was able to use them for her own ends. She also started the OU course on the invitation of a friend: 'A Jewish friend of mine ... she said: "Oh I'd like to ... have someone to go with" ... so I thought I'll have a go'. The difference for Nora was that she already had her own sense of agency based on earlier successes, in particular educational achievement. One would feed the other.

Social contacts were often transient and simply based on geographically bound community associations (Fukuyama, 1995). Elsie for instance, obtained her old job as a legal secretary after becoming widowed, simply because the firm had heard about it: 'When the barristers heard that I was a widow on the grapevine in Cardiff, they wrote to me asking me if I'd like to go back so I did'. In this respect social capital seems to be a more fluid and changing process than indicated in the literature. Putnam (1995) suggests that there has been a decline in social capital for all education groups over the years. But in many ways the Bridge Centre and the course itself re-created those reciprocity behaviours, irrespective of educational background. Within the Bridge Centre itself, people would exchange interests in a form of mutual reciprocity, as Bernadette showed:

> What I did was to help Nora, I said: 'Would you like me to?', because er newspaper cuttings, I had two friends who give me ... I have a friend who took the Times and one who took the Daily Mail and there was always an art section ... so I used to cut pictures out and give them to Nora and I helped her that way ... I love poetry so she recites poetry for me.

Like Nora's earlier office exchanges with her colleagues, education was being used here as a non competitive sharing activity. Its value was in the creation of social support rather than some form of individualistic gain. Education itself was a form of social capital - its human capital value only drawn on at selected moments. It also served a form of economic 'good housekeeping' value - as newspapers were only bought once but served three different people. It is perhaps the change in educational purpose which determines how social capital develops.

The Bridge Centre performed a similar role to the centres for the other groups. It acted as a communication hub for information exchange via friends or its own publications which people happened to notice in public places. Some people found out about the art classes because they attended the Bridge Centre for Tai Chi classes. Two others made contact via its creative writing classes and Catherine found out via another senior citizens club.

The Bridge Centre therefore acted as a networking resource on several fronts rather like a spiders web:

> The Bridge Centre has people coming everyday ... its an absolute lifeline for them. They sit around, they have their lunch, they chat to their friends ... there are others who like to learn something .. but we all talk ... I used to go the art in the afternoon on Mondays (Nora).

The success of this Centre in attracting a wider range of educational backgrounds suggests it had a different infrastructure than the two smaller organisations. As a local branch of Age Concern it interlaced with other public and voluntary agencies, as Catherine and Hilary proved. It may be that Age Concern benefits from an essentially middle class infrastructure with national connections. So even though the local branch was primarily working class in composition, it sustained a slightly wider circle of social bonds within the mainstream of society.

The way education was used in the DAB Centre, East Lancs and at the Bridge Centre meant that it became almost a general consumer item which could be shared and passed round friends and relatives - as something of value, but not necessarily something which had to be claimed for individual gain. The expansion of informal education into other forms of support groups or activities is as common a feature of community courses for adults (Jamieson et al., 1998) as it is for other social groups (McGivney, 1990; Preece, 1999). Only Hilary seemed not be part of this market place (though she did appropriate the learning gained from the art course for her own public speaking activities). For members of the Bridge Centre their acquired learning for the most part had been gained during adulthood, often in spite of earlier prejudices about girls education and opportunities. So, as for the East Lancs women, knowledge was perhaps something which the women would use as a form of shared power, rather than a means of accumulating authority to know more than someone else. It was also something which had to be acquired when other forms of support were already in place and could not be age bound. Furthermore it depended on the strength and status of individual identities at any point in time.

Subjectivities

As in the other groups the Bridge Centre participants' subjectivities were shaped by gender power relations regarding educational entitlement. These were influenced by pre, during and post war events and the women's own learning experiences at school and as adults. Family expectations, as usual, had the most effect on how people performed at school. But for many, their sense of social class and gender constraints continued to shape how they would access education in adulthood. This was an ongoing process of defining the self, based on an understanding of the past and present (Maierhofer, 1999).

Those who went to grammar school (Nora, Hilary, Mary, Frances) generally did so because their parents supported the move. The women reinforced this perception with memories of books in the home and that they were often read to as children. Many carried with them images of a denied self in terms of educational ability. Liz and Catherine both felt disadvantaged by their impoverished schooling opportunities of the school war years: 'I bet if I was going to school now I could have gone forward'; while Elsie bitterly regretted the denial of a grammar school place she had gained as a scholarship: 'My father didn't believe in education for women, its heartbreaking, heartbreaking, because the headmaster wrote especially to my parents'. Nora, too, regretted the lost opportunities during her youth: 'Nobody suggested going and working at the university, nobody ... I didn't know anybody who went to university'. Although she made up for it in adulthood, she still somehow felt disadvantaged: 'A general feeling that I've missed out on something, quite honestly'.

Frances's parents did want her to go to university but she chose not to, partly through lack of confidence and partly because she felt her parents could not afford it, but also because the trend was not to go: 'I've regretted it after, I wished I had gone as I got older, but there you are, when you are 16 you sort of want to get earning'. She had been trapped in the conforming discourse of her peers which had already shaped her identity as a working class girl.

Patricia did not get a grammar place. She defined herself accordingly. She felt on the whole she was too slow and too shy to have taken the pressures of academic study as a young person:

I don't think I was the type of person who would have enjoyed going away to college or university ... I much prefer doing it now, I'm much less afraid of meeting people; I was very shy and I would have been utterly devastated thrust into a strange place with loads of strangers.

The Bridge Centre course in some ways, then, was a leveller - an opportunity for people to liberate themselves from the confining social boundaries of the past that defined them according to gender and age (Maierhofer, 1999). Their realisation of themselves as individuals meant they could nurture their educational potential instead of being confined to nurturing others.

Perhaps because of the opportunity to recycle and reshape their lives - and the added factor that few had followed conventional family lives - the Bridge Centre women were different from the East Lancs women in how they saw themselves. In spite of regrets and frustrations - and Bernadette's acknowledgement that she was a nervous person - the women did not indicate the same sense of depression exhibited by some of the East Lancs women. These women were more independent selves. Their present exclusion from the discourse of employability and pressures to conform meant they were not having to compete with their own generation. In East Lancs the women were comparing their existing, gendered lives with their more Westernised peers and pressures to be part of the social world of qualifications and employment.

Nevertheless the fragility of the Bridge Centre women's academic identity was often apparent. Nora, the most confident of all ('I used to be ... an extrovert at school'), withdrew her first application for teacher training because of the interviewer's construction of her as a mature woman: 'He said: "You do realise that you will be with youngsters" ... he said he thought I'd be completely out of my depth ... I let it go at that'. Liz constructed a different kind of identity - one which enabled her to feel she had ability but without putting it to the test: 'If I didn't feel as though I was cheating young ones out of going to university I wouldn't mind doing that, either ... I'd think it was wasting the country's money'. In different ways they internalised the discourses around them which excluded them from the opportunity to develop the abilities they obviously had. In contrast, Hilary, having achieved her ambitions and with an MA to her name was able to produce a more dispassionate assessment of her ability, which justified where she was without leaving a desire for more:

I'm sort of mid level academically and if its a higher level then I get put off ... I do question sometimes, but on the whole I tend to accept rather than question (academically) ... On the other hand I've always quite enjoyed listening to things that I have to struggle to understand.

Each participant constructed her sense of self according to the values of those around her and through interfaces with difference experiences. Most of them positioned themselves as active learners and educational participants in their immediate social world. They consistently reported they were always interested in books and quite often writing as well: 'I'd like to write a novel or my autobiography' (Liz); and in spite of their age, most of them were still keen to study in some way - though disability or illness was affecting some of the women and those over 77 were simply more interested in 'living a little bit longer'.

The art course gave them a sense that they were being valued and gave some of them new opportunities to gain qualifications. The extent to which they were typical of their generation is difficult to say in view of the limited research on older adults. Withnal and Percy (1994) suggest that some older adults will pursue multiple goals and take part in different activities at the same time: 'The meaning of later life is what we choose it to be' (p.152). It might be added that the meaning of later life is linked to how personal identities interface with the discourses of the present and internalised discourses of the past.

Although the women seemed less constrained by the influences of immediate family - physically and emotionally, there were indications that it was the interconnectedness of their association with other active learners' past events which enabled them to participate. The Bridge Centre or other organisations that they were associated with created the discourses and spaces for the learning to happen if it built on activities and practical interests which had been stimulated in childhood: 'I adored art classes ... I used to go into competitions' (Nora); 'I always liked colour' (Bernadette); 'I'm always looking in encyclopaedias' (Liz). The CAP course then was itself a form of social capital which interlaced with the Bridge Centre's own social capital. From here the course outcomes facilitated new networks and fed into old ones: 'Aspects of society mutually act upon each other' (Bradley, 1996: 27). As Jamieson et al (1998) said, educational activities have many social meanings with outcomes which are difficult to measure. But there are indications that the relationship between education and social capital is a two way process, and depends on structures which enable people to re-negotiate their identities in contradistinction to stereotype norms of the past and present. In addition, there are indications that learning will never be linear in a world of flux. It is the responsibility of providers to provide educational opportunities that have to compete with more powerful obstacles - of power, of language, of social behaviour. Whilst progression from those opportunities may not be linear, the new experience and new power relationship will be absorbed into the discourses of the moment. Their value lies in the latent opportunity for people to draw on those experiences later when circumstances change. Higher education has a responsibility to be part of those experiences - particularly as it has the most work to do in reconstructing itself to become relevant and useful to those denied in the past.

11 But is it Higher?

> The wider world is looking for three things from its universities: a continuing flow of new stories ... a critical interrogation, and even rebuttal, of existing ideas; and the development of human capacities to live both at ease and purposively amid such uncertainty. All this the university can provide; but first, it needs to rid itself of its being an authority on matters and of its tendency to conduct inner conversations of the intellect. We live in a perplexing world ... the university had better help us to live in that world (Barnett, 2000: 71).

Academics often question whether university community provision is of an acceptable 'higher' level. The question is perhaps rather unfair if it places the burden of defining 'higher' on the learner. After all, universities are constantly redefining themselves and it is difficult to come up with a single definition of 'higher' as earlier chapters have shown. If we were to scrutinise university provision more closely, it would be singularly difficult to apply any consistent criteria for higher across the university sector. So in a sense the question is both unfair and unanswerable. Nevertheless, since we have staked our claim that both our students and their learning material are worthy of higher education status, we must seek to identify why and how we make this claim.

This chapter summarises the main arguments across the book. It argues two things. Firstly, learners who are currently excluded by virtue of previous qualifications, focus of interest or simply lack of opportunity to study at a fixed time, pace and place, can and do study at university level if these barriers are minimised. Secondly, the broadening concept of higher education and its societal role create new opportunities for engaging with the social wealth of different communities. In themselves these arguments are not new. What is new, in the UK at least, is the current political and economic climate for change, inclusion and recognition of difference. The challenge lies in embracing these concepts alongside the global rapidity of new technological advances, drive for competitiveness, convergence and corporatism. These competing elements can have the effect of silencing difference and individual identity - and potentially restrict Barnett's search for new stories. What we have attempted to do, therefore, is demonstrate that, given the space and time to do so, the university can help the most vulnerable in society to live in a perplexing world. Many of the participants in this project used their own experience of being different to develop new knowledge and critique existing values. This often meant re-appraising their own identities which gave them a sense of purpose and direction amidst the uncertainty of their changing environments (see for example, Kevin from the DAB Centre and Mumtaz and Farida from East Lancs in chapters four and five).

The other questions often asked of university community provision are - 'Could a further education college do better? Why should universities be involved in this kind of work?' We feel that the students and community tutors themselves have already answered this question by identifying distinctive aspects of teaching style and learning demands in the CAP courses. Colleges and other providers could, and do, engage with this kind of work, of course - but in those circumstances they are offering higher, rather than further education. Further education is usually constrained by external agencies whose funding and regulatory mechanisms promote a more top-down curriculum and epistemology. Higher education institutions on the other hand ostensibly adhere to a rationale and autonomy that looks beyond pre-defined learning outcomes. In higher education there is an assumption that we are dealing with multiple 'frameworks through which we interrogate the world' and engage with 'critical scrutiny' (Barnett, 2000: 76). However, we also need to understand how to interact differently with existing frameworks, otherwise the stories will remain with the same people, building the same frameworks and drawing comparisons against the same criteria as they have always done, thus ignoring and therefore silencing those outside the familiar. Barnett (2000) argues that: 'There is no framework that we can hang on to with security: all are fragile' (p. 84). If this is the case, we claim, then higher education is about a process, rather than a place of learning. This argument is supported, albeit for different reasons, by those involved in promoting new HE technological stories. Arguably university should not be the only place for studying higher education, particularly since the university already has self defining frameworks whose internalised values automatically exclude different ones. So we take Barnett's position that there can be no disciplinary givens, but we also take earlier lifelong learning arguments (Longworth, 1997; Knapper & Cropley, 1995; McNair, 1998; Watson and Taylor, 1998) that higher learning must take its place on the learner's terms.

In doing so, we are fighting an educational trend which has endured a long history of normalisation and silencing of difference in order to create the citizen:

> National education was a massive engine of integration, assimilating the local to the national and the particular to the national consciousness which would bind each to the state and reconcile each to the other, making actual citizens out of those who were deemed such in law by virtue of their birth or voluntary adoption (Green, 1997: 134).

Green goes on to argue that the idea of citizenship as a form of social cohesion has become increasingly confused and neglected in the context of modern, pluralistic society. So our goal has been to explore how education can be both higher in a modern, pluralistic sense and how it can make new knowledge challenges by building new frameworks for the modern citizen, irrespective of class, race, gender or physical condition.

Chapter one looked at the purpose of higher education. It discussed how the literature makes links between higher education and lifelong learning in the context of applied learning and interpretation of knowledge within the wider world and in anticipation of the world of risk and uncertainty. This book contests the discipline focus of knowledge which ignores different and socially situated forms of understanding. Similarly the idea of higher education as a level of learning is re-appraised as a learning stage (McPherson, 1991). The concept is offered as a way of coming to being for critical citizenship through depth of analysis and complexity of interpretation, rather than extended textual knowledge. Such a learning process requires the individual to be self reflexive and critically aware. Greater awareness of the self, it is argued can bring about more coherent identities and more cohesive communities. The role of the teacher in this context needs to focus on facilitating the development of learning. The quality of such learning might be defined more by the learning achievements for the learner, rather than their educational attainments at the point of entry. For such open ended styles of learning to be effective the teaching process must be learner-centred, requiring an ongoing means of support and guidance and development of curriculum materials which can be accessed in flexible ways. The essence of such changes should ensure that higher education will make learning accessible to a wider range of people and take account of localised needs and identities, in order to meet the global concerns of international markets.

Chapter one also discussed the tension between participation in higher learning and participation in broader society. So, whilst education provides an increasingly essential skills resource for employability (human capital), it is also perceived as having a direct relationship to social capital – nurturing certain forms of social behaviour and ability to take part in a democracy. (These might also be interpreted to include the local values of different communities.) In this respect chapter two emphasised how the action research methodology aimed to give voice to marginalised values and explore how a holistic approach to curriculum and participation might maximise the benefits of a higher education process for the learner. The following chapter explained how such engagement between higher education and marginalised social groups also required us, as HE providers, to interact with the social networks of those groups. This would ensure a build up of sufficient trust to extend, rather than cut off, their communication structures and information channels. Such links would be necessary for nurturing the sense of mutuality that is regarded as central to broader notions of social capital. The suggestion was that conventional patterns of university communication need careful review if HE is to connect and interact effectively with different groups of learners. This may mean that information about educational opportunities has to be filtered through networks at the local level. By starting from this point it may be easier to give value to social capital which is grounded in the reality of people's lives. It is only by doing this that we can recognise and accept the appropriate exchange value for different forms of capital.

The second part of the book looked more closely at aspects of a higher education which might engage with the idea of nurturing the critical being but also offer a transparent learning framework with practical applicability in different situations. Whilst the concept of key skills is acknowledged to be a contested discourse, it was interpreted holistically and differentially from the more dominant, vocationalist discourse for skills. An attempt was made to describe and analyse transparent ways of developing higher learning behaviours and attitudes whilst simultaneously drawing on the non discipline specific knowledge of local cultures, experiences and interests. In this context the idea of learning level became a process rather than body of content. The students revealed a number of distinctions between university and college learning processes - such as the way the CAP courses encouraged independent inquiry and critique, making informed and comparative choices in order to build up new knowledge. From this base they would then start making their links with wider society and develop a critical awareness of themselves and their place within that society. Farida, for instance, discussed how she wanted to start writing about Islamic women in society in Britain, Kevin talked of how he was now developing links with disability societies following his own validation of himself as an individual with rights and skills.

Chapter five pursued this critical, self reflective theme, but expanded on Cherryholmes' (1988) notion of a curriculum 'off limits'. Here the curriculum design process and teaching relationship privilege the marginalised voice and in doing so challenge the authoritative text by drawing on experience as a basis for 'situated knowledge'. The issue here is how knowledge is critiqued. The chapter takes on board Barnett's emphasis on questioning all forms of knowledge. The difference for the CAP students is that their knowledge is given privileged status in the desire to create a level playing field for questioning dominant knowledge. In other words the point of critical neutrality is re-positioned to privilege the marginalised. This shift in values is needed, it is argued, for the development of trust and mutual respect for the socially excluded. The CAP experience of developing learning opportunities from the marginalised perspective is a means of stimulating a new kind of higher education - one that can be developed at higher and more complex levels of debate once the principles of difference are acknowledged as central, rather than marginal (or non existent) in the process of critical inquiry. Hooks (1994) called this 'coming to voice' for the marginalised - the realisation and self actualisation of learning on the learner's terms, enabling them to shape what they consume. A practice of critical analysis, student voice and reflexivity - the process of constructing new knowledge - is done from this base.

In order to provide a safe learning environment for developing the critical learner, however, you must also allow space for the individual to have a sense of self. The level playing field of higher learning comes not from the university as a source of learning, but from the learner's validation of him/herself within the learning environment. Making the curriculum culturally and socially relevant, therefore, demands more than just listening to people on the margins. It requires providing an opportunity for exploration, and repositioning, of self in different social contexts. The Muslim women, for instance, repositioned themselves as Muslims in a Western world, critiquing their religion, but from the standpoint of Islam, rather than a Western notion of neutrality.

In such a fluid system of learning the conventional support systems of discipline structures and authoritative text are vulnerable, making it more, rather than less, difficult to guide the learner. This is especially so when learners are not building on earlier foundations where their learner identity was secure. Strategies for guidance and learner support then become blurred with the processes of teaching and nurturing of study skills. The CAP provision would often deconstruct conventional guidance boundaries for pre, on-course and end of course support. The activity of learning integrated guidance with tutoring and the higher learning process of critical self awareness. Guidance was an educative activity which contributed to critical development, autonomy, an awareness of citizenship rights and ability to make decisions.

The role of technology, as chapter seven showed, also had to be interpreted differentially in the teaching design. Where ICT might sometimes contribute to social cohesion, it could also facilitate the very social exclusion that had marginalised these learners in the first place. The tension between IT which represents global learner identities and the needs of local individuals challenges notions of flexibility as driving forces for participation. Nevertheless the learners did use technology in different ways - to enhance their voice, presentation and access to inaccessible resources. But they were used as part of a group experience and learning enhancement rather than as a technique to replace other forms of teaching. Technology, the flagship of globalisation's constriction of time and space with concepts of flexibility, is therefore a discourse that does not always engage with those most in need of its ideology. To contribute to the building of communities, ICT must be part of a wider, integrative education strategy.

This second section explored 'higher' education in the context of contemporary explorations of the future university as a learning organisation for the majority. The research showed that the practicalities of those ideals might need to be re-thought. The challenge of criticality in an age of supercomplexity is to avoid the danger of silencing the very opportunities to engage with that complexity. The attractions of a global market and globally constructed resources need to be understood in the context of local identities and differential perspectives. The third part of the book attempted to demonstrate why this is so. We talked in depth to three groups of learners, whose backgrounds and personal histories had already excluded them from the university of today. Their stories were contextualised by the themes of chapter one: human capital; social capital; citizenship and a related issue - subjectivity.

The learner stories emphasised that experiences of displacement - in terms of time, health and space - meant that people needed to regroup and re-shape aspects of the new converging world. This meant in some cases that old notions of citizenship required re-conceptualising to take account of new rights and responsibilities, especially for women and minorities. Similarly, social capital as a localised means of exchanging knowledge, skills and power could become a form of social wealth through educational practices which nurtured self help in communities. The way in which social capital could be further developed through new HE learning experiences was by means of educational providers making direct links with the existing social networks and communication channels in those local communities. Both these issues were closely linked to the relationship between a sense of self and educational participation - how we position ourselves in relation to others. People can sometimes re-construct their identity by shifting the balance of power between discourses. Given the opportunity and relevant help they can start to critique the way others define their role and status in society. Individuals can then have those new identities validated by those around them in a supportive atmosphere. The additional validation of their experiences by university representatives as authoritative knowledge holders could be significant in the transformation process. The relationship between personal biographies and current participation, therefore, is complex, made more so by differential power relations regarding disability, race, gender, class. We tried to identify these community strengths and what the CAP courses tapped into to enhance those strengths. We sought to find out how the higher learning was a contributory factor to enhancing social capital and identity formation.

The East Lancs women were struggling with the tensions and opportunities of diasporic existences - as bearers of past certainties and advocates for new possibilities. They demonstrated that culture is constantly in progress by rooting cultural positions in new locations and shifting new values in the context of time and place. Their private, local networks were subliminated beneath more dominant voices, leaving some of their citizenship roles apparently in a state of compulsory altruism, rather than a self selection of public services. The courses validated their group mutuality and reciprocity and helped to give their achievements a public place through certification and engagement with a public institution. At the same time their shared values and cultural differences were accommodated through single sex provision and other services which supported the complexity of their multiple identities as mothers, daughters, carers and housekeepers. By combining these worlds, the courses enabled the women to manage the unpredictability of their changing identities through the learning process. The courses made links with their existing social capital enabling them to build on that capital for wider social purposes. In some cases this shifted the women's power relations in their own communities, in other cases it opened up ideas for what might be possible in the wider world. Frequently the women started to actively re-negotiate their social boundaries. The university involvement gave them space to reconstruct a new self around reflexivity, rather than simply banking of old knowledge. As a consequence the women re-grouped, reconstructed and re-asserted themselves, building new local identities but in a re-awakened global context.

Similarly the DAB Centre students re-positioned their disabled selves in the context of wider political movements and local initiatives to make their activities public and accessible. ICT was an enabling tool in relation to different aspects of their lives, but it was done in the context of local, face to face support and alongside a reciprocally enhanced system of social interaction. The increased peer support, engendered through the courses, strengthened existing social capital and broadened its links, building new trust, using new knowledge and strengthening the inner self. A significant feature for the DAB and East Lancs groups of their enhanced learner identities was the way individuals emphasised how they were now able to help their children - creating another form of family mutuality. Again the university's involvement in that process created further communication flows which would otherwise not have been established.

The DAB group also used their new identities to re-construct ways of being a citizen, contesting the normative notion of disability as a state of being in need of welfare. The critical self became a more constructive and stronger self enabling the participants to challenge the images others had bestowed upon them. In some respects this process of criticality reflects Kolb's (1984) learning cycle of experience, reflection, re-application of new learning and continued reflection. It is a learning process advocated in higher education, particularly through the enterprise education movement. For minority and marginalised groups, such a process enables individuals and groups to re-position themselves in opposition to dominant images.

Such progression did not always mean that people underwent a continuous, linear learning journey. The outcome could simply mean greater engagement in society. For people whose lives remained largely hidden, this is an outcome of higher education which makes difference more visible and provides long term messages for the development of human as well as social capital. The long term outcome of such developments is beyond the scope of this project but it has implications for how and why higher learning is offered to society as a whole.

The last group, the Bridge Centre, offered us the opportunity to explore how people might learn over a lifetime without a proactive interface with higher education. It was apparent that many in this group had undertaken several initiatives to learn at various points in their lives. But only two people engaged with higher education independently. One was the daughter of a school master. The second was a woman whose grammar school scholarship place eventually gave her the confidence to take up teacher training as a mature student. From there she took an open university degree during its first wave of publicity in the 1970s. The remaining seven people did not attempt study beyond or even up to 'O' level. Yet five of them chose to tackle the foundation credit assignment as a result of the CAP involvement. All of the women interviewed emphasised their interest in the CAP art courses was because of the opportunity to study locally at a time and place to suit them. As with the other groups, their experience on the courses meant they increased their existing social networks and citizenship activities, ranging from organising art appreciation societies, to giving art talks in existing organisations.

Social capital, then, is in a state of flux and contingent upon circumstances past and present. For all the groups, their learning experiences contributed to their evolving lives. The courses emphasised non competitive, reciprocal activities, rather than competitive individualism or personal gain. People's subjectivities - the way they defined themselves based on the past in the present - were influenced by the way learning provision was offered and also by the nature of that provision. This suggests that higher education needs to build on the past in order to engage with the present. If so, then this is likely to influence the teaching and learning provision since there must be a mutual enactment of different aspects of society on each other. Education and social capital mutually act upon each other.

Not all the courses demonstrated the same level of criticality and not all individuals manifested the same level of personal growth. The courses demanded no prior qualifications or experience and participants brought with them a vast range of educational backgrounds. Similarly, not every tutor found it easy to adopt the teaching styles we were asking of them. The programme required ongoing staff development and dialogue before, during and after the courses. Our own action research and partnership strategy facilitated this dialogue. Our analysis of the project's overall success in achieving a higher learning experience in community settings comes from the interviews and group discussions. There was the added enjoyment of seeing people gain credits which would not otherwise have been available to them. Equally the realisation that higher education is an achievable goal would influence generations and others in their immediate surroundings far more effectively than any targeted marketing strategy. We argue, therefore that it is the responsibility of higher education to be a part of the experiences of everyone's life - not just for those already connected with higher education. By interacting with those most on the margins and sharing their knowledge perspectives, hopefully HE will begin to explore new forms of knowledge that may enhance its role in those communities. There are constraints, however, both political and financial, on how universities choose to position themselves in this arena.

Political and Financial Implications for Higher Education which Engages with Social Capital

Current Government widening participation strategies are moving in two directions. On the one hand the digital age is generating a competitive drive towards the 'e' university (HEFCE, 2000). Global learning delivered through electronic means, will have its own potential impact on the teaching and learning curriculum. The 'e' university is influenced by world markets and a consequent race to capture financial and political status.

Whilst it might be claimed that future generations may gain from the university's technological advances, on the whole it is not a measure which will have immediate impact on those already excluded. Some reinvestment of subsequent financial gains towards social goals might be possible if an economic argument can be found to justify this. but on the whole, the 'e' university is serving a different, more lucrative market.

On the other hand, there are plans to provide a two year flexibly delivered foundation degree (DfEE, 2000a), achievable in small bites through credit accumulation and transfer. This is a style of learning that might well appeal to people seeking recognition for 'really useful' learning. If one acknowledges the personal growth manifested amongst the community learners then it may be that any higher learning achievement might stimulate an enhanced sense of self with consequent benefits for social cohesion. Some would argue that a vocational qualification has a sound economic rationale, suggesting a direct gain for the local or national economy. It may be that such a degree, delivered through local colleges will provide new learning routes for normalising the socially excluded. Courses delivered at an appropriate time, pace and place are certainly required features of a new kind of higher education.

Whilst the economic rationale for the above initiative may fit the current discourse for inclusion, the rationale is not necessarily proven. Indeed, there were features of our programme which suggest something more needs to be done if education is to be higher *and* socially inclusive. Part of the problem lies in the hidden economics of providing a service that is not directly linked to employment. Most of the participants in CAP courses had little or no immediate prospect of labour market activity. Furthermore, their personal circumstances meant that participation in the courses was only possible if they were free or heavily subsidised. The economic rationale for this kind of provision has to be read in the small print. Primarily it is this. Increased participation will have the long term effect of helping people re-position themselves as active, rather than passive, members of society. By nurturing self help networks the participants will become less dependent on welfare services. Whilst the economic savings from welfare dependency are also not proven in this model of HE, there are clear indications in this project that individuals and groups were seeking increased independence for themselves and on behalf of others.

The kind of HE which nurtures social capital in excluded communities engages with the values of those communities but does not lose sight of the goal to develop critical thinkers. Investment in the learning needs of those communities may pave the way for participation in emerging models of higher education; it will also enable people to make informed choices about the social fabric of their lives. Higher education that expects participants to make this cultural leap for themselves is unlikely to reach those communities it most needs to reach.

So what features of our kind of higher education would need to be incorporated into the new learning agendas? We suggest the following:

- Firstly there is a need to create a climate of mutual respect by concentrating on redressing the balance of power between those with authority to know and those with different kinds of knowledge.

- One mechanism for bridging social and cultural divides is to foster role model advocates who can act as mediators/translators between the expectations and values of different communities.

- The nurturing of an appropriate climate of mutuality and trust for widening participation is dependent on long term investments in marginalised communities.

- There also needs to be a recognition that people have a right to do what they want with their learning. For some the notion of progression may not be a linear move towards further qualifications. Indeed, the hidden economy may benefit more readily from a more lateral view of progression – which feeds directly into community regeneration.

- Higher education providers should not rely on a front-loaded model of encouragement and support for new learners. For integration between current higher and local communities to be effective this requires the building of mutual understanding and support throughout and beyond the first stages of participation.

- Part of this integration strategy will be facilitated by interactive teaching styles and methods which allow space for the marginalised voice to be heard – in the curriculum, in the classroom and throughout the learning community.

- Widening participation is also not just about engaging with individuals at the point of entry. It includes a holistic commitment to understanding community and family cultures and exploring with them what value HE has for their lives, as well as exploring what the economic gains might be for society as a whole.

Taking on board these issues will facilitate understanding of a broader picture of the essential qualities of HE for everyone. These will hopefully be seen as an investment in society as well as contributing to the current goals of investment in lifelong learning leading to wealth creation. Furthermore, by nurturing the social capital of excluded communities it will enrich the stories available within higher education in the twenty first century.

APPENDICES

APPENDICES

Appendix 1:

Community Access Course Proposal Form Requirements

Date: Level: Pre Access   Access   Year 1
Tutor Name (attach application form & CV if new to dept.)
Working Title
Start Date & Day; Class Times (eg. 2-4pm or 7-9pm)
Number of Meetings; Maximum Student Numbers

Location; Who are the Intended Participant Group?

Evidence of Community Consultation (any discussions with people, organisations and why it was decided to do this course).
How is this course part of any progression, or long term plan, for the participants?

Educational Goals of Course (what do you hope the participants will learn, gain or do by the end of the course?) **By the end of the course the students will:**

What 'Employability' Qualities or Further Learning Interests is this Course Intended to Develop?

Syllabus (weekly breakdown or timetable of topics)

Educational Guidance Plans for this Course

Teaching Methods: Please identify rough % of time for each: Group work, Role play, Discussions, Visits, Instructions, Demonstrations, Talks, Other.

Assessment (To be completed for Foundation Credit Courses)

Resources Required – OHP, flip chart etc. How will these be obtained?

Will Participants be Expected to do Work Beyond Course Attendance?
(for example: reading/visits/writing etc.)

Please Identify any Special Circumstances Which Need to be Taken into Account for this Group e.g.

Bilingual Support	Literacy Support
Disability Access	Transport
BSL Support	Single Sex Provision
Other (please state)	

Give Examples of How Course Material or Content is Being Adapted to Suit the Particular Needs of this Group (eg. Cultural issues, relevance, language, braille etc.)

Any Other Comments About this Group's Needs or Why You Are Doing this Course

Approved by: Details of Discussion
Date of Meeting   No. Present   Outcome
Community Access Committee
Departmental Advisory Group

Appendix 2:

Example Assessment Criteria for Investigation Skills Assignment

Analysis (insight and interpretation - 30% of grade)
Grade 1: Able to show:
a) main research question which has been justified and followed through logically in the investigation
b) fieldwork appendix (e.g. questionnaire, sub questions) which are very relevant to the main question
c) evidence that writer has identified patterns from the data
d) interpretation/analysis of what these patterns mean in relation to the question
e) evidence of background information gathered in addition to the fieldwork which can support or be challenged by the new data, with a conclusion or summary
f) thoughtful identification of areas of weakness and ways in which the investigation could be improved next time.

Grade 2: Able to show:
a) main research question which relates to the field work questions and why writer has chosen it
b) fieldwork appendix (e.g. questionnaire, sub questions) which are relevant to the main question
c) evidence that the writer has identified patterns from the data and drawn some conclusions
d) identification of areas of weakness or ways in which the investigation could be improved next time.

Grade 3: Able to show:
a) main research question
b) fieldwork appendix (e.g. questionnaire, sub questions)
c) evidence that writer has identified patterns from the data and attempted to draw some conclusions from this.

Organisation (coherence and logical development - 30% of grade)
Grade 1: Able to show clearly and neatly the five different sections of the report: introduction, methods used, results, analysis, conclusions.

Grade 2: Able to show evidence that all five sections have been signposted in some way.

Grade 3: Some evidence that the report has been tackled in a logical way and that at least 4 of the five sections are easy to identify.

Relevance (personal or work related - 10% of grade)
Grade 1: Clear evidence that the writer has identified a good/personal reason for doing the investigation.

Grade 2: Some evidence as to the usefulness of the investigation to the writer and the general public.

Grade 3: Some evidence that the investigation has some point to it.

References (range and appropriateness of sources/examples - 10% of grade)
Grade 1: Signposted (annotated) evidence of additional reading or use of additional information beyond the fieldwork/activity/survey.

Grade 2: Some evidence that additional material has been used/read in addition to the survey/fieldwork (for e.g. reference to other evidence but no source stated).

Grade 3: Some evidence that the writer has thought about the possibility of additional evidence (e.g. hearsay material).

Presentation (readability - 10% of grade)
Grade 1: Very clearly presented and easy to follow, with few or no spelling mistakes or other punctuation errors.

Grade 2: Carefully prepared with some evidence of attempts to correct punctuation and spelling.

Grade 3: Material is readable and shows evidence of careful preparation.

Overall comments (effort, distinguishing aspects etc. - 10% of grade)
Grade 1: A piece of work which the writer has taken considerable time to prepare and think about and identifies a topic which will be of interest to others.

Grade 2: A piece of work which the writer has taken time to prepare and identifies a topic which is of some use to others.

Grade 3: A piece of work where the writer has put in a certain amount of effort and which will be of minor interest to others.

Bibliography

Ackers L (1998) *Shifting Spaces: women, citizenship and migration within the European Union,* Cambridge: Polity.

Alfonsi A (1997) Citizenship and National identity: the emerging stirrings in Europe, in T K Oommen (ed), *Citizenship and National Identity: from colonialism to globalism,* London: Sage.

Allen P (1997) Black Students in Ivory Towers, *Studies in the Education of Adults* 29 (2): 179-190.

Apple M W (1993) *Official Knowledge: democratic education in a conservative age,* London: Routledge.

Aronowitz S & Giroux H A (1991) *Postmodern Education: politics, culture and social criticism,* London: University of Minnesota Press.

Ashton D (1999) Skill Formation: redirecting the research agenda, in F Coffield (ed), *Learning at Work: the learning society,* Policy Press/ESRC.

Ashworth P D & Saxton J (1990) On Competence, *Journal of Further and Higher Education* 14 (2): 3-25.

Bailey D (1993) Gender and Educational Guidance: questions of feminist practice, *British Journal of Guidance and Counselling* 21 (2): 161 - 174.

Ball S J C (1990) *More Means Different: widening access to higher education,* London: Industry Matters.

Barnes M (1997) *Care, Communities and Citizens,* Harlow: Addison Wesley Longman Ltd.

Barnett R (1988) Does Higher Education Have Aims? *Journal of Philosophy of Education* 22 (2): 239-250.

Barnett R (1990) *The Idea of Higher Education,* Buckinghamshire: SRHE/Open University Press.

Barnett R (1994) *The Limits of Competence,* Bucks: SRHE/Open University Press.

Barnett R (1997a) Beyond Competence, in F Coffield and B Williamson (eds), *Repositioning Higher Education,* Buckinghamshire: SRHE/Open University Press.

Barnett R (1997b) *Higher Education: a critical business,* Buckinghamshire: SRHE/Open University Press.

Barnett R (1998a) In or For the Learning Society? *Higher Education Quarterly* 52 (1): 7-21.

Barnett R (2000) *Realizing the University,* Buckinghamshire: SRHE/Open University Press.

Baron S, Stalker K, Wilkinson H and Riddell S (1999) The Learning Society: the highest stage of human capitalism? in F Coffield (ed), *Learning at Work: the learning society*, Bristol: Policy Press/ESRC:

Barrow R (1987) Skills Talk, *Journal of Philosophy of Education* 21 (2): 187-195.

Barton D and Hamilton M (1998) *Local Literacies: reading and writing in one community*, London: Routledge.

Battersby D (1990) From Andragogy to Geragogy, in F Glendening and K Percy (eds), *Ageing Education and Society*, Keele: Association for Educational Gerontology.

Bauman Z (1998) *Globalization*, Cambridge: Polity.

Beck U (1998) *Democracy Without Enemies*, Cambridge: Polity.

Beinart S and Smith P (1998) Education, Globalisation and Economic Development, in A H Halsey, H Lauder, P Brown and A S Wells (eds), *Education: culture, economy, society*, Oxford: Oxford university Press.

Benn R & Fieldhouse R (1997) The Role of Adult Learning in Promoting Active Citizenship in Britain in the twentieth century, in C Thorne (1998) Democratic Deficit, *Adults Learning* 10 (3): 23-25.

Bhachu P (1993) Identities Constructed and Reconstructed: representation of Asian women in Britain, in G Buijs (ed), *Migrant Women: crossing boundaries and changing identities*, Oxford: Berg.

Bird J (1996) Black Students and Higher Education: rhetoric and realities Buckinghamshire: SRHE/Open University Press.

Blair A, McPake J and Munn P (1998) The client's perceptions of guidance, in R Edwards R Harrison A and Tait (eds), *Telling Tales: perspectives on guidance and counselling in learning*, London: Routledge.

Blass E (1999) Changing the Concept of Skill in Higher Education in the UK: is it progress in the current environment? *European Journal of Education* 34 (2): 237-248.

Blissand V (1999) *Storming Lifelong Learning*, Unpublished Paper, University of Strathclyde.

Blunkett D (1999) *Tackling Social Exclusion: empowering people and communities for a better future*, London: DfEE.

Boddy G (1997) Tertiary Educators' Perceptions of and Attitudes Toward Emerging Educational Technologies, *Higher Education Research and Development* 16 (3): 343-358.

Boud D Cohen R & Walker D (eds) (1993) *Using Experience for Learning*, Bucks: SRHE/Open University Press.

Bourgeois E, Duke C, Luc-Guyot J, Merrill B (1999) *The Adult University*, Buckinghamshire: SRHE/Open University Press.

Bourke J (1994) *Working Class Cultures in Britain 1890-1960*, London: Routledge.

Bradley H (1996) *Fractured Identities*, Cambridge: Polity.

Bradshaw D (1985) Transferable Intellectual and Personal Skills, *Oxford Review of Education* 11 (2) 210-215.

Brah A (1996) *Cartographies of Diaspora: contesting identities*, London: Routledge.

Brennan J, Fedrowitz J, Huber M and Shah T (eds) (1999) *What Kind of University? International Perspectives on Knowledge, Participation and Governance*, Buckinghamshire: SRHE/Open University Press.

Brindley J (1995) Learners and Learner Services: the key to the future in open distance learning, in J Roberts and E Keough (eds), *Why the Information Highway? Lessons from Open and Distance Learning*, Toronto: Trifolium Books Inc.

Brine J (1999) *UnderEducating Women: globalizing inequality*, Milton Keynes: Open University Press.

Brown J (1991) What is Educational Guidance? *Adults Learning* 2 (10): 277-278.

Brown J S and Duguid P (1996) Organisational Learning and Communities of Practice: toward a unified view of working, learning and innovation, in M Choe and L Sproull (eds), *Organisational Learning*, London: Sage Publications.

Brown P (1997) Cultural Capital and Social Exclusion: some observations on recent trends in education employment and the labour market, *Work Employment and Society* 9 (1): 29-51.

Brown P and Lauder H (1997) Education, Globalization and Economic Development, in A H Halsey, H Lauder, P Brown and A S Wells (eds), *Education: culture, economy, society*, Oxford: Oxford University Press.

Brunt J M (1997) Can You Put Your Arm Around a Student on the Internet? In J Field (ed), *Electronic Pathways: adult learning and the new communication technologies*, Leicester: NIACE.

Buck M (1997) The Global Demands for Change in J Field (ed), *Electronic pathways: adult learning and the new communication technologies*, Leicester: NIACE.

Burgess R G (1982) The Unstructured Interview as a Conversation, in R G Burgess (ed), *Field Research: a sourcebook and field manual*, London: Unwin Hyman Ltd.

Burgess T (ed) (1986) *Education for Capabilit,y* Berkshire: NFER-Nelson.

Carlton S & Soulsby J (1998) *Learning to grow older: the importance of learning in later life*, Leicester: NIACE.

Castells M (1996) *The Rise of the Network Society*, Oxford: Blackwell.

Challis S (1997) Rural Broadnet in Shropshire, in J Field (ed), *Electronic Pathways: adult learning and the new communication technologies*, Leicester: NIACE.

Cherryholmes C H (1988) *Power and Criticism: poststructural investigations in education*, London: Teachers College Press.

Chertos C (1987) In Praise of Useable Research, in C Bose and G Spitze (eds), *Ingredients for Women's Employment Policy*, Albany: State University of New York Press.

Chrisholm L (1997) *Getting In, Climbing Up and Breaking Through: women returners and vocational guidance and counselling*, Bristol: Policy Press.

Clare M (1990) *Developing Self-Advocacy Skills with People with Disabilities and Learning Difficulties*, London: Further Education Unit.

Clarke A (1999) Achieving Core Competencies in the Digital Society, *Adults Learning*, 11 (3): 16-17.

Code L (1991) *What Can She Know? Feminist Theory and the Construction of Knowledge*, London: Cornell University Press.
Code L (1995) *Rhetorical Spaces*, London: Routledge.
Coffield F (1999) Introduction: lifelong learning as a new form of social control? in F Coffield (ed), *Why's the Beer Always Stronger Up North?* – Studies of Lifelong Learning in Europe 2, Bristol: The Policy Press.
Coffield F & Williamson B (1997) *Repositioning Higher Education*, Bucks: SRHE/Open University Press.
Coffield F & Williamson B (1997) The Challenges Facing Higher Education, in F Coffield and B Williamson (eds), *Repositioning Higher Education*, Buckinghamshire: SRHE/Open University Press.
Cohen L and Manion L (1989) *Research Methods in Education*, London: Routledge.
Coleman J S (1988) Social Capital in the Creation of Human Capital, *AJS Supplement*, 94: S95-S120.
Coleman J S (1994) *Foundations of Social Theory*, Harvard University Press.
Coleman J S (1997) Social Capital in the Creation of Human Capital, in A H Halsey, H Lauder, P Brown and A S Wells (eds), *Education: culture, economy, society*, Oxford: Oxford University Press.
Council for Industry and Higher Education (CIHE) (1997) *Widening Participation in Lifelong Learning: a progress report*, London: CIHE.
Cronin C, Foster M and Lister E (1999) Set for the Future: working towards inclusion in science, engineering and technology curricula in higher education, *Studies in Higher Education* 24 (2): 165-181.
Cruikshank J (1994) The Consequences of our Actions: a value issue in community development, *Community Development Journal* 29 (1): 75-89.
Cryer P (1998) Transferable Skills, Marketability and Lifelong Learning: the particular case of postgraduate research students, *Studies in Higher Education* 23 (2): 207-216.
Dadzie S (1990) *Educational Guidance with black communities*, Leicester: NIACE/REPLAN.
Daniels J (1995) Preface, in J Roberts and E Keough (eds), *Why the Information highway? Lessons from open and distance learning*, Toronto: Trifolium Books Inc.
Dearing R (1996) *The Review of Qualifications for 16-19 olds*, London: SCAA.
Dearing Sir R (1997) *Higher Education in the Learning Society*, National Committee of Inquiry into Higher Education, London: HMSO.
Deem R (1996) The Gendering of Educational Organisations, in R Cosslett, A Easton and P Summerfield (eds), *Women, Power and Resistance*, Milton Keynes: Open University Press.
DfEE (Department for Education and Employment) (1998) *The Learning Age: a renaissance for a new Britain*, Green Paper, London: HMSO.
DfEE (1999) *Learning to Succeed: a new framework for post 16 learning*, White Paper, London: HMSO.
DfEE (1999a) *The Wider Benefits of Learning* - invitation to tender for a research centre, London: DfEE.

DfEE (2000) *Learndirect,* http://www.dfee.gov.uk/adlearners/Pages/PAGES_NF/LearnDir.html.
DfEE (2000a) *Foundation Degrees: a consultation document,* www.dfee.gov.uk/heqc/fdcd.htm.
Directorate General 22 (DGXXII) (1995) White Paper: *Teaching and Learning, Towards the Learning Society,* www.cec.lu/en/comm/dg22/ dg22.html.
Duke C (1992) *The Learning University,* Buckinghamshire: SRHE/Open University Press.
Ebbutt D (1985) Educational Action Research: some general concerns and specific quibbles, in R G Burgess (ed), *Issues in Educational Research: qualitative methods,* Lewes: Falmer Press.
Edwards M (1998) Commodification and Control in Mass Higher Education: A Double Edged Sword, in D Jary and M Parker (eds), *The New Higher Education: Issues and Directions for the Post-Dearing University,* Staffordshire: Staffordshire University Press.
Edwards R (1997) *Changing Places? Flexibility, Lifelong Learning and a Learning Society,* London: Routledge.
Elliott J, Francis, Humphries R and Istance D (eds) (1966) *Communities and Their Universities: the challenge of lifelong learning,* London: Lawrence and Wishart.
Elsdon K T with Reynolds J and Stewart S (1995) *Voluntary Organisations: citizenship, learning and change,* Leicester: NIACE.
Etzioni E (1995) *The Spirit of Community: rights responsibilities and the communitarian agenda,* London: Fontana Press.
Fazey D (1996) Guidance for Learner Autonomy, in S M McNair (ed), *Putting Learners at the Centre: reflections from the guidance and learner autonomy in higher education programme,* Sheffield: DfEE.
Field J (1997a) Telematics for Education: the policies and programmes of the European Union, in J Field (ed), *Electronic Pathways: adult learning and the new communication technologies,* Leicester: NIACE.
Field J (1997b) The Adult Learner, Listener, Viewer and Cybersurfer, in J Field (ed), *Electronic Pathways: adult learning and the new communication technologies,* Leicester: NIACE.
Field J and Spence L (2000) Informal Learning and Social Capital, in F Coffield (ed), *The necessity of informal learning,* Bristol: Policy Press.
Fieldhouse R and Associates (1996) *A History of Modern British Education,* Leicester: NIACE.
Finkelstein V (1993) Disability: a social challenge or an administrative responsibility? in J Swain, V Finkelstein, S French and M Oliver (eds), *Disabling Barriers: enabling environments,* London: Sage.
Fordham P, Poulton G and Randle L (1979) *Learning Networks in Adult Education: non formal education on a housing estate,* London: Routledge and Kegan Paul.
Foucault M (1980) *Power/Knowledge,* London: Harvester Wheatsheaf.
Freire P (1972) *Pegagogy of the Oppressed,* London: Penguin.
Friedman J (1994) *Cultural Identity and Global Process,* London: Sage.

Fryer R (1997) *Learning for the Twenty-first Century: first report of the National Advisory Group for Continuing Education and Lifelong Learning*: Sheffield: NAGCELL.

Fryer R (1999) *Creating Learning Cultures: next steps in achieving the learning age: second report of the National Advisory Group for Continuing Education and Lifelong Learning*, Sheffield: NAGCELL.

Fukuyama F (1995) *Trust: the social virtues and the creation of prosperity*, London: Penguin.

Further Education Unit (1994) *Initiating Change: educational guidance for adults 1988-93. The Final Report of the National Educational Guidance Initiative*, Northants: Further Education Unit.

Gain M and Cicco E D (1999) Putting the Learning Back into ILT, *Adults Learning* 11 (3): 23-25.

Gibbons M (1999) Changing Research Practices, in J Brennan, J Fedrowitz, M Huber and T Shah (eds), *What Kind of University? International Perspectives on Knowledge, Participation and Governance*, Buckinghamshire: SRHE/Open University Press.

Giddens A (1991) *Modernity and Self Identity: self and society in the late modern age*, Cambridge: Polity Press.

Giddens A (1998) *The Third Way*, Cambridge: Polity.

Glover R J (1998) Perspectives on Ageing: issues affecting the latter part of the life cycle, *Educational Gerontology* 24 (4): 325-332.

Goduka I N (1998) Educators as Cultural Awakeners and Healers, *South African Journal of Higher Education* 12 (2): 49-59.

Gore J M (1993) *The Struggle for Pedagogies*, London: Routledge.

Gosden C (1994) *Social Being and Time*, Oxford: Blackwell.

Green A (1997) *Education, Globalisation and the Nation State*, Hants: Macmillan.

Hake B (1997) Lifelong Learning and the European Union: a critique from a 'risk society' perspective in J Holford, C Griffin & P Jarvis (eds), *Lifelong Learning: reality, rhetoric and public policy, conference proceedings*, Surrey: University of Surrey.

Hall S (1990) Cultural Identity and Diaspora, in Rutherford J (ed), *Identity, Community, Culture, Difference*, London: Lawrence & Wishart.

Harvey L & Knight P (1996) *Transforming Higher Education*, Bucks: SRHE/Open University Press.

Harvard M, Hughes M and Clarke J (1998) The Introduction and Evaluation of Key Skills in Undergraduate Courses, *Journal of Further and Higher Education* 22 (1): 61-68.

HEFCE (Higher Education Funding Council for England) (1994/95) *Special Initiative to Encourage Widening Participation for Students with Special Needs*, Circular 8/94, Bristol: HEFCE.

HEFCE (1995/96a) *Widening Participation - Continuing Education*, Circular 9/95, Bristol: HEFCE.

HEFCE (1995/96b) *Widening Participation - Non Award Bearing Continuing Education*, Circular 7/95, Bristol: HEFCE.

HEFCE (1998) *Widening Participation in Higher Education: funding proposals*, Circular 98/39, Bristol: HEFCE.

HEFCE (1999) *Widening Participation in Higher Education: request for initial statement of plans; invitation to bid for special funds*, Circular 99/33, Bristol: HEFCE.

HEFCE (2000) *'E' University Project*, Circular letter 04/00, Bristol: HEFCE.

Heinz W (1999) Lifelong Learning; learning for life? Some Cross National Observations, in F Coffield (ed), *Why's the Beer Always Stronger Up North? The Learning Society*, Bristol: Policy Press/ESRC.

Held D, McGrew A, Goldblatt D, Perraton J (1999) *Global Transformations*, Cambridge: Polity.

HEQC (Higher Education Quality Council) (1995) *A Quality Assurance Framework for Guidance and Learner Support in Higher Education: the guidelines*, London: HEQC.

HEQC (1996) *Understanding academic Standards in Modular Frameworks*, London: HEQC.

Hill Collins P (1990) *Black Feminist Thought*, London: Routledge.

Hillier Y (1990) How Do Adult Students Learn About Educational Opportunities? *New Era in Education*, 71 (1): 6-10.

Hirst G and Thompson G (1996) *Globalization in Question*, Cambridge: Polity.

Hoatson L, Dixon J and Sloman D (1996) Community Development, Citizenship and the Contract State, *Community Development Journal: an international forum* 31 (2): 126 - 136.

hooks b (1994) *Teaching To Transgress*, London: Routledge.

Houghton A-M (1997) Learning How to Work as Partners: the 3 MP's, meeting as partners and making plans for mutual progress, Unpublished Conference Paper, *Empowering Education: student diversity, tutor training and part time HE students*, UACE Empowering Education and Training Network: Sussex.

Houghton A-M (1998a) Guidance as Research, Teaching and Learning, in R Benn (ed), *Research, Teaching, Learning: making connnections in the education of adults*, Exeter: SCUTREA.

Houghton A-M (1998b) Extending the Guidance Boundaries: an exploration of educative and empowering guidance strategies for learners who have been long term unemployed, in J Preece (ed), *Beyond the Boundaries: exploring the potential of widening provision in higher education*, Leicester: NIACE.

Houghton A-M (1999) Confidence, Communication and Citizenship: enterprising community learning. Unpublished Conference Paper, *Social Change and Active Citizenship in the Learning Society*, Posnan: Adam Mickiesvick University, ESREA.

Houghton A-M and Ali H (1999) Voices from the Community, *Widening Participation and Lifelong Learning* 1 (3): 45-46.

Houghton A-M and Bokhari R (1997) Creating an Environment for Enabling and Empowering Students in the Community: guiding differently, in K Hurley (ed), *University Continuing Education in Partnership for Development*, Unpublished Conference Paper, Dublin; UACE.

Houghton A-M and Bokhari R (1998) Guiding Differently, *Adults Learning* 9 (7): 15-17.

Howarth C and Kenway P (1998) A Multi-dimentional Approach to Social Exclusion Indicators, in C Oppenheim (ed), *An Inclusive Society: strategies for tackling poverty*, London: IPPR.

Hudson B (1993) Michael Lipsky and Street Level Bureaucracy: a neglected perspective, in M Hill (ed), *The Policy Process: a reader*, London: Harvester Wheatsheaf.

Hunjan I and Kent K (1997) Access and support for black and ethnic minority people, in R Taylor (ed), *Opportunities for Black People in Higher Education*, Unpublished Conference Paper, Education for Transformation, Leeds: School of Continuing Education, Leeds University.

Hunt M (1998) British Systems of Careers Software: past and present, in M Crawford, R Edwards and L Kydd (eds), *Taking Issue: debates in guidance and counselling in learning*, London: Routledge and Open University Press.

Hunter L (1995) *Open Studies Survey: deciding factors, factors affecting the enrolment decision*, Unpublished Report, Lancaster: Lancaster University.

Hunter L, Nelson J and Tait J (1995) *Credit for All: a marketing research report into credit bearing courses*, Unpublished Report, Lancaster: Lancaster University.

Hurst A (1996) Reflecting on researching disability and higher education, in Barton L (ed), *Disability and Society: emerging issues and insights*, Harlow: Addison Wesley Longman Ltd.

Hyland T (1994) Experiential Learning, Competence and Critical Practice in Higher Education, *Studies in Higher Education* 19 (3): 327-338.

Hyland T & Johnson S (1998) Of Cabbages and Key Skills: exploding the mythology of core transferable skills in post-school education, *Journal of Further and Higher Education* 22 (2): 163-172.

Imeson R and Wyatt J (1996) Pre-Entry Guidance and Admission, in S McNair (ed), *Putting Learners at the Centre: reflections from the guidance and leaner autonomy in higher education programme*, Sheffield: DfEE.

Jackson K (1980) Forward, in J Thompson (ed), *Adult Education for a Change*, London: Hutchinson.

Jamieson A, Miller A, Stafford J (1998) Education in a Life Course Perspective: continuities and discontinuities, *Education and Ageing* 13 (3): 213-228.

Jansen J D (1998) Curriculum Reform in South Africa: a critical analysis of outcomes-based education, *Cambridge Journal of Education* 28 (3): 321-332.

Jarvis P (1992) *Paradoxes of Learning: on being an individual in society*, San Francisco: Jossey Bass.

Jarvis P (1996) The Public Recognition of Lifetime Learning, *Lifelong Learning in Europe* Vol 1: 10-17.

Johnston R (1992) Education and Unwaged Adults: relevance, social control and empowerment, in Garth A and Martin I (eds), *Education and Community Practice: the politics of practice*, London: Cassell.

Johnstone B (1999) The Future of the University: reasonable predictions, hoped for reforms or technological possibilities? In J Brennan, J Fedrowitz, M Huber and

T Shah (eds), *What Kind of University: international perspectives on knowledge participation and governance*, Buckingham: SRHE/Open University Press.
Jordan B (1996) *A Theory of Poverty and Social Exclusion*, Cambridge: Polity.
Jordan B (1997) Citizenship, Association and Immigration: theoretical issues, in M Roche and R Van-Birkel (eds), *European Citizenship and Social Exclusion*, Hants: Ashgate.
Kelly A (1985) Action Research: what is it and what can it do? In R G Burgess (ed), *Issues in Educational Research: qualitative methods*, Lewes: Falmer Press.
Kennedy H (1997) *Learning Works: widening participation in further education*, Coventry: FEFC.
Killeen J (1986) Vocational Guidance: a study of demand, *British Journal of Guidance and Counselling* 14 (3): 225 - 239.
Kirkpatrick D and Jakupec V (1999) Becoming Flexible: what does it mean? in A Tait and R Mills (eds), *The Convergence of Distance and Conventional Education: patterns of flexibility for the individual learner*, London: Routledge.
Knapper C & Cropley A J (1995) (2nd edition) *Lifelong Learning and Higher Education*, London: Kogan Page.
Kolb D A (1984) *Experiential Learning*, New Jersey: Prentice Hall.
Korsgaard O (1997) The Impact of Globalization on Adult Education, in S Walters (ed), *Globalization, Adult Education and Training: impacts and issues*, Leicester: Zed Books/NIACE.
Lather P (1988) Feminist Perspectives on Empowering Research Methodologies, *Women's Studies International Forum* 11 (6): 569-581.
Lather P (1991) *Getting Smart: feminist research and pedagogy with/in the postmodern*, London: Routledge.
Leicester M (1993) *Race for a Change in Continuing and Higher Education*, Buckingham: SRHE/Open University Press.
Lister R (1997) *Citizenship: Feminist Perspectives*, Basingstoke: Macmillan.
Llewelyn S and Haslett A (1986) Factors Perceived as Helpful by the Members of Self-Help Groups: an exploratory study, *British Journal of Guidance and Counselling* 14 (3): 252 - 262.
Longworth N (1997) Higher Education Responding to a Lifelong Learning World, *Higher Education in Europe* XXII (4) 517-524.
Lovett T (1982) *Adult Education, Community Development and the Working Class* (2nd edition), Nottingham: University of Nottingham.
Lynch K & O'Riordan C (1998) Inequality in Higher Education: a study of class barriers, *British Journal of Sociology of Education* 19 (4): 445-478.
McGivney V (1990) *Education's For Other People: access to education for non participant adults*, Leicester: NIACE.
McGivney V (1999) *Informal Learning in the Community: a trigger for change and development*, Leicester: NIACE.
McMahon B (1996) The Meaning and Relevance of Education for Working Class Mature Students: a personal view, Conference Proceedings, *Mature Students in Higher Education*, Ireland: Athlone Technical College, pp 28-34.

McNair S (1995) Commentary: adults in a changing higher education, *Studies in the Education of Adults* 27 (1): 1-8.

McNair S (1997a) Changing Frameworks and Qualifications, in F Coffield and B Williamson (eds), *Repositioning Higher Education*, Buckinghamshire: SRHE/Open University Press.

McNair S (1997b) Is There a Crisis? Does it Matter? in R Barnett & A Griffin (eds), *The End of Knowledge in Higher Education*, London: Cassell.

McNair S (1998) The Invisible Majority: adult learners in English higher education, *Higher Education Quarterly* 52 (2), 167-178.

McNair S with Cara S, McGivney V, Raybould F, Soulsby J, Thomson A and Vaughan M (1999) *Non Award Bearing Continuing Education: an evaluation of the HEFCE programme 1995-1998*, Report 99/19, Bristol: HEFCE.

McPherson A (1991) Widening the Access Argument, in T Schuller (ed), *The Future of Higher Education*, Buckinghamshire: SRHE/OUP.

Maierhofer R (1999) Desperately Seeking the Self: gender, age and identity in Till Olsen's Tell me a Riddle and Michelle Herman's Missing, *Educational Gerontology* 25 (2): 129-142.

Manning J and O'Hanlon C (1995) *Students with Disabilities and Special Needs: applications for higher education in 1993/4* - Leverhulme Project Report, Birmingham: The School of Education, University of Birmingham.

Mansell R and When U (1998) *Knowledge Societies: information technology for sustainable development*, Oxford: Oxford University Press.

Marks G (1994) 'Armed Now with Hope': the construction of the subjectivity of students within integration, *Disability and Society* 9 (1): 71-83.

Mayo M & Thomson J (eds) (1995) *Adult Learning, Critical Intelligence and Social Change*, Leicester: NIACE.

Meekosha H and Dowse L (1997) Enabling Citizenship: gender, disability and citizenship in Australia, *Feminist Review* 57 (Autumn): 49-72.

Merton B (1997) Still Disaffected After All These Years? *Adults Learning* 8 (6): 153-4.

Middlehurst R (1997) Enhancing Quality in F Coffield and B Williamson (eds), *Repositioning Higher Education*, Buckinghamshire: SRHE/Open University Press.

Miller T (1998) Shifting Layers of Professional, Lay and Personal Narratives: longitudinal childbirth research, in J Ribbens and R Edwards (eds), *Feminist Dilemmas in Qualitative Research: public knowledge and private lives*, London: Sage Publications.

Moore R and Muller J (1999) The Discourse of 'Voice' and the Problem of Knowledge and Identity in the Sociology of Education, *British Journal of Sociology of Education*, 20 (2): 189-206.

MORI (1996) *Summary Report: state of the nation poll*, London: MORI.

National Curriculum Council (1990) *Curriculum Guidance 8: education for citizenship*, York: NCC.

NIACE (1993) *An Adult Higher Education: a vision*, Policy Discussion Paper, Leicester: NIACE.

OECD (1999) *Overcoming Exclusion Through Adult Learning*, Paris: OECD.

Oglesby L and Houghton A-M (1997) Exploring Threshold Standards for Guidance and Learner Support in HEQC (ed), *Managing Guidance in Higher Education: using quality assurance guidelines - selected case studies*, London: HEQC.
Oliver M (1990) *The Politics of Disablement*, London: Macmillan.
Oliver M (1996) Education for All? A Perspective on an Inclusive Society, in M Oliver (ed), *Understanding Disability: from theory to practice*, London: Macmillan.
Oommen T K (ed) (1997) *Citizenship and National Identity*, London: Sage.
O'Rourke J (1999) Canaries in the Mine? Women's Experience and New Learning Technologies, in A Tait and R Mills (eds), *The Convergence of Distance and Conventional Education: patterns of flexibility for the individual learner*, London: Routledge.
Pahl R (1990) *Prophets, Ethnographers and Social Glue: civil society and social order*. Mimeo: ESRC/CNRS Workshop on Citizenship, Social Order and Civilising Processes, Cumberland Lodge.
Paquette-Frenette D and Larocque D (1995) A Collective Approach to Distance Education, in J Roberts and E Keough (eds), *Why the Information Highway? Lessons from Open and Distance Learning*, Toronto: Trifolium Books Inc.
Payne J and Edwards R (1997) Impartiality in Pre-entry Guidance for Adults in Further Education Colleges, *British Journal of Guidance and Counselling* 25 (3): 361 - 375.
Peters S (1999) Transforming Disability Identity Through Critical Literacy and Cultural Politics of Language, in M Corker and S French (eds), *Disability Discourse*, Buckingham: Open University Press.
Phillips M (1998) Learning How to Learn: a cross curricula approach to key skills in access to higher education, *Journal of Access and Credit Studies* 1 Winter: 113-119.
Preece J (1997) Making Credit Work for Communities, Unpublished Conference Paper, *Empowering Education: student diversity, tutor training and part-time higher education students*, UACE Empowering Education and Training Network: Sussex.
Preece J (1999) *Combating Social Exclusion in University Adult Education*, Aldershot: Ashgate.
Preece J (1999a) *Using Foucault and Feminist Theories to explain why some adults are excluded from British University Adult Education*, Edwin Mellen Press.
Preece J (1999b) Making the Curriculum Culturally Relevant through a Higher Education Core Skills Framework, *South African Journal of Higher Education* 20 (3): 89-96.
Preece J and Bokhari R (1996) Making the Curriculum Culturally Relevant Through a Higher Education Core Skills Framework, *Journal of Further and Higher Education* 20 (3): 70-80.
Purvis J (1991) *A History of Women's Education in England*, Milton Keynes: Open University Press.

Putnam R D (1995) Tuning in and Tuning Out: the strange disappearance of social capital in America, *Political Science and Politics* 18 (4) 664-683.

Qualifications and Curriculum Authority (1999) *Qualifications 16-19: a guide to the changes resulting from the qualifying for success consultation*, London: QCA.

Rees T & Bartlett W (1999) Adult Guidance Services in the European Learning Society: a Scottish case study, *Studies in the Education of Adults* 31 (1): 21-34.

Reinharz S (1992) *Feminist Methods in Social Research*, Oxford: Oxford University Press.

Ritzer G (1998) *The McDonaldisation* Thesis, London: Sage.

Roberts E (1984) *A Woman's Place: an oral history of working class women 1890-1940*, Oxford: Blackwell.

Roberts E (1995) *Women and Families: an oral history 1940-1970*, Oxford: Blackwell.

Roberts J and Keough E (1995) *Why the Information Highway? Lessons from Open and Distance Learning*, Toronto: Trifolium Books Inc.

Robertson D (1997) Social Justice in a Learning Market, in F Coffield & B Williamson (eds), *Repositioning Higher Education*, Buckinghamshire: SRHE/Open University Press.

Robertson R (1992) *Globalization: social theory and global culture*, London: Sage.

Robinson A (1997) Adult Learning by Videoconferencing, in J Field (ed), *Electronic Pathways: adult learning and the new communication technologies*, Leicester: NIACE.

Rosenau J N (1997) Citizenship without Moorings: American responses to a turbulent world, in T K Oommen (ed), *Citizenship and National Identity: from colonialism to globalism*, London: Sage.

Sadlack J (1998) Globalization and Concurrent Challenges for Higher Education, in P Scott (ed), *The Globalization of Higher Education*, Buckingham: SRHE/Open University Press.

Sadler J and Atkinson K (1998) Managing Guidance in Further Education, in R Edwards, R Harrison and A Tait (eds), *Telling Tales: perspectives on guidance and counselling in learning*, London: Routledge.

Sargant N (1991) *Learning and Leisure: a study of adult participation in learning and its policy implications*, Leicester: NIACE.

Sargant N, Field J, Francis H, Schuller T and Tuckett A (1997) *The Learning Divide: a study of participation in adult learning in the United Kingdom*, Leicester: NIACE.

Schuller T (1995) *The Changing University?* Buckinghamshire: SRHE/Open University Press.

Schuller T and Field J (1998) Social Capital, Human Capital and the Learning Society, *International Journal of Lifelong Education* 17 (4) 226-235.

Scott P (1995) *The Meanings of Mass Higher Education*, Buckinghamshire: SRHE/Open University Press.

Scott P (1997) The Changing Role of the University in the Production of New Knowledge, *Tertiary Education and Management* 3 (1), 5-14.

Skeggs B (1997) *Formations of Class and Gender*, Sage: London.

Skillbeck M & Connell H (1996) Lifelong Learning: a missing dimension in undergraduate education, in F. Coffield (ed), *Higher Education and Lifelong Learning*, Department of Education, Newcastle Upon Tyne: University of Newcastle Upon Tyne.

Smail B, Whyte J and Kelly A (1982) Girls into Science and Technology: the first two years, *SSR* 64: 620-630.

Sparrow J (1992) The Need to Work with Perceptions, in J Sparrow (ed), *Knowledge in Organisations*, London: Sage Publications.

Standing K (1998) Writing the Voices of the Less Powerful: researching lone mothers, in J Ribbens and R Edwards (eds), *Feminist Dilemmas in Qualitative Research: public knowledge and private lives*, London: Sage Publications.

Stephens J, Hall R, Knowles V and Stewart J (1998) Exploring Business Skills: an innovative approach to promoting lifelong learning, *Journal of Further and Higher Education* 22 (3): 329-340.

Storan J (1999) A View to Learn, *Adults Learning* 11 (2): 13-14.

Stuart M (1996) Working with the Enemy? Responding to Social Change through Partnerships, in J Elliott, H Francis, R Humphries and D Istance (eds), *Communities and Their Universities: the challenge of lifelong learning*, London: Lawrence and Wishart.

Stuart M and Thomson A (eds) (1997) *Engaging with Difference: the other in adult education*, Leicester: NIACE.

Tait A and Mills R (eds) (1999) *The Convergence of Distance and Conventional Education: patterns of flexibility for the individual learner*, London: Routledge.

Tallantyre F (1996) Guidance and the Institution in S McNair (ed), *Putting Learners at the Centre: reflections from the guidance and learner autonomy in higher education programme*, Sheffield: DfEE.

Thompson D (1999) From Marginal to Mainstream: critical issues in the adoption of information technologies for tertiary teaching and learning, in A Tait and R Mills (eds), *The Convergence of Distance and Conventional Education: patterns of flexibility for the individual learner*, London: Routledge.

Thorne C (1998) Democratic Deficit, *Adults Learning* 10 (3): 23-25.

Torkington N P K (1996) *The Social Construction of Knowledge: a case for black studies*, Liverpool: Liverpool Hope Press.

Trotman C and Pudner H (1998) 'What's The Point?' in J Preece (ed), *Beyond the Boundaries: exploring the potential of widening provision in higher education*, Leicester: NIACE.

Tuijnman A & Van der Kamp (eds) (1992) *Learning Across the Lifespan*, Oxford: Pergamon.

UDACE (1986) *The Challenge of Change: developing educational guidance for adults*, Leicester: NIACE/UDACE.

Vandenbroucke F (1998) *Globalisation, Inequality and Social Democracy*, London: IPPR.

Walker A (1998) Speaking for Themselves: the new politics of old age in Europe, *Education and Ageing* 13 (1): 13-36.

Walters P and Baldwin E (1998) Complicated Money: funding student participation in mass higher education, in D Jary and M Parker (eds), *The New*

Higher Education: issues and directions for the post-Dearing university, Staffordshire: Staffordshire University Press.

Wann M (1995) *Building Social Capital*, London: IPPR.

Ward K (1996) Community Regeneration and Social Exclusion: some current policy issues for higher education, in J Elliott, H Francis, R Humphries and D Istance (eds), *Communities and Their Universities: the challenge of lifelong learning*, London: Lawrence and Wishart.

Ward K and Taylor R (1986) *Adult Education and the Working Class: education for the missing millions*, Kent: Croom Helm.

Waters M (1995) *Globalization*, London: Routledge.

Watson D & Taylor R (1998) *Lifelong Learning and the University: a post Dearing agenda*, London: Falmer.

Watts A, Hawthorn R, Hoffbrand J, Jackson H and Spurling A (1997) Developing local lifelong guidance strategies, *British Journal of Guidance and Counselling* 25 (2): 217 - 227.

Watts A and Young M (1998) Models of Student Guidance in a Changing 14 - 19 Education and Training System in R Edwards, R Harrison and A Tait (eds), *Telling Tales: perspectives on guidance and counselling in learning*, London: Routledge.

Watts T (1999) Mind Over a Matter of Exclusion: social and moral dilemmas lie at the heart of social exclusion, *Careers Guidance Today* 7 (1): 18 - 26.

West L (1997) *Beyond Fragments*, London: Taylor and Francis.

Whitlock Q (1999) Author! Author! *Adults Learning* 11 (3): 14-15.

Whitston K (1998) Key Skills and Curriculum Reform, *Studies in Higher Education*, 23 (3): 307-319.

Williams J (1998) What is a Profession? Experience Versus Expertise, in R Edwards, R Harrison and A Tait (eds), *Telling Tales: perspectives on guidance and counselling in learning*, London: Routledge.

Williamson B (1998) *Lifeworlds and Learning: essays in the theory, philosophy and practice of lifelong learning*, Leicester: NIACE.

Williamson B & Coffield F (1997) Repositioning Higher Education, in F Coffield & B Williamson (eds), *Repositioning Higher Education*, Buckinghamshire: SRHE/Open University Press.

Wills M (1999) Bridging the Digital Divide, *Adults Learning* 11 (4): 10-11.

Wilson P (1999) *Lifelong Qualifications: developing qualifications to support lifelong learners*, Leicester: NIACE.

Withnal A & Percy K (1994) *Good Practice in the Education of Adults*, Hants: Arena/Ashgate.

Woodrow M (1998) *From Elitism to Inclusion: good practice in widening access to higher education*, London: CVCP.

Woodward K (ed) (1997) *Identity and Difference*, London: Sage.

Wynne A (1999) A Learning City, *Adults Learning* 11 (3): 18-20.

Yuval-Davis N (1992) Fundamentalism, Multiculturalism and Women in Britain, in J Donald and A Rattansi (eds), *'Race' Culture and Difference*, London: Sage/Open University Press.

Yuval-Davis N (1994) Women, Ethnicity and Empowerment, in K K Bhavnani and A Phoenix (eds), *Shifting Identities, Shifting Racisms*, London: Sage.

Yuval-Davis N (1997) Women Citizenship and Difference, *Feminist Review* 57 Autumn: 4-27.

Zriny Long N A (1997) Minority Students Success Through an Integrated Curriculum, *National Association for Development Education* volume 3, 21st Annual Conference Proceedings, Colorado.

Zuber-Skerritt O (1996) *New Directions in Action Research*, London: Falmer Press.

Index

ACACE 92
Access 5, 11, 18, 19, 30, 48, 52, 77, 113, 116, 119, 122, 133, 150, 154, 158, 163, 179
Ackers L 10, 129, 130,137, 164
Action research 21, 27-35, 33, 98, 176
Adult 6, 12, 15, 17, 18, 51, 90, 92, 107, 111, 138, 139, 161
Adult learners 17, 18, 23-24, 29, 30, 31, 33-35, 40, 47, 49, 99, 108, 111, 112, 113, 114, 146
Age 130, 141, 160, 171
Agency 10, 27, 97-98, 131, 133, 140, 143, 144, 153, 168
Alfonsi A 129
Allen P 80
Apple M W 81
Aronowitz S 79
Ashton D 60
Ashworth P D 61
Asian 24, 27, 33, 38, 44, 49, 51, 52, 116, 133, 135, 143-144
Assessment 120
Autonomy 97-98, 107

Bailey D 92, 99, 101
Ball S J C 64
Barnes M 43, 118, 151, 152
Barnett R 12, 13, 14, 16, 17, 18, 61, 64, 65, 67, 72, 73, 79, 81, 90, 174, 175
Baron S 60
Barrow R 60, 71
Barton D 27, 31
Battersby D 79
Bauman Z 149
Beck U 8, 9, 10, 11
Beinart S 40, 95, 96
Benn R 165
Bhachu P 141
Bird J 82

Blair A 95
Black 11, 86, 95
Blass E 61, 67
Blissand V 60
Blunkett D 145
Boddy G 109
Boud D 64
Bourgeois E 6, 15, 18
Bourke J 161
Bradley H 160, 172
Bradshaw D 61
Brah A 89, 127, 131-132, 133, 137, 141
Brennan J 18
Bridge Centre 72, 74, 84-85, 115-116, 119, 142, 150, 160-173, 181
Brindley J 111
Brine J 10, 129, 131
Brown J S 22, 54, 92
Brown P 148
Brunt J M 111
Buck M 110, 114
Burgess R G 32
Burgess T 64, 72

Carlton S 160
CASCAID 94
Castells M 6
CD ROM 115-116
Challis S 112
Cherryholmes C H 79, 80, 177
Chertos C 29
Chrisholm L 48, 97, 99
CIHE 40
CITINET 112
Citizenship 3, 6, 8-11, 33, 43, 49, 52, 55, 80, 88, 89, 90, 92, 97-98, 108, 117, 118, 127, 129-130, 132, 137-139, 148, 151-153, 164, 165-167, 176, 178, 179, 180, 181
Clare M 95

211

Clarke A 108, 110
Code L 131
Coffield F 13, 15, 17, 60, 65, 72
Coleman J 9, 45, 48, 53, 140
Collaboration 17, 21, 24
Community 3, 4, 7, 8, 9, 11, 12 18, 25, 27, 31, 43, 50, 54, 59 37-42, 81, 82, 95, 97, 98, 106, 111, 112, 113, 114-123, 116, 117, 122, 129, 137, 139-140, 152, 153, 156, 159, 165, 180 gatekeepers, 54 47 capacity 11, 113, 145 adult education 17 communities 6-8, 33-35, 77, 91, 98, 108, 127, 131, 145, 179, 182-184
Community Access Programme, CAP 21, 23-26, 54, 62, 64-67, 71, 82, 91, 108, 111, 114-123, 118, 132, 137, 146, 150
Community organisations 37-42
Competitiveness 5, 108, 174
Complexity 5, 10, 15, 16, 74, 76
Computers 114
Consultation 25, 118
Convergence 10, 59, 62, 76, 127, 131, 136, 137, 143, 149, 174
Cost/s 40, 110, 112
Cottle 33
Course, Courses 21, 22, 24, 25, 31, 34, 52-3, 71, 73, 74-76, 83, 89, 94, 104, 115, 118, 122, 133, 135, 136, 137, 140, 142, 164, 166, 169, 172, 175, 180, 182 development 22, 23, 59 evaluation 26
Credit 3, 5, 17, 18, 19, 23, 25, 33, 34, 59, 63, 74, 149
Critical thinking, analysis, 13, 14, 16, 17, 18, 59, 69, 76, 86, 178
Cronin C 78
Cruikshank J 26, 47
Cryer P 62
Culture 8, 84, 127, 129, 130, 141, 155, 180
Cultural 4, 6, 7, 19, 13, 29, 78, 108, 116, 118, 131, 135, 136, 137, 141, 144, 166, 184 cultural relevance 77, 80-90, 104, 113
Cultural capital 45

Curriculum 4, 17, 18, 19, 21, 25, 28, 33, 54, 61, 62, 72, 73, 77, 107, 115-120, 122, 143, 176, 177, 182, 184 content 79-83 off limits 19, 76, 77-90, 177

DAB Centre 70, 73, 74, 84-85, 88, 117, 145-159, 180-181
Dadzie S 48, 95, 99
Daniels J 111
Dearing R 14, 17, 46, 60, 63, 91, 108, 151
Deem R 78
DfEE 8, 11, 13, 46, 91, 183
Diaspora 89, 128, 131, 135, 141
Difference 70, 78, 82, 84, 86, 90, 127, 130, 131, 174, 178, 181
Disabled, disability, disabilities 10, 24, 27, 33, 34, 38, 44, 50, 52, 80, 85, 88, 90, 95, 101, 102, 109, 117, 120, 127, 131, 135, 141, 145-159, 172, 177, 181
Discourse, discourses 10, 82 79, 89, 127, 131, 132, 133, 136, 141, 143, 158, 164, 168, 171, 172, 177, 179
DOTS 106
Duke C 6, 12, 65, 71, 72

E-mail 1, 10
E University 182-183
East Lancs 74, 83-85, 118, 133-144, 150, 168, 171, 180
Ebbutt D 12
Economic 8, 9, 12, 14, 44, 128-129, 132, 139, 140, 152, 163, 164, 169, 183, 184
ECTIS 94
Edwards M 5, 14, 93
Edwards R 18, 19, 59
Elliott J 22
Elsdon K 39, 151
Employability 10, 11, 14
Employment 8, 15, 34, 113, 134, 146, 150, 154
Engaged Pedagogy 79, 82, 83-84
Ethnicity 39
Etzioni E 128-129, 141
European 14, 35
European Social Fund 23

Exclusion 78 82 (see also social exclusion) 107
Experience 16, 17, 18, 19, 25, 27, 32, 53, 63, 64, 69, 70, 76, 79, 80, 82, 86, 88, 89, 90, 101, 133, 145, 157, 159, 175, 177, 182

Fazey D 102
FE colleges 38
FECIS 94
Feminist 10, 85
Field J 9, 10, 44, 108, 109, 110, 119
Fieldhouse R 166
Finkelstein V 145, 152
Focus group 30, 51, 52, 98
Fordham P 11
Foucault M 78, 144
Foundation credit 25, 66, 142, 147, 151, 164, 181
Foundation degree 183
Fragmentation 7
Freire P 65
Friedman J 7
Fryer R 48, 60, 91, 95, 97, 102, 108
Fukuyama F 128-129, 141, 167, 168
Further Education 136, 175

Gain M 113
Gender 10, 89, 127, 128, 130, 131-132, 136, 141, 146, 157, 162, 164, 166, 170
Gibbons 80
Giddens A 8, 9, 131, 136, 141
Global 4, 5, 6, 7, 8, 14, 21, 39, 84, 90, 108, 111, 132, 138, 145, 174, 176, 179, 182 global village 7
Global/local 38, 47, 48, 90, 116, 118, 127, 135-137, 144, 145, 149-151, 156, 163-164, 179, 180
Globalisation 3, 5, 6, 8, 11, 33, 59, 95, 107, 108, 129, 130, 132, 136, 137, 143, 162, 163, 164
Glover R J 165
Goduka I N 78, 80, 81
Gore J M 79
Gosden C 87
Green A 130, 176

Guidance 18, 19, 23, 25, 27, 28, 29, 30, 33, 46, 48, 62, 90, 91-107, 118, 146, 176, 178 holistic 9, 92, 98-104 group 99, 104-106 peer 99, 104-106

Hake B 14
Hall S 131
Harvey L 64
Harvard M 62
HEFCE 11, 22, 28, 35, 46, 146, 182
Heinz W 60
Held D 7
HEQC 93, 94
Higher education 3, 5, 11, 12, 20, 27-28, 29, 32, 33, 34, 45, 48, 54, 59, 63, 74, 75, 90, 108, 109, 113, 127, 132, 151, 159, 160, 173, 174-185
Hill Collins 81-82, 85, 90
Hillier Y 48, 94
Hirst G 7
Hoatson L 106
Holistic 9, 92, 177, 184 (see also guidance)
hooks b 77, 79, 81, 83, 84, 85-87, 178
Houghton A-M 30, 48, 95, 105, 118, 156
Howarth C 11
Hudson B 26
Human capital 8, 10, 23, 26, 34, 44-45, 59, 77, 108, 117, 127, 132, 134-135, 140, 145, 147-149, 155, 161-162, 168, 176, 181
Hunjan I 99
Hunt M 94
Hunter L 22
Hyland T 60, 61, 62

Identity 19, 77, 79, 80, 81, 82, 83, 84, 89, 90, 112, 116, 127, 129, 130-132, 133, 141-144, 153, 157-159, 167, 170, 171, 174, 178, 179, 180
Imeson R 48
Inclusion 6, 8, 11-12, 77, 81, 174
ITC 19, 108-123 ICT 148, 149, 178
Insiders, insider 31, 81, 82, 86-88, 90
Interviews 32

Jackson K 80
Jamieson A 169, 172

Jarvis P 60, 69
Johnston R 22
Johnstone B 18
Jordan B 10, 43, 88, 98

Kelly A 29
Kennedy H 46, 48, 91, 95, 108
Killeen J 105
Kirkpatrick D 112
Knapper C 13, 59, 64, 72, 175
Knowledge 13-15, 16-17, 18, 1, 54, 64, 77, 78, 79, 80, 81, 90, 109, 113, 119, 128, 136, 140, 149, 152, 154, 169, 175, 177-178, 179, 180, 182, 184
Kolb D A 69, 181
Korsgaard O 14

Lather P 29, 32
LAWTEC 94
Learning 15, 17, 69, 72, 74, 76, 77, 79, 82, 83, 91, 109, 155, 160, 166, 168, 172, 175, 176, 183 (see also teaching) learning society 14, 37 learning organisation 15
Learndirect 94, 97, 121
Leicester M 82
Level 69-72, 176, 177
Liberal adult education 22
Lifelong learning 7, 12, 12-15, 59-76, 91, 92, 93, 95, 97, 113, 119, 175, 176, 185
Lister R 10, 43, 97, 107, 129, 137, 151
Llewelyn S 104, 105
Local 6, 7, 14, 19, 20, 25, 38, 54, 77, 81, 83, 94, 100, 108, 111, 112, 113, 128, 134, 136, 151, 153, 165, 169, 176, 177, 180
Longworth N 15, 17, 175
Lovett T 80
Lynch K 80

McGivney V 24, 40, 45, 46, 47, 83, 169
McMahon B 81
McNair S 11, 13, 16, 18, 48, 49, 62, 64, 70, 77, 175
McPherson A 14, 176
Maierhofer R 170, 171
Manning J 99

Mansell R 109, 119
MARIS 94
Marks G 80
Mayo M 81, 84
Meekosha H, 43, 151, 152
Merton B 65
Metacognition 64
Middlehurst R 15
Miller T 31
Minority 10, 127 minority ethnic 24
Moore R 78
MORI 50
Muslim 89, 133, 140, 178

NAEGS 92
National Curriculum Council 151
NEGI 92
NERIS 94
NIACE 18, 49
NICEC 92
NVQ 60, 63

OECD 11
Oglesby L 93, 95
Older adults 24, 27, 33, 115, 160, 172
Oliver M 145-146
Oommen T K 10, 129
O'Rourke J 109, 112
Outreach 22, 81

Pahl R 151
Participation 8, 21, 26, 35, 37, 42, 45-55, 77, 80, 98, 112, 129, 133, 145-146, 152, 153, 155, 158, 161, 166, 176, 177, 179, 180, 183
Partnership/s 22, 33, 38, 119, 147, 150, 152, 153, 182
Paquette-Frenette D 123
Payne J 99
Peters S 156
Phillips M 62
Policy 29, 108, 109 policies 11-12, 91, 92-95, 161
Power 44, 77, 78, 89, 127, 128, 131, 132, 140, 141, 143-144, 155, 158, 160, 163, 164, 167, 169, 172, 179, 184
Praxis 17

Preece J 11, 13, 24, 32, 69, 78, 79, 83, 89, 131, 134, 161, 169
Private sphere 130
Progression 19, 25, 26, 29, 33, 46, 50, 74, 91, 148, 172, 181, 184
Providers
Purvis J 137, 142
Putnam R D 9, 44, 45, 119, 140, 168

QCA 108
Qualifications 134, 136
Quality 15, 18, 21, 111, 152
Questionnaire 27, 37, 42-45, 49, 54

Reflexivity 16, 76, 86 reflexive 79, 88, 89, 131, 132, 157, 176, 178, 180
Reinharz S 28, 29, 30
Roberts E 137, 142, 161
Roberts J 109
Robertson D 16
Robertson R 7
Robinson A 110, 113
Role model 24, 26, 101, 184
Rosenau J N 129

Sadler J 95, 106
Sargant N 34, 37, 40, 50, 51, 91, 95, 96
Schuller T 9, 45, 48, 53, 141
Scott P 14, 15
Situated knowledge 82, 87, 177
Skeggs B 82, 131
Skillbeck M 64, 72
Skills 7, 8, 13, 17, 18, 22, 25, 33, 34, 59-76, 80, 92, 95, 107, 140, 143, 145, 150, 151, 176 ITC skills 108-123, 128, 134, 136, 154, 157, 160, 166, 167, 178
Smail B 29
Social capital 8-11, 12, 33, 37, 39, 43, 44-55, 77, 90, 108, 117, 118, 119, 122, 127, 128-129, 132, 139-141, 148, 153-156, 160, 167-170, 172, 176, 177, 179, 180, 181-182, 183
Social exclusion 6, 8, 11-12, 65, 108, 145, 179
Society 15, 17, 169, 176, 181, 184, 185
Standing K 30
Stephens J 62
Storan J 119

Stuart M 22
Subjectivities 131, 132, 133, 141-144, 156-159, 170-172
Supercomplexity 11

Tait A 109, 12
Tallantrye F 104
TAPS 94
Teaching 17, 30, 59, 61, 62, 63, 71, 73, 74-76, 81, 82, 83-86, 90, 109, 111, 112, 175, 176, 178, 179, 182, 184 (see also learning) teaching relationship 77, 78-79, 177
Technology 94-95, 107, 108-123, 136, 149, 163, 178, 179
Telephone 114, 121
Television, TV 114, 119
Thompson D 109, 110, 112
Thorne C 165
Torkington N P K 80
Transferable, transferability 67-69
Transformative learning 64
Trotman C 11
Trust 9, 45, 54-55, 73, 82, 84, 128-129, 139, 140, 141, 143, 154, 157, 177, 178, 180, 184

UCAS
UDACE 92
Ufi 94, 113
Unemployment 11 unemployed 23, 24, 34, 38, 99

Vocationalism 14, 15
Voice 80-81, 85, 86, 127, 176, 177, 178
Voluntary activity 117, 165 work 139, 159
Voluntary groups, organisations 8, 151, 152 agencies 22

Walker A 165
Waters M 7, 162
Walters P 40
Wann M 128, 140
Ward K 11, 22
Watson D 17, 62, 175
Watts A 95, 105
Watts T 100

WEA 75, 165
Wealth 7, 8, 60, 128, 129, 140, 174, 179, 185
Welfare 23, 129, 156, 181, 183
West L 131
Whitlock Q 111
Whitston K 61, 67
Widening provision, widening participation 48,184
Williams J 54, 95
Williamson B 5, 15, 17
Wills M 113
Wilson P 63
Withnal A 172

Women 10, 24, 33, 34, 53, 97, 112, 116, 129 136, 137, 141, 160, 161, 166, 170, 171, 179 migrant women 129, 131
Woodrow M 46
Woodward K 130-131
Working class 24, 80, 134, 137, 146, 147, 157, 164, 167, 170
World Wide Web 111, 114
Wynne A 112

Yalom 104, 105
Yuval-Davis N 134, 135, 137

Zriny Long N A 78